Routledge Revivals

Rebuilding the Ancestral Village

Originally published in 2000, this second edition was first published in 2010. This is a discussion of the relationship between one group of Singapore Chinese and their ancestral village in Fujian in China. It explores the various reasons why the Singapore Chinese continue to want to maintain ties with their ancestral village and how they go about reproducing Chinese culture (in the form of ancestor worship and religion) in the village milieu in China. It further explores the reasons why the Singapore Chinese feel morally obliged to assist their ancestral village in village reconstruction (providing financial contributions to infrastructure development such as the buildings of roads, bridges, schools, hospitals) and to help with small scale industrial and retail activities. Related to this is how the village cadres and teenagers, through various strategies, managed to encourage the Singapore Chinese to revisit their ancestral village and help with village reconstruction, thereby creating a moral economy. The main argument here concerns the desire of the Singapore Chinese to maintain a cultural identity and lineage continuity with their ancestral home. Ethnographically, this anthropological study examines two groups of Chinese separated by historical and geographical space, and their coming together to re-establish their cultural identity through various cultural and economic activities. At the theoretical level, it seeks to add a new dimension to the study of Chinese transnationalism and diaspora studies.

Rebuilding the Ancestral Village
Singaporeans in China

Khun Eng Kuah

First published in 2000 by Ashgate Publishing
Second edition published in 2010
by Hong Kong University Press

This edition first published in 2022 by Routledge
4 Park Square, Milton Park, Abingdon, Oxon, OX14 4RN

and by Routledge
605 Third Avenue, New York, NY 10017

Routledge is an imprint of the Taylor & Francis Group, an informa business

© 2010 Hong Kong University Press

All rights reserved. No part of this book may be reprinted or reproduced or utilised in any form or by any electronic, mechanical, or other means, now known or hereafter invented, including photocopying and recording, or in any information storage or retrieval system, without permission in writing from the original publishers.

Publisher's Note
The publisher has gone to great lengths to ensure the quality of this reprint but points out that some imperfections in the original copies may be apparent.

Disclaimer
The publisher has made every effort to trace copyright holders and welcomes correspondence from those they have been unable to contact.

ISBN: 978-1-032-26121-8 (hbk)
ISBN: 978-1-003-28686-8 (ebk)
ISBN: 978-1-032-26160-7 (pbk)

Book DOI 10.4324/9781003286868

Rebuilding the Ancestral Village
Singaporeans in China

Khun Eng Kuah

香港大學出版社
HONG KONG UNIVERSITY PRESS

Hong Kong University Press
14/F Hing Wai Centre
7 Tin Wan Praya Road
Aberdeen
Hong Kong
www.hkupress.org

© Hong Kong University Press 2011

ISBN 978-988-8028-81-8

All rights reserved. No portion of this publication may be reproduced or
transmitted in any form or by any means, electronic or mechanical,
including photocopy, recording, or any information storage or
retrieval system, without permission in writing from the publisher.

British Library Cataloguing-in-Publication Data
A catalogue record for this book is available
from the British Library.

Printed and bound by Liang Yu Printing Factory Limited, Hong Kong, China

Contents

Preface to the Second Edition		vii
Acknowledgements to the Second Edition		xi
Note on Romanization		xiii
List of Illustrations		xv
1	Introduction	1
2	Constructing a Singapore Chinese Cultural Identity	29
3	The Ancestral Village in Anxi County	55
4	Negotiating Collective Memories and Social Experiences	71
5	The Moral Economy of Rebuilding the Ancestral Village	101
6	The Bond of Ancestor Worship	131
7	Religious Revivalism	163
8	Rewriting Genealogy and Reclaiming One's Cultural Roots	189

9	Chinese Lineage as a Cultural Network: A Model	217
10	Conclusion: From Lineage to Transnational Chinese Network	241
	Notes	251
	Glossary	255
	Bibliography	263
	Index	275

Preface to the Second Edition

Since the publication of the first edition of this book in 2000, the relationship between the Chinese Diaspora and their *qiaoxiang* has intensified and the transnational linkages have grown stronger. Such relationship has spread to the north where new migrants from such places as Wenzhou, Hubei and Hunan have also returned to their ancestral villages and helped with village reconstruction. There is no doubt that Chinese lineage as a social organization has progressed into a cultural network that encompasses members scattered throughout the Diaspora in which some members are able to form a community while others remain isolated individuals. Nevertheless, they continue to look to their ancestral home as their source of origin.

The intensification of the transnational linkages is a result of the global migration and return migration. It is also motivated by the migrants who want to help rebuild their ancestral homes irrespective of whether they are wealthy or are primarily labouring in an overseas environment. There are many rural villages that still experience abject poverty and migration continues to be seen as a route out of poverty. Once out, these migrants, in addition to paying their debts, are expected to send remittances back to their home villages, as in the nineteenth century, and help to rebuild their family home. For those who have made some fortune, it is expected that they contribute to village reconstruction, help fund schools, clinics and hospitals as well as construct roads, bridges and other infrastructure, in addition to create jobs for their village kin. These new *qiaoxiang*, not unlike the old ones, have become prosperous with new buildings dotting the rural landscape.

One key issue in my book is to explore the link between ancestor worship and the creation of a moral economy that propels Chinese overseas to visit their ancestral homes and help with reconstruction. Since the 1978 reform, there has been a gradual relaxation of policies pertaining to religious activities and ancestor worship. Ancestor worship is specifically listed as an integral part of Chinese culture and hence divorced from religion. As such, it is not subjected to the stringent control of the state. From the 1990s onwards, there has been a proliferation of large-scale communal ancestor worship throughout Guangdong and Fujian in South China. In Guangdong, wealthy Hong Kong Chinese have provided funds to help rebuild their ancestral villages. They also help revitalize the economy by relocating or setting up factories in key townships where many of the ancestral villages are located. The villages have become more urbanized as most of the agricultural lands are now being appropriated for other uses. On the whole, Guangdong has become very prosperous. The same is also true of Fujian. The process of urbanization has encroached into the rural areas as well. In the *qiaoxiang* districts, agricultural lands are being used for residential and economic purposes. The cultural concession granted in the form of large-scale ancestor worship and other religious celebrations has created a workable moral economy that enables these villages to benefit from the flow of capital into the region. The money thus helps rebuild the villages and transforms them into modern market towns. The creation of a moral economy has now spread to other parts of China where new migrants have rebuilt and revitalized their villages after they migrated overseas in the 1970s.

The fluidity of migration, circulatory and return migration and settlement in the Diaspora has impacted on how we look at the identity issue of these Chinese. My argument that these Chinese continue to hold various sets of identities is even more relevant today as they try to make sense of the rapidly changing world and position themselves within different polities. While Chinese individuals locate themselves in the Diaspora, they are confronted with a set or sets of identities that they want and choose to align with. At the same time, they are also confronted with the issue of home and where home is. In this search for an identity and home, I argue that both home and identity lie in a continuum where the source of origin locates in one pole and the nodes on the other. Where one decides to locate oneself, either closer to the nodes, at midpoint, or closer to the source, will enable us to understand how the person views his/her status and identity. Such identity is not necessarily a fixed one, but is shifting depending on context and situation.

This book thus aims to fill an important gap—an attempt to understand the transnational relationship of a group of people who were separated by time and space but have come together again as a result of shared memories, sentiments and emotions, facilitated by the changing political climate in China. In the process of reunion, these two groups of Chinese have renewed their kinship and re-established their cultural identity. In so doing, they have established the lineage as a transnational cultural network that binds members of a lineage from various nodal points scattered throughout the world to the source.

In the twenty-first century, this transnational cultural network will become more crucial because it does not only bind and bring together those members physically to their ancestral village, it also serves as a resource network for all to communicate with one another through various forms without physical contact. The cyberspace, twitterspace and telecommunicative space are all new media that the Chinese in the Diaspora could use to communicate with one another for different purposes. In this sense, the transnational cultural network provides an imagined space for individuals to forage for information. It is also a space for expressing their memories and sentiments to their ancestral home and their present home, to their status as part of their ancestral village community and that of a migrant, to their new identity and citizenship of a new polity, and as a global citizen. All these open up new spaces and challenges for us to understand the complexity of the relationship between the ancestral home and the Diaspora home as well as the individuals within the two places.

Khun Eng Kuah
July 2010

Acknowledgements to the Second Edition

I am grateful to Hong Kong University Press for their support in publishing the second edition of this book.

I am indebted to a lot of people who have been most helpful and made it possible for me to carry out the research and see the completion of this book. I would like to record my gratitude to the informants in both Singapore and Anxi for opening their hearts and doors to constant questionings and probing. They have been most gracious in their answers. The names appeared in this book have been changed to protect the privacy of these individuals who have openly shared their views with me.

In addition, I would like to acknowledge the institutional support provided by the University of Hong Kong and my colleagues within and outside the university. I am especially grateful to Professors Wang Gungwu and Arthur Kleinman who have provided much support for this work, and to the three reviewers, Professors Richard Madsen, James Watson and Yan Yunxiang, who have provided valuable comments and supported the publication of this second edition. I would also like to thank Michael Duckworth of Hong Kong University Press for his whole-hearted support and patience in this work, to researchers at Xiamen University for assisting with data collection, John Thorne for editing the manuscript, Ying Xiaofei for her thorough and meticulous efforts in updating the data in this second edition, Ke Jianyuan for taking the new photos, and Clara Ho and staff at Hong Kong University Press for their efforts in bringing this book to fruition.

Last but not least, I would like to express my gratitude to my mother and late father for the assistance that they have provided me. They have been very generous with their time and patience, and to my husband and our daughter whose unfailing support has made my intellectual pursuits a joyous experience.

Needless to say, any shortcoming remains my sole responsibility.

The author acknowledges the following journals and publishers for their kind permission to reproduce portions of her articles in this book:

(1) For Chapter 5:
Kuah, Khun Eng (1998). Rebuilding their ancestral villages: The moral economy of the Singapore Chinese. In G. W. Wang and J. Wong (eds.), *China's Political Economy*. Singapore: University of Singapore Press and World Scientific, pp. 249–276.

(2) For Chapter 6:
Kuah, Khun Eng (1999). The changing moral economy of ancestor worship in a Chinese emigrant village. *Culture, Medicine and Psychiatry* 23(1): 99–132.

(3) For Chapter 9:
Kuah-Pearce, Khun Eng (1998). Doing anthropology within a transnational framework: A study of the Singapore Chinese and emigrant village ties. In S. Cheung (ed.), *On South China Track*. Hong Kong: Institute of Asia-Pacific, the Chinese University of Hong Kong, pp. 81–109.

Note on Romanization

Chinese terms and place names are transliterated using the Hanyu Pinyin system in the text. Some terms and names commonly used by the informants are romanized according to the Fujian dialect and are identified with an [H] immediately following the term. A list of the romanized terms and names, their corresponding Chinese characters and meanings is provided in the glossary.

Illustrations

Tables
1	Strength of sentiments in relation to knowledge of kinship	87
2	Sex and distribution of education and literacy	113
3	Age groups and educational attainment	113
4	Attitudes of cadres towards ancestral house and ancestor worship	158
5	Reasons for supporting ancestor worship by cadres at different levels	159

Diagrams
1	Lineage network: Relationship between source and nodes	232
2	Intra-lineage networking and relationship between individuals and source	235
3	Inter-lineage networking: Cross-lineage and source relationship	237

Maps
1	Location of Anxi County in Fujian Province	56
2	Administrative units of Anxi County, Fujian	57
3	Penglai Zhen, Anxi County	59

Photos

Front Cover
Offerings of soul house to the ancestors by individual families (top)
Kuitou Keshi Lineage Ancestral House (bottom)

After p. 129
1   Old and new houses
2   New homes and renovated traditional home in the foreground

3 Qingshuiyan Bridge in Penglai
4 Pedestrian bridge
5 Tea plantation producing the famed 'Iron Goddess' tea
6 No. 8 Secondary School
7 Jinlai Secondary School teachers' dormitory
8 Retail shops
9 A new and prosperous Xiancheng

After p. 162
10 The Buddhist monks perform 'the rite of ancestor spirit recalling'
11 The sedan chairs carrying the ancestors' spirits
12 Monk giving a ritual bath to the ancestral spirits
13 A group of monks chanting sutras
14 Communal ancestor worship
15 Villagers offering food to the ancestors
16 Offerings of soul house to the ancestors by individual families
17 Preparing big-bowl noodles for the guests
18 The black-faced Qingshui zushigong
19 Qingshuiyan Temple

1
Introduction

This book is a study of the relationship between two groups of Chinese, the Singapore Chinese and their village relatives in Anxi County, Fujian. It covers the Singaporeans' search for their cultural roots in their ancestral home villages in Anxi, which has resulted in the revival of their Chinese lineage. Anxi County is popularly known as a district of emigrant villages—a *qiaoxiang* (侨乡)—from which people emigrated to various parts of the world, especially to Southeast Asia, during the nineteenth and the first half of the twentieth century. The discussion here specifically focuses on the relationship between members of Xitou, or *kway-tau* [H] (溪头), Ke lineage in Singapore and Penglai.

Since the early 1990s, there has been much interest in the study of *qiaoxiang* and of the Chinese in overseas communities. While some literary works have focused on the attempts of 'overseas Chinese' to trace their roots back to their home villages in China, there has been very little systematic work done on the relationship between Chinese overseas and their *qiaoxiang* connections.

The focus of this study is to address the question of why the Singapore Chinese continue to be interested in their ancestral home villages and, more specifically, why they, especially those born in Singapore, have become involved in the life and socio-economic reconstruction of their ancestral villages, as well as in the revival of their traditional culture. This study is thus about the creation of a moral economy, which has incidentally resulted in the general prosperity of the ancestral villages within the county.

Central to this focus is an examination of how collective memory serves as a powerful force in pulling the Singapore Chinese back to their ancestral villages. Through this collective memory, the Singapore Chinese have been able to revive their lineage and reinvent socio-cultural and religious roles. The involvement of Singapore Chinese in village activities has resulted in a need to reinvestigate the role of lineage structure in both contemporary urban Singaporean and rural Chinese village societies, and this will be discussed in the following chapters. The way in which a sense of moral responsibility has helped the Singaporeans to redefine their roles within the Chinese village milieu will also be discussed.

At a broader conceptual level, this study looks beyond the Singapore Chinese/*qiaoxiang* connection and seeks to link it up with phenomena involving Chinese communities elsewhere.

Finally, this is also a study of the positions of the Singapore Chinese and their *qiaoxiang* relations within a cultural network, and of the transformation of the Chinese lineage from a parochial structure to a transnational network structure.

Establishing a Moral Economy

Why do Singapore Chinese feel morally obligated to assist their ancestral homes? To understand their motives and actions we need to explore their understanding of, and their identification and affinity with, their ancestral villages and specific ancestral homes (*laojia*, 老家), as well as their understanding of their moral duty and the level of their moral consciousness. It is imperative to do this from an inter-generational perspective in order to understand the continuities and discontinuities between the Singapore Chinese and their *qiaoxiang* kin. Thus it is also important to understand the Anxi Chinese and their actions to create an environment which binds the Singapore Chinese to the villages and brings the moral economy into existence and maintains it.

From the inter-generational perspective, it is often the case that migrants who moved to Singapore maintain strong sentimental ties with their ancestral villages, and this includes the majority of first-generation migrants from Anxi. Such immigrants feel morally obliged to assist their immediate village kin financially and materially. They have also contributed substantially to infrastructure development and socio-religious activities in the ancestral village. Even during times of political restriction, members of this first generation managed to send small remittances, medicines and other material goods to their village kin. Among other things, they have been motivated to do this by their knowledge of what poverty is, as their ancestral districts have, throughout history, been some of the poorest in China.

But what about the Singapore-born Chinese, especially those of Anxi descent? How do they look at their ancestral villages, and what moral demands do they feel? A common view is that these Singapore-born Chinese have less emotional attachment and interest in their ancestral villages than do generations born in Mainland China, and are hence less likely to assist in village reconstruction or participate in village activities. According to this view, they do not see the ancestral villages as having any great significance; they are merely the places where their ancestors came from. They therefore want to have very little dealing with their ancestral villages.

In fact, Singapore-born Chinese of Anxi descent have substantial interest in their ancestral villages. A sizeable number of them have visited their ancestral villages and have participated in various socio-religious activities there. They have also contributed significantly to the infrastructure development in the villages.

Several factors account for this. The first is the strength of the lineage structure in Singapore in binding younger members to their primordial kinship networks. The fact that younger members of the lineage continue to socialize and have links with one another demonstrates that the lineage creates a critical group of younger members within itself. These younger members are then drawn into participating in village activities by the older members. Another factor is the strength of the family. Older members often encourage younger ones to visit the ancestral village, and to participate in and contribute to village development in Anxi. Finally, in recent years the (Singapore) Anxi Association has also played an instrumental role in encouraging younger lineage members to participate in the activities of their ancestral villages and of Anxi County.

In the village, the Anxi Chinese draw on existing social lineage ties, or *guanxi* (关系), to extract monetary and material benefits from their Singapore kin. They use moral arguments and persuasion to encourage the Singapore Chinese to become more involved in village affairs. By recalling their kinship ties and insisting on the moral duties of their Singapore relatives, the Anxi Chinese have managed to tap into the sentiments, including guilt, harboured by the Singapore Chinese, and are thus able to create a moral economy based on a sense of moral responsibility.

The Anxi Chinese publicly display various types of social recognition which they bestow on their Singapore kin for contributing to village development. By honouring them, the Anxi Chinese further strengthen the moral economy.

However, this moral economy is not a harmonious one; it is imbued with tension, conflict of interests, rivalry and resentment between the two groups of Chinese. Tension and resentment are most acutely felt by the younger generation of Singapore Chinese who, as the common view outlined above holds, in fact often do *not* feel that they belong to the ancestral village.

Collective Memories and Nostalgic Sentiments

A second major theme to be explored is that of the collective memories and nostalgic sentiments that the Singapore Chinese continue to hold for their ancestral homes. These are especially strong among the immigrant generation. Many of this generation are unable or unwilling to erase their memories and have passed them on to their children, grandchildren and great-grandchildren. Their early experiences in their home villages in China have thus become a sort of collective memory for them and for their descendants.

What concerns us here is the social and historical memories of groups of people. According to Le Goff, memory is an essential element of any individual or collective identity (Le Goff, 1992: 98). Each society has its own forms of memories. Some aboriginal communities in Australia and Africa have no written records but only oral collective memories in the forms of songs and stories. Other societies have their memories written down so that their members and their future generations can turn to them for guidance. Through historical development, social and collective memories undergo changes. Depending on the social conditions and expectations of each historical epoch, collective memory undergoes change through, according to Le Goff, a process of divinization, secularization and rationalization. The focus on mythology and religious activities, in some societies, has led to emphasis on divine ideologies and religious structures and rituals. Many of these have been written into the collective memory of these societies (Le Goff, 1992: 58–64).

Memory is a subjective thought-process. It is the events and situations which individuals have experienced that constitute personal memories. These memories are passed on to others in various ways; these include recording in diaries, memoirs, letters; storytelling; and other forms of oral transmission. Those that are not recorded in any form are often lost permanently (Watson, 1994: 8). These are the individual memories. Apart from them, there are also collective memories. According to Halbwachs, 'while the collective memory endures and draws strength from its base in a coherent body of people, it is individuals as group members who remember' (Halbwachs, 1992: 22). Thus, there are as many collective memories as there are groups and institutions in a society (Halbwachs, 1992: 22). Collective memories are usually shared experiences of individuals within a group, who have 'remembered' events, in a sense that, although they may not have experienced the actual events, they are well versed in the images and imagery of them. These events are often represented in various forms—in historical monuments, stories, paintings, rituals, poetry, music, photographs and films (R. Watson, 1994: 8).

The remembering of events is never systematic. Memories are not logically presented; nor do individuals usually intellectualize them. Representations of collective memory—whether in visible form, as in monuments, paintings, and rituals, or in documented form as in diaries—remain fragmented. Nevertheless, they provide groups of people with images to rely on, when they are in search of the events that affected the life of their ancestors, their society and/or their country. Collective memories allow individuals to reconstruct 'their' collective past—the past of the groups to which they consider themselves to belong—by thinking about what the collective events were like at crucial historical moments. But history and historical events are not snapshots and cannot be seen as such; it is the fluidity of events and their representations that allows for the corresponding flow of images and imagery that is encapsulated as collective memory. History records the interpretation of memories in various contexts—public, private and personal—but memories remain on the individual level.

Collective memories are derived from a collection of individual memories grounded in a particular social context, and therefore represent social memory. However, they are the products of individual understandings and are subject to personal and varying interpretations that change through time and space. Thus, it is not uncommon to have several variants of collective memories.

Historical and social memories are important in helping individuals to establish themselves in relation to the past and to provide anchorage in their search for self-identity in contemporary society, in which the past and the present have become increasingly separated. They provide continuity from the past to the present and into the future, and help to shape present actions and reactions in relation to past and present events, and to permit individuals or groups to use existing knowledge and recollections to pursue future goals. Thus the Singapore Chinese from Anxi 'remember' their ancestral or home villages and the social events there, and these memories help them decide 'who they are' and where they 'come' from, and in turn push them to react to (for example) calls for help from their ancestors' villages.

Since 'while the collective memory endures and draws strength from its base in a coherent body of people, it is individuals as group members who remember' (Halbwachs, 1992: 22), individual memory must be located within the thought of the relevant social group of people in order for it to become meaningful and relevant to all within it. In many societies without written traditions there are 'memory specialists, memory men', who are similar to the 'genealogists, guardians of the royal lawbooks, historians of the court, traditionalists' (Le Goff, 1992: 56) of literate society. Their main preoccupation is to maintain the cohesion of the group through a continuous reminder of the commonality of its members. Le Goff considers this to be 'ethnic memory' (Le Goff, 1992: 55), and argues that 'the accumulation of elements within memory [are] part of everyday life' of individuals (Le Goff, 1992: 55).

In collective memory, family plays an important role in establishing the framework for the types of memories to be included and for the transmission of such memories to its members. Because certain activities and ideas are repeatedly transmitted to family members, they become deeply embedded in their minds and are reproduced for future use. Part of this involves the reproduction of the past.

The significance of collective memory lies in the roles which it plays within a society. It does not only help people to understand certain historical events but also present ones. Collective memories are known as historical facts, which embody a set of values that society once upheld. While some of these values are still held by the group concerned, others are, or have been, discarded. However, collective memories may also be reinvented, and attempts may be made to revive traditional values to assist the group in attempting to deal with social change.

Memory is seen as an instrument and an objective of power. As such, a struggle for domination over remembrance and tradition involves the manipulation of memory (Le Goff, 1992: 98). Types of memory that are reconstructed and/or censored are deliberately and consciously chosen in contemporary society in order to assert authority and/or to legitimize one's position. To understand how this works for a community or an individual, it is important to position collective memories within a relevant social framework. Halbwachs looks at the initial preservation of collective memory as the primary domain of the elite class, which has an entrenched tradition and sits atop a class hierarchy. Since it is the elite version of the collective memory that dominates society, it is also the elite version of social values that is dominant within society. However, when a group of non-elite enter the elite class, the society needs to reorganize and modify, to some degree, the frameworks of its memory, either by distorting its past or by limiting the field of memory in order to screen out less desirable elements. Often, such a reorganization is required because the new elite demand that their actions and values be incorporated into the collective memory. In this process, it is not uncommon for societies to 'forget' their remote past and only concentrate on the recent past contiguous with the present.

Additionally, Halbwachs argues that when a certain category of people have been conferred higher prestige and when this is collectively recognized by society, it is because these people and their activities are believed to have contributed most to the entire social body (Halbwachs, 1992: 138). Thus collective memories of the contributions of these people, in the forms of socio-political or economic functions and philanthropic and charitable acts, are based on the judgement that society makes of its members (Halbwachs, 1992: 144). In traditional societies, these are often associated with a gentry-elite class and it is institutions involving these factors that have become established. It is this elite class that is subjected to challenges by new groups. The moral tradition of the elite is therefore part of the established social value system. Halbwachs argues that it is the rich who are responsible for imparting the moral tradition to the poor, for they do not have a moral tradition. However, with changing social order, moral traditions are subjected to challenges from the newly-rich-turned-elite, and there is thus an emergence of a new morality. The new members of the elite may comprise an assortment of people ranging from artisans to merchants and others. Today, the moral traditions that have emerged from the villagers are also significant in restructuring the social order of the Chinese society.

In modern society, the idea of virtue of the wealthy is that each family head has amassed wealth through his or her own efforts—an obvious ploy to justify one's position. To a large extent, Halbwachs equates the scale of wealth with the scale of perceived personal merit, and the moral value of the possessor of quantities of goods can be evaluated through this equation. However, such a person and his or her qualities have to endure the scrutiny of his or her society over a passage of time in order for the society to evaluate his or her contributions. Thus, his or her contributions to society, rather than the scale of his or her wealth, are the basis for his or her moral standing. After a considerable length of time, and if his or her qualities and contributions can make an imprint on the memory of the society, memories will serve to perpetuate the legacy of such a person or class of persons. In traditional society, the conferring of titles provides recognition of the desirable social qualities and virtues.

What happens with the emergence of new wealth and a new elite? Within the new moral tradition, wealth remains an important social asset, and those with wealth, irrespective of their occupational categories, assume high social status. Members of this new elite do not fit into the traditional framework of 'success'—wealth and money now become important yardsticks to measure their achievement. They therefore need to modify the existing social order to create an elite space for themselves. At the same time, the tradition must recognize them as the new successful elite.

Inevitably, the modification of tradition and the creation of new tradition come into conflict with existing tradition. The relationship between tradition and morality also comes into question. In Halbwachs' view, the old tradition continues to be seen as one that corresponds to morality, while the new tradition is associated with immorality or, at best, with utilitarian morality. Utilitarian morality is used by the new elite, in a society experiencing a rise of commercial activity, to justify its commercial moneymaking activities, and it presupposes the need to contribute something back to society, such as philanthropic actions, perhaps involving an element of altruism.

As changes occur within a society, it is thus forced to adopt new values, and this involves consulting alternative collective memories and frameworks of social values in order to establish a new tradition and a new order of social values. Here, in addition to the dominant elite tradition and the elite version of collective memories that the society has been exposed to, alternative collective memories of various groups—not only of the new elite, but also of various existing social groups such as lineage, family and minority groups—become important. These groups begin to exert their presence and demand that their memories and social histories be incorporated into the mainstream societal thought process.

An anthropological discourse on collective memory and nostalgia is therefore important in attempting to understand a group of people—be it an extended family, a lineage, or a community—who are seeking to re-explore their cultural roots and identity. It is possible to see the pursuit of memory as promoting and maintaining cultural formations in all their fullness and complexity.

Kuchler and Melion (1991: 7) argue that memory is characterized as follows:
(1) it is an actively constructed social and cultural process;
(2) it operates through representations;
(3) the modalities of recollection are historically based and the project of understanding is a historical one; and
(4) forgetting and recollecting are allied mnemonic functions where forgetting is a selective process through which memory achieves social and cultural dimensions.

Memory can be tapped and activated through processes of philosophical inquiry, but it does not itself generate these processes (Kuchler and Melion, 1991: 3). It is thus significant to understand the ways in which experience shapes and reshapes the collective memory. For example, nostalgia is seen as a response to dissatisfaction with one's immediate situation. Such dissatisfaction provides an individual with a motivation to idealize past events as, by looking towards an idealized past, one can momentarily disengage oneself from the immediate, less-than-enchanting present (Nosco, 1990: 4). Nostalgia is thus one way in which collective memories can allow individuals or social groups to recreate the past to satisfy their present needs for identity and for interaction.

In understanding memory and its recollection, the accuracy and exactness of each event has become a subject of contention by scholars of inquiry, especially those practising psychology and psychiatry. Lengthy works have been written on this issue. However, it is not the objective of this work to discuss the scientific inquiry into memory and of the accuracy of recollection. We are interested not so much in what is 'true', but rather, in the process of recollection and in the events, images and representations that are recalled as important. This involves selection (Fentress and Wickham, 1992).

The role of women is particularly important here. Geary (1994) argues for the need to study the 'memory of women' who are active in remembering, preserving and transmitting the past. It is through such acts of preservation, structuring and moulding that the past, along with its institutions, is remembered and its dynamics brought to knowledge in the present. Here, both women as rememberers and women who are remembered are important issues. However, while women as rememberers take a front seat in this area of collective memory, women tend to pale into insignificance in patriarchal social structures and are less likely to be remembered than men. Such is true in Chinese society, where remembered women are few. It remains to be seen whether, at the level of oral history, the prominence of women is more readily articulated than in the written tradition (Geary, 1994: 51–73).

This issue of the role of women is related to the issue of the professionalization of the carriers of memory. Oral transmission was and is still an important method of imparting memories to future generations, especially at individual and familial levels. At lineage and other social levels, however, there is a tendency, particularly in Chinese society, to establish memory on a permanent basis. Oral transmission here gives way to written records, which are kept by men. Genealogies, as official records, serve to formalize present events and preserve them as memories for future generations. Such texts maintain a high level of accuracy, which is important for future reference. Such documents and records of the past enable us to reconstruct it and to revive the memories associated with it, thus providing continuity from past to present. This allows for the development of two streams of memories. One is the official version, as represented by genealogies and written records. The other is the unofficial oral stream at individual and folk levels. These two may converge or diverge. Convergence and divergence spell out the emphases on different materials that different groups make in conscious remembering. This differential selection of material is very much influenced by the social, cultural, or political environment during the time and at the place when the collective memory was transmitted and documented and, obviously, by the different positions of groups within the current society.

In the daily discourse of individuals, from storytelling to the reproduction of cultural items and rituals, it is the personal version of memory that we are confronted with. What is articulated consists of individual, personal and fragmented accounts of what individuals can remember, what they choose to remember and what they want to remember. These accounts come in the forms of stories, reminiscences and matter-of-fact statements. These are usually told to members of the inner kinship network, and children hear them from their elders. Such stories form part of the oral history of the early emigrants who arrived and settled in Singapore.

The operation of collective memory can help us to further understand the emotions and attachment of the migrants and their descendents to their ancestral home villages, and can also help us to comprehend, for instance, the eagerness of the first-generation Singapore Chinese to visit them, as well as to impart large sums of money and other contributions to help with village reconstruction.

Singapore Anxi Chinese and Their Collective Memory

The collective memory of the Singapore Anxi Chinese is tied to their shared understandings of their ancestral home, their past experiences and their present expectations. The crux of it lies in their desire to perpetuate a cultural identity. These cultural memories—including bittersweet ones of great difficulties, individual memories of first-generation migrants themselves, etc.— include an awareness of their ancestral home. This collective memory propels the migrants-turned-citizens to visit their ancestral villages, and pushes them to contribute financially to the socio-cultural and economic life of the villages. However, this collective memory may have a negative impact on some, who do not wish to visit their home village.

The collective memories of these Singapore Chinese are thus selective. In reconstructing past events, the collective memory of most Singapore migrant Chinese is one of poverty. Early experiences of poverty pushed many migrants to endure great difficulties and to work hard. Many recount the great difficulties and poverty that they were in, their fear of the unknown when they set sail for Singapore, and their eventual success, however modest, in Singapore. They also remember their struggle for survival in their villages before migrating. It is this memory that they have kept alive and that they choose to pass on to their descendants.

Today, even as many Anxi migrants to Singapore have become relatively successful and have accumulated modest wealth, they continue to work hard. This form of work ethic is now widely studied and debated. Neo-Confucian scholars have argued that it is attributable to the existence of a Confucian Ethic, citing the economic success of Taiwan, South Korea, Hong Kong and Singapore, all of which have been influenced by Confucian ideology.

In Singapore, the state has consciously used various elements of Confucian ideology for purposes of economic and social engineering.[1]

Be that as is may, this collective memory of poverty is instrumental and has become, in part, a tool in dealings between the Singapore migrant Chinese and their village counterparts. By recalling the poverty that they have undergone, Singapore migrant Chinese may adopt a liberal, humane attitude towards the existing poverty experienced by their village kin in their ancestral villages. Gradually, after initially helping members of their immediate families and lineage, many became involved in village reconstruction, and since the 1978 reform years, they have become involved in county-level financial, technical and informational activities. In doing so, they have helped transform the emigrant villages from extreme poverty to relative prosperity.

The collective memory also provides the Singaporeans with a sense of identity, based on common cultural roots: 'who they are' is related to 'where their ancestors came to Singapore from', and the social customs, rituals and religious elements, now routinized as part of the communal social fabric in Singapore, which they brought with them. When visiting the ancestral village, they thus bring along their own understandings of these. Their strong sense of affinity (*ganqing,* 感情) for their ancestral home (*zuxiang,* 祖乡) allows them to locate their identity within a known and manageable social framework grounded in kinship ties.

Recalling collective memory and transmitting it to younger generations serve to keep alive the experiences of the ancestors and remind them of their ancestral villages and wider kinship networks. Most of these elements of the collective memory are transmitted, through oral stories and reminiscences, in a spontaneous and fragmented manner. Nevertheless, they remind them of their ritual obligations and duties to ancestors and encourage them to engage in cultural reproduction.

The Ideology of Moral Duty

This all brings us to consider the role of ideology in shaping the attitudes of the Singapore Chinese towards their ancestral villages and the effect this has on cultural identity. Although they have experienced various phases of change in Singapore, they continue to be governed by a sense of moral duty to their ancestral villages. What is this sense of moral duty? Is it related to Confucianism, Buddhism or what?

Halbwachs sees the preservation of collective memory as an important *moral* duty, irrespective of whether it belongs to an individual, family, lineage or a social group, arguing that it is the desire to preserve this memory that leads group members to embark on philanthropic or charitable acts. Such acts are a tangible outcome that preserves the memory of the giver after his or her death. Such philanthropy thus aims for future gratification after the passing away of an individual or group, but also consolidates the socio-moral fabric of a society.

Weber (1966) argued that such creation and giving-away of wealth, involving a sacrifice of enjoyment, are grounded in one's moral duties. Weber considered specifically Christian calls for an inner-worldly asceticism in one's spiritual development. Thus, although the creation of wealth is important, the giving-away of this wealth is more important. This sense of moral duty is a matter of fulfilling God's calling, towards ultimate salvation and the giving-away of wealth is done in devotion to God Himself. In this Christian model of moral duty, Perry (1909) argues for the uncomplicated good nature of human beings as the key to moral duty to a community by individuals. The actions are altruistic, for the individuals desire neither fame nor social reward.

In Confucianism, the moral duty of an individual is governed by the observance of the five moral values. They are: *ren* (仁), or humanity; *yi* (义), righteousness; *li* (礼), rituals; *zhong* (忠), loyalty; and *xiao* (孝), filial piety. In the ideal-type situation, a person who has perfected all five moral values is a 'gentleman', or *junzi* (君子). Such a gentleman commits himself totally to the cultivation of these moral values as second nature. For an individual to attain the highest level of moral cultivation, he or she has to routinize moral practices as part of his or her daily routine.

To achieve moral and spiritual perfection, *ren* (仁) is most important. Tu argues that human nature is perfectible and that perfection can be achieved through a continuous process of 'inner illumination and self transformation' (Tu, 1985: 19) of a moral and spiritual kind (Tu, 1985: 22). According to Tu, self-knowledge of one's mental state and inner feeling is the key to this process of inner illumination and transformation (1985: 19). This self-knowledge will enable an individual to act, create and transform his or her self into a perfect self (Tu, 1985: 19–20). It is 'an objectless awareness, a realisation of the human possibility of "intellectual intuition"' (Tu, 1985: 20). One's true or real nature is thus 'a self-creating and self-directing process' (Tu, 1985: 20). It is also a liberating process, freeing oneself from the trappings of human desires. It is this that is considered becoming human.

In the book of Mencius, according to Tu, human beings are endowed with moral sense, which consists of four basic human feelings: commiseration, shame and dislike, deference and compliance, and right and wrong (Tu, 1985: 24). It is these feelings that push individuals to learn and refine the 'self', a term which refers to both conscience and consciousness. Interestingly, and revealingly, the character *xin* (心) represents both 'moral sense' and 'self'—

i.e., the conscious self is thus essentially a moral entity (Tu, 1985: 24). Imbued with the four basic feelings, which serve as imperatives for moral cultivation, human beings are able to cultivate and attain perfection. Thus, Confucian teaching sees altruistic motivation as an important force for the perfection of the self.

Morality and moral actions are to be found in daily social intercourse. The *Book of Filial Piety* (Xiaojing, 孝经) stresses the moral responsibility of an individual to his or her parents, to family, and to other lineage members, including the dead ancestors. To neglect them is to be unfilial, *buxiao* (不孝); consciously to neglect one's parents or ancestors is to descend to the lowest level of moral irresponsibility. Thus, a consciousness of the responsibility to one's parents is a moral requirement. Aged parents should be regarded with high esteem, and an individual is expected conscientiously to look after the spiritual and material well-being of his or her parents. There are two reasons for this, the first being that the individual is indebted to his or her parents for the gift of life, the second being that the individual is indebted to his or her parents for raising him or her from infancy to adulthood. This form of indebtedness is incurred irrespective of the treatment the person has received during the various stages of growth and development. In the *Xiaojing*, individuals are expected to transcend personal feelings in carrying out filial duty and becoming morally worthy.

Buddhism has also influenced Chinese moral beliefs. The Buddhist notion of karma and merit-making shapes the way in which adherents devote themselves to cultivating moral good in order to achieve spiritual enlightenment. The Buddhist notion that one can realize one's self serves to encourage individuals to cultivate their spiritual being (*xiuxin*, 修心) through this-worldly asceticism. This involves a willingness to sacrifice immediate material enjoyment to prepare for otherworldly spiritual achievement. In particular, *xiuxin* involves doing good and depriving oneself of all material and sensual pleasures. The ultimate goal is to attain Buddha-hood, of becoming a Buddha, *chengfo* (成佛).

Within the Mahayana Buddhist tradition, the concept of the bodhisattva reveals the ultimate path towards Buddhist morality. Differing from Theravada Buddhism, which focuses on self-enlightenment, Mahayana Buddhism stresses mass salvation through the help of the bodhisattva, a perfected being who postpones his or her attainment of nirvana indefinitely in order to help all sentient beings to attain enlightenment. This altruism of the bodhisattva is something that those who aspire to Buddhahood will attempt to emulate. The taking of the bodhisattva vow by adherents is an important step in this process of self-realization. Hence, the bodhisattva is an excellent example of a superior altruistic being—total devotion to the welfare of others and different from the many who desire to help someone in order to fragrance the name of the individual family on the lineage.

Buddhist doctrine declares that the heart of every individual is capable of doing good deeds. Within the mundane world, 'doing good' is translated into practical selfless actions that are aimed at assisting the welfare of others, in both spiritual and material senses. Good deeds and works of charity are regarded as important social actions.

Other key concerns of Buddhist behaviour are the notions of karma and merit-making. Every individual is subjected to karmic influences, and the situation of an individual is the result of accumulated individual acts during both past and present lives. There are both good and bad karma. The main purpose of performing good deeds is merit-making, as an accumulation of merit and good karma in this life can cancel bad karma previously accumulated. Since good merits can be transferred from one person to another, individuals can engage in meritorious deeds to help the dead to increase their store of good merits. It is thus a common sight to see charity being carried out in the name of the dead in order to provide them with a sufficient store of merits and good karma (the latter is also essential for ultimate enlightenment). Charity work and good deeds may likewise be carried out for the living, so as to ensure that in the after-life, and/or in future lives, individuals will be relieved of extreme suffering. A store of good karma will also enable the dead to move swiftly from the netherworld to the human plane. This is important, for it is only when one is reborn on the human plane of existence that there is hope for the ultimate cessation of rebirth.

Finally, Daoist morality considers that goodness and compassion are parts of human nature. Daoism sees moral good as the flow of nature. To do what is not good is to be unnatural and against the Dao. Moral good and moral duty are thus essential parts of human nature.

Reinventing a Chinese Culture

A fourth theme that will be investigated in this study is that of cultural reinvention and cultural reproduction. Hobsbawm defines 'invented tradition' as 'a set of practices, normally governed by overtly or tacitly accepted rules and of a ritual or symbolic nature, which seeks to inculcate certain values and norms of behaviour by repetition, which automatically implies continuity with the past' (Hobsbawm and Ranger, 1983: 1). The term 'inventing traditions' is taken to mean a 'process of formalisation and ritualisation, characterised by reference to the past' (Hobsbawm and Ranger, 1983: 4). The invention of tradition is required under three circumstances: the first is a need to establish social cohesion and membership of a group within a real or imagined community; the second is a need to legitimize the institutions and authority structures of a given society; and the third is the need to provide a set of values and beliefs for members of a community (Hobsbawm and Ranger, 1983: 8).

In the process of reinventing a culture, the significant elements that a group of people consider as representational of their culture are selected. These include material icons, ritual functions, ritual behaviours and social customs. During the process of reinvention, there are two groups of players. One group is engaged in the decision-making process. Its task is to detail the elements that are to be reinvented. This group comprises the elite and dominant members of a society, who have the resources and intellectual and cultural depth to engineer the reinvention of selected cultural elements that they see as significant for portraying their culture and cultural identity. The second group consists of those engaged in the actual process of reinventing these cultural elements and acts. These players lack the resources and administrative skills needed to initiate the process of cultural reinvention, but they are active participants in carrying it out. The culture that is reinvented within a society can thus be seen as the idealized and imagined culture of the dominant group. Through time, this invented culture disseminates into the wider community and becomes accepted as the culture. Under such an ideal situation, no one within the community would question its origin.

The timing and the socio-political context in which cultural invention takes place are important factors to consider. Success in cultural reinvention can only be realized when the timing is correct and when the political climate is conducive to reproduction. It is important that members of the group share a collective need for such a reinvention and believe that such action is necessary for the survival of their social collectivity. A conviction of such need will push the members to group together and engage in this process of reinvention. However, success can only be achieved if there is no hostile political climate to interfere with cultural reproduction. A relaxed and liberal climate will enable the group to engage in the reproduction of cultural elements without fear of reprisal for its members and without the suppression of its cultural practices. In many cases, it is important that the state supports such reinvention.

Within a migrant society where there are numerous groups in existence, each group attempts to reinvent its own culture. Within the Singapore Chinese community there are numerous groups based on dialect and territorial affiliations. These have brought varieties of cultural elements and have placed varying degrees of significance on the various cultural elements brought from their ancestral villages. Thus, there are several subcultural systems among Chinese subgroups.

However, for the Singapore Chinese, the ancestral village may provide a physical space in which elaborate socio-religious activities that are no longer fashionable within Singapore society are carried out. Functions conducted in the ancestral village are either religious or have strong religious overtones. Communal religious fairs and ancestor worship have become two important types of activity and the *raison d'etre* for village visits, and are conducted with great elaboration.

In the ancestral village, such socio-religious activities were not the central focus of village life until the early 1980s, when economic liberalization brought about some socio-cultural liberation. Formerly, from about 1950 to 1980, traditional practices had not been regarded as significant by the younger generation, and older villagers had come to realize their inability to carry out many of these activities. Only with the return of Singapore lineage members did attempts to revive and reproduce certain aspects of socio-religious practices begin. Thus, their reproduction within the village milieu can be seen as an outcome of a process of negotiation between the Singapore Chinese and the villagers.

When the Singapore Chinese began to visit their ancestral villages, they brought along the knowledge and cultural practices that they were familiar with in Singapore, and sought to reproduce them in the ancestral village. Within these and other Chinese villages, many of the cultural practices of the pre-Communist era were considered a waste of precious resources, and this was true of religious practices, as religion was considered superstition and was officially banned.

However, since the 1978 reform, the Chinese state has formally recognized the existence of institutional religions. Although religious practices continue to be low-key affairs, and, any form of organized religious function still continues to receive close attention of Communist officials, within the ancestral villages such functions have received a more liberal treatment. However, the villagers are forced to rely on their collective memories to reconstruct them, while ritual practices must be consciously constructed to suit the political ideology in order to safeguard the interests of the villagers and not to offend the state.

As a result of the differences in the social environments and political requirements experienced by the two groups of lineage descendents, those in the village and those from Singapore, there exists a great gulf between them in the understanding and interpretation of cultural and religious practices. What we see today in the ancestral village is thus a tradition negotiated and invented by the two groups, based on a shared understanding of what constitute the core elements of the culture and of what can be practised within the existing socio-political framework without arousing official dissatisfaction.

The content of this negotiated culture is geared towards ancestor worship and folk religion. These practices are known to both the Singapore and Anxi Chinese. However, there remain differences between them as to the style, ritual content and elaboration of these activities. An agreement on practice has been reached, and so today we see each lineage conducting ancestor worship and folk religious practices according to its own internally-agreed-upon agenda.

The invention of tradition is thus an outcome of a process of negotiation between various elements found within the social group of the community at large, and what are seen to be common and shared cultural elements are reproduced and accepted by all, while elements that do not have the support of the majority will either be eliminated or confined to subgroups and reflective of the particularistic values of those subgroups.

'Foreign' elements of culture may be introduced when inventing tradition. Cultural elements also undergo change and adaptation to new situations, resulting in new forms of practice and new interpretations despite the continued use of the old contents. Hybridization of old and new contents occurs, as culture changes. Thus, a quest for cultural authenticity becomes less useful than a study of how groups develop and interpret their cultural practices.

Bourdieu argues that possession of cultural capital by an individual will place his or her in a high position within society, thus allowing him or her a position in the social structure that would otherwise be inaccessible. Cultural capital, although it is symbolic capital, thus acts to enhance the economic status of individuals, groups or societies that possess it (Bourdieu, 1993: 75). Persons in possession of cultural capital who are able to make names for themselves and attain social prestige are called cultural bankers (Bourdieu, 1993: 75).

During the process of cultural reinvention in ancestral villages, selected members of both Singapore and Anxi Chinese groups are seen to be such cultural bankers. They possess the knowledge of ancestor worship and religious practices and help to reproduce them, so that the rituals are once again practised within the village structure. These practices bring the Singapore and village lineage members together in ritualistic fashion to acknowledge their shared identity.

Chinese Overseas and the China Connection

A study of the Singapore Chinese and their ancestral villages would not be complete without an understanding of their positions within the global history of Chinese overseas. Lately there has been great interest in the study of the global spread of Chinese overseas, as well as of their communities and their links with China in general. This has been in part due to the economic success of the 'little dragons' of Asia (including Hong Kong, Singapore and Taiwan), where large Chinese populations reside. In this book, we will term the Chinese in the Diaspora as "Chinese overseas", in order not to confuse with the term "overseas Chinese" which has political overtones.

Two main streams of thought exist concerning the increasing economic integration between Mainland China, Hong Kong, Taiwan, Macau, and the Chinese communities overseas, the first being *Da Zhonghua* (大中华), or the 'Greater China' thesis,[2] and the other *Wenhua Zhongguo* (文化中国), or the 'Cultural China'[3] model. Both approaches attempt to explain the continued cultural links among Mainland China; the peripheral areas of Hong Kong, Taiwan and Macau; and the Chinese communities overseas.

The idea of Greater China, according to Harding (1993: 660–686), can be seen at three levels. One level is manifested in the emergence of a transnational Chinese economy, involving the rapid rate of economic growth and integration of China with Hong Kong, Macau and Taiwan, and with other Chinese communities. The interlocking relationships and the rapid growth are attributed to economic complementarities and cultural similarities among these regions, as well as the political integration of the first two. These developments have led to calls for the formation of a single economic bloc that would include all of the Chinese communities.

A second level of the Greater China idea is that of a globalized Chinese culture. The 'Greater China' thesis assumes that there is increased cultural interaction between people of Chinese descent internationally. Currently, many Chinese from Taiwan, Southeast Asia and many Western countries visit Mainland China. There are also visitors from the integrated regions of Hong Kong and Macau, and the number of Chinese from China who visit Chinese communities overseas has increased. Communication between these areas has grown with better and more open telecommunication, and the flow and interaction of both popular and traditional forms of culture between China and Chinese communities elsewhere is on the increase.

On yet another level, 'Greater China' is associated with the idea of a reunified Chinese state including Mainland China, Hong Kong, Macau, Taiwan, Tibet and Xinjiang. Harding suggests the ways which a reunified Chinese state might be governed. Should it be governed according to a 'One Country, Two Systems' policy, as Hong Kong is? Or should the 'reunified Chinese state' or 'Greater China' be governed as a 'Chinese Federal Republic'?

In the twenty-first century, as Hong Kong and Macau have returned to Chinese rule since 1997 and 1999 respectively and both regions have continued their capitalist economic system with great success and have achieved greater economic and social integration with the Mainland, such a model is regarded as a possibility for Taiwan although there continues to be resistance from the democratic camp. However, with the election of Ma Ying-jeou of the China-friendly Kuomintang (KMT) Party as Taiwan president in 2008, there are great hopes that Taiwan would consider reunification with the Mainland under either the 'One Country Two Systems' model or a variant of it.

A central criticism of the 'Greater China' thesis is its failure to account for the status of the overseas Chinese communities scattered throughout the world. Wang Gungwu (1993a: 926–948) has argued that the use of 'Greater China' should be context-specific. When 'Greater China' is used to refer to a transnational economic system, it is important to point out that the 'economic integration' refers more to the 'South China Economic Periphery', where economies have been booming and where there are links among Hong Kong, Macau, Taiwan and other southern areas of China. When 'Greater China' implies a political concept, it refers simply to those regions within the PRC. In the sense of a 'globalized culture', the term includes overseas Chinese communities, where older Chinese values have undergone changes due to modern influences and adaptations with which those who live in them might find it possible to identify (Wang, 1993a: 926).

Chinese overseas have political allegiance and national loyalty to their nation-states, and increasingly have developed nationalist feelings for their countries. By confirming their loyalty to these nation-states (Wang, 1993a: 940), they have gained the trust of their respective national governments. The participation of Chinese overseas in the economic development of South China has gradually come to be accepted by the national leaders of the countries where the overseas Chinese live, and their actions are not considered to be disloyal to their nations (Wang, 1993a: 940). Wang argues that it is the acceptance of the Chinese as full-fledged, loyal citizens that has led to the possibility of their push for cultural autonomy and for its acceptance by the nation-state. Such is now the situation in Singapore, but other countries have yet to adopt such an attitude fully. An example of this is Indonesia, where Indonesian Chinese investments in the PRC continue to be viewed with suspicion by the Indonesian government.

The other main model that attempts to explain the increasing economic and cultural integration between Mainland China and Chinese communities elsewhere is the 'Cultural China' model or thesis initiated by Tu Weiming. The Cultural China thesis offers three symbolic universes. The first of these includes Mainland China, Taiwan, Hong Kong and Singapore, which are populated primarily by ethnic Chinese. To the second universe belong the Chinese communities that form significant political minorities within their 'adopted' countries—Malaysia and the United States are parts of this universe.

The third symbolic universe consists of individual men and women—mainly scholars, teachers, journalists, industrialists, traders, entrepreneurs and writers—who attempt to understand China and bring their understanding of China to their own linguistic communities (Tu, 1994: 13–14). According to Tu, this universe membership in the global Chinese culture is defined in terms of cultural understanding and acceptance, rather than ethnicity.

Tu argues that the increasing influence of the overseas Chinese communities has created a situation where the periphery has become a centre in its own right, with much power and influence. He writes that 'it is unprecedented for the geopolitical centre to remain entrenched while the periphery presents such powerful and persistent economic and cultural challenges' (Tu, 1994: 13), and that 'the centre no longer has the ability, insight or legitimate authority to dictate the agenda for "Cultural China"' (Tu, 1994: 34).

Chinese overseas communities have attracted much attention among scholars who study the 'Chinese Diaspora' phenomenon. In one study, a group of scholars called for the study of Chinese overseas as part of 'Chinese Transnationalism' (Ong and Nonini, 1997). In another, Peter Van der Veer (1995) explored the 'politics of space' as a mediating factor between a displaced population's relation to a homeland and its relation to the nation-state of the displaced population. As he studied Indian populations living in different places around the world, his research can be classified as concerning a South Asian Diaspora. According to him, it is the 'politics of space' that connects Indian populations regardless of where they live. This is a politics by which the migrants, or the diaspora ethnic community, contest with the nation-state for a place to live and for a space to express their cultural and ethnic identities. Van der Veer sees space as the alienating property of the nation-state and not as a property of the Diaspora. The migrant communities thus continue to experience marginalized positions and retain marginal spaces.

In Van der Veer's work, this politics of space has grown as a result of two primary factors: British colonialism and the emergence of indigenous Indian culture and religion. He argues that it was British colonialism that brought about the sensitivity, which resulted in a search for an indigenous ideology to compensate for the British ideology. The result was, according to Van der Veer, the emergence of an indigenous Indian culture and religion, which has formed the ideological basis for Indians overseas to reproduce their cultural identity.

Not only space but also time is an important factor in the study of diasporas. According to Van der Veer, there are two types of time. One is 'structural time'; its starting reference point is the beginning of colonialism, from which it gradually moves to post-colonial time, then on to contemporary time, and ends with nation-state time. The second type is the so-called 'cultural time' which involves moving back in history to the source of an indigenous culture and its religion, the purpose being to answer contemporary cultural and religious needs. In so doing, cultural reproduction becomes the key concern. Today, the mobility of the Chinese has ushered in a new phase of development where circulatory migration and return migration have been the norm. No longer are the Chinese contended to stay in one place, they move for a variety of reasons. Hence, locating the diaspora self in a transnational environment becomes an important consideration where territorialization and deterritorialization are two counter-movements working in tandem (Kuah-Pearce, 2006).

How relevant are these models to this study of the Singapore Chinese and their *qiaoxiang* connections? I find that the labels are less important than some ideas that have grown out of these various discourses. An important aspect of the Greater China thesis, as well as of the Cultural China thesis, is the concept of a globalized Chinese culture which is important to our understanding of the links between China and Chinese overseas communities. For the Cultural China thesis, the strength of the periphery dictating the agenda of Mainland China has some merit in discussing the contemporary relationship between China and the Chinese overseas. Likewise the issues of structural and cultural time help us to understand the significance of memories, social experiences and the acts of cultural reproduction, while the issue of territorialization and deterritorialization helps us to locate the individuals in a fluid transnational environment.

In searching for an appropriate framework to understand the social relationship of the Singapore Chinese with their *qiaoxiang* counterparts, I feel that the migration/diaspora framework is useful for evaluating the emotions and actions of the community. This framework also allows us to look at various disparate overseas communities from a global-historical perspective.

Therefore, we need to take into consideration the following factors: (i) the migration history; (ii) the changing status of the Chinese overseas from migrant to citizen of the adopted country; (iii) the formation of the Singapore nation-state, with its citizenship and the corresponding question of allegiance either to a national entity, to an ethnic entity, or to both; (iv) and the transnational cosmopolitan environment.

Conceptually, the formation of the Chinese community in Singapore can only be understood as part of the wider global migration history of the Chinese. Globally, the Chinese create physical spaces with which they come to identify, within which they reconstruct their socio-cultural structures. However, they maintain links with their ancestral villages through occasional letters and regular remittances.

Early Chinese sojourners to Southeast Asia went in search of economic opportunities and employment and, as sojourners—mostly were temporary traders or labourers—rarely considered settling as an option. Social and political forces were hostile towards their settling permanently. In the event, however, many settled down as permanent or semi-permanent migrants.

Although the concept of 'sojourning' was traditionally defined to refer to temporary movement to an unfamiliar place, Wang has considered sojourning not only as a temporary phenomenon, but also as a settlement for a lifetime, which might stretch over generations. Such sojourning is taken to mean 'that a highly particularistic loyalty towards family and the clan-based village formed the basis of linked space over a great distance. Under these circumstances, it was possible to create small independent groups, which were later supported by the advancement in technology and information. Sojourning for them was based on physical and trading ties with their ancestral homes' (Wang, 1993b: 138).

Today, the telecommunication revolution provides quick information and allows individual Chinese to communicate and travel at ease. This access to modern technology has brought individuals together (Wang, 1993b) and has made it possible to create an intensive network of linkages for Chinese in different countries, irrespective of their locality. What lies between those in overseas communities and those in their ancestral villages is the social distance between them.

After the formation of the Singapore nation-state, the Chinese in Singapore were given a choice of citizenship. Those who opted to remain permanently adopted Singapore as their home and assumed Singapore citizenship. This issue of loyalty to China or to Singapore remained important as a contest of allegiance until the 1980s. Only in the 1990s was there an acceptance of a Singapore Chinese identity by the Singapore state, a development which has created less suspicion within Singapore and between it and its geopolitically sensitive neighbours. In addition, globalization has also restructured the government mentality towards the mobility of its citizens in the global sphere.

The conceptual transition from temporary sojourner to Singapore citizen and now to global citizen is an important factor to consider in our attempt to study the Singapore Chinese and their *qiaoxiang* connections. It allows us to understand the sentiments that the Singapore Chinese continue to attach to their ancestral homes, and their present actions and participation in village reconstruction and cultural reproduction.

Contest of Identities

An underlying theme throughout this study is the issue of identity among the Singapore Chinese. Contests of identities occur at various levels. There is a contest of identity between the Singapore and the Anxi Chinese at the lineage level. On the state level, there is a contest between Chinese ethnicity and Singapore national identity. At the global level, there is a contest among Singapore Chinese identity, Mainland Chinese identity and global Chinese overseas identity as well as a global citizen identity.

At the lineage level, the issue of identity is a crucial one. By acknowledging the existence of the ancestral village and participating in village affairs, Singapore Chinese affirm that they are part of the lineage structure. They become insiders to the activities of the village and lineage. Inducting the younger generation of Singapore Anxi Chinese into the lineage structure becomes crucial, as in many Chinese overseas communities, a permanent break in lineage structure has already occurred. Chinese communities in the United States, Australia and Europe have entered their third, fourth and fifth generations, and most Chinese have very little knowledge of their ancestral villages, much less active interaction with relatives in the villages. In contrast to this, the Anxi Chinese in Singapore have consciously maintained lineage continuity and have ensured that a permanent break has not occurred.

The Anxi example thus illustrates the point that migration does not necessarily lead to the cessation of contacts with ancestral villages, and that ultimate integration with adopted countries, as in the nation-state, does not have to mean a discontinuity with the ancestral villages from whence the migrants, or their ancestors, first emigrated.

However, some Singapore Anxi Chinese may be viewed as 'others'. The list of differences between the Singapore Chinese and the Mainland Anxi villagers is a long one, and there are tensions between them. Contact between younger Singapore-born Chinese with Anxi lineage members has been very recent, notably from the 1980s onward and their feeling for 'their' ancestral home is very ambiguous. The great differences in attitudes and general lifestyle make them feel alien to the village members, and both groups are inclined to draw a dividing line between the two groups. Younger Anxi lineage members often feel that the younger Singapore members are arrogant and proud, and so tend to treat them as 'outsiders' and 'others'. Indeed, some younger Singapore members do not want to be seen as 'insiders', and so consciously behave as 'outsiders' when in the village.

However, for some Singapore Chinese, visiting the ancestral village is a return to their cultural roots, serving to reaffirm their Chinese identity as well as helping them to locate themselves within the Singapore polity. Thus, by going to their ancestral base, they come to grips with a hybrid identity that they come to possess.

As citizens of Singapore, Singapore Anxi Chinese are very much influenced by the operation of the policies of multi-ethnicity and nation-building of the Singapore state. Their change of status from migrant to full-fledged citizen has involved a change in identity—they have become Singapore Chinese. On arrival in Singapore, the identity of the Chinese migrants was closely tied to their lineages, villages and territorial boundaries. They were differentiated according to dialect groups. Now, this identity is constantly contested with their national identity, and their cultural practices have been challenged and altered by the forces of modernity.

The creation of a national identity is part of the nation-building process. In Singapore, the state policy has been to create a set of common values among the different ethnic groups in Singapore. This relates to Anderson's (1986) 'imagined community' of the nation-state. The shared values which the Singapore state has, since independence, conscientiously attempted to create for its multi-ethnic population have been to shape them into people who would call themselves 'Singaporean'. To a large degree, this process has been successful, and citizens identify themselves as Singaporean.

Thus the Singapore Chinese today have multiple identities—both as Chinese and as Singaporean. Within their own world, they, as the case of the Anxi Chinese, further identify themselves according to their different dialect and territorial, *tongxiang* (同乡) affiliations. Within the Singapore polity, they are Chinese, an ethnic group within the national boundary of the Singapore nation-state. In the twenty-first century, they also see themselves a part of the globalized citizen identity.

Within a Global Chinese Cultural Network

A final consideration is the study of the globalization of the Singapore Chinese–China connection. One key factor here is the role played by the lineage structure and other traditional institutions in providing an interconnecting network structure for members scattered throughout the world. By exploring the lineage structure as a cultural network and resource base, it is possible to map out the linkages among disparate groups of lineage members. The Singapore Anxi Chinese and their village counterparts have begun to create a network to help bring together lineage members from all over the world. Through their formal institution, the Anxi Association, they consciously search for members, whom they invite to participate in various activities that the Association organizes. Modern information technology has allowed the association to establish a database of membership and to provide a communication channel for its members.

There were early migrations of Chinese to Singapore and other Southeast Asian countries and later migrations to the United States, Australia and Canada, and other countries. In these countries, numerous Chinese communities have thus been created and Chinese associations based on territorial origin or lineage/surname origin have also been formed. The lineage association has been important as a cultural network, and has thus remained a key social institution in contemporary Chinese society.

Lineage organization has created a globalized space for members to interact with one another socially, economically and culturally. Important for this has been the encouragement of lineage members to visit their ancestral villages and to participate in their cultural and religious activities. The lineage has also become actively involved in both economic development of the ancestral home and in trade between China and the rest of the world. In recent years, Ke lineage members have operated businesses in both the ancestral village and in other parts of China. For this and other purposes, the lineage provides necessary social connections (*guanxi*) and helps its members to venture into new economic areas in China and Southeast Asia. In this manner, the lineage has extended its socio-economic space.

The contemporary expanding globalized roles of the Chinese lineage should be conceptualized as a cultural network. With the ancestral village as the conceptual point of origin or source, continuous regional and peripheral interaction takes place through the nodes of this network and its regional and peripheral organizations scattered throughout the world. By belonging to this lineage cultural network, members in various parts of the world are brought together to acknowledge their ancestors and their ancestral home and village; by participating and involving in socio-religious activities and village development, they renew both their lineage and cultural identities.

Methodology

In Singapore, research was conducted in various stages. Participant-observation started in 1991 and was easily conducted, as the author herself is part of the Anxi community and of the Ke lineage, and there was much interest in her work. Non-intrusive participant-observation was conducted on numerous communal socio-religious activities in Singapore. Conversations among lineage members were recorded. Collection of this data was unstructured, but this was followed by 20 interviews with selected members, especially with those actively involved in activities in Singapore and in the development of

Anxi. Two sets of questionnaires were also issued to a random sample of 40 Singapore Anxi lineage members, one for first-generation migrants and the other for those with Anxi ancestry only, in order to provide greater quantitative breadth. The questionnaire interview was conducted with the help of a research assistant. This part of the research was conducted from February to March 1995.

Fieldwork in Anxi did not follow the conventional village-study pattern. It was conducted in Penglai Town (Penglai Zhen), of Anxi County, Fujian, in a manner that I thought would provide me with the most opportunities to interact and to observe the socio-religious functions and decision-making processes. I usually followed Singapore Chinese back to Anxi whenever there were major events that they had organized, and when they were returning to participate in. In such cases I was able to participate and observe as a member as well as a researcher. I followed the conventional anthropological method of participant-observation. I observed, participated and recorded detailed accounts of the social, economic and religious activities of the villagers. I also participated in meetings of the village elders pertaining to their organization of the various functions as well as their meetings with the schools and village cadres. The first trip was made in 1988. I talked extensively to the villagers of various age groups. I also issued two sets of questionnaires in Anxi, one to tap the views and attitudes of the villagers and the other to tap the views of the official cadres. This questionnaire survey was conducted with the help of four researchers from Xiamen University. The two sets of questionnaire were issued to the villagers and cadres primarily in the Kuitou precinct in Penglai where there were a large number of Ke members of the various emigrant villages. These were Penglai Market Town, Lianzhong Village, Lianmeng Village, Lingdong Village, Lingnan Village and Pengxi Village as well as the neighbouring Kuidou Market Town and Kuidou Village. The total number of questionnaire interviews conducted on the villagers was 200; those conducted on cadres at various levels totalled 98. These interviews were conducted in April 1995. Further updates were observed when I visited Anxi on various festive occasions, the last being in 2003.

In addition to the above, I have collected letters from both Singapore and village Chinese and this has provided me with additional information, particularly concerning the livelihood of lineage members during earlier periods.

In conducting this research, I was confronted with several problems. One was the dichotomy insider/outsider. As a member of the community, I am an insider and so was given access to much information. The members were usually friendly and open to me. In this sense I had a great advantage, which made my research much easier. Another advantage is that there had been, on the whole, no desire on the part of informants to 'please' me by saying only things that they thought I wanted to hear. Most of the time, in both Singapore and Anxi, I was regarded as an insider, and a high level of trust was lavished on me.

This brought me to a major dilemma: with so much trust lavished on the researcher, there was an expectation to write only the good and not the bad. To a large degree, the interpretation and the presentation of the data reflects the intersubjective views of the researcher and her informants. While I have consciously attempted to distance myself from my informants, it is inevitable that such subjectivity can intrude into the analysis.

Outline of the Book

In this research, I attempt to bring together various theoretical understandings to the study of the relationship between Singapore Chinese and the emigrant villages, and especially of the continuity between the two. In Chapter 1 I have explored the various themes that are conceptually significant to the understanding of this relationship. Chapter 2 examines how the Singapore Chinese attempted to establish a cultural identity within the Singapore polity, using their experiences in both China and Singapore. It is a multiple identity that they have assumed. Chapter 3 provides some background information about the state of poverty that Anxi experienced during the early years, and even today. Chapter 4 looks at how the Singapore Chinese remember their ancestral village and how their collective memories and early social experiences have played a large role in their way of looking at village life today, thereby influencing their participation in village development.

Chapter 5 examines the role of the Singapore Chinese in village reconstruction, explains why they are primarily involved in the development of infrastructure in the village, and discusses the strategies adopted by the villagers and the village and county-level cadres to encourage them to do so. It also shows how the Singapore Chinese use their contribution to infrastructure development to bargain for concessions in the area of cultural reproduction.

Chapters 6 and 7 look specifically at cultural reproduction—namely, ancestor worship and religious revivalism. Chapter 6 investigates why ancestor worship is significant for both the Singapore Chinese and the villagers, while Chapter 7 explores the extent to which religion and religious fairs have been revived in the village since the mid-1980s.

Chapter 8 examines the rewriting of the genealogy and how, through the genealogy, the two groups reclaimed their social identities and re-established their lineage links. This brings to mind an important conceptual issue—

that of how we should conceptualize the Chinese lineage, given the fact that migration, in both historical and contemporary times, has led to the creation of new Chinese communities around the world. Here I attempt to locate this study within an understanding of the wider Chinese overseas community and to reconceptualize and argue that in contemporary world, we are confronted with a globalized Chinese structure.

Building on the arguments and information of the other chapters, Chapter 9 provides a theoretical conceptualization of the Chinese lineage, arguing for the need to look at Chinese lineage as a cultural network rather than as a social institution.

The concluding Chapter 10 draws together the various themes and explores possible future directions for Chinese overseas communities and the process of maintenance and change of their identities.

2
Constructing a Singapore Chinese Cultural Identity

The changing political and moral order has brought about a renewed search for individual identity, be it ethnic or cultural. As migrant communities throughout the world settle into their countries of adoption and as younger generations become identified with these countries, diaspora experiences are replaced by a sense of affiliation within the boundaries of nation-states. Yet the question remains whether migrant groups can become fully integrated into their adopted nation-states. Violence and tension have become hallmarks of contemporary ethnic politics, and separatism is on the increase—phenomena which sometimes involve migrants. Amidst these developments, the maintenance of a Chinese cultural identity in Singapore, 'Within the four seas, we are brothers' (*sihaizhinei jiexiongdiye,* 四海之內皆兄弟也). This old Chinese saying continues to hold relevance for the Chinese overseas today. The urgency of the search for cultural roots and identity on the part of Chinese in various parts of the world has never been more intense than at the present time. Throughout the world, Chinese community members are becoming more confident of their own communities, irrespective of their minority statuses, as well as more vocal and assertive in their quest for an identity of their own within the nation-states of which they are citizens. They have also participated in mainstream politics, thereby further elevating the statuses of their communities within their nation-states.

In Singapore, the search for cultural identity has pushed the Chinese to re-evaluate their cultural and religious practices to maintain their sense of cultural continuity. Despite the fact that the Chinese constitute the dominant ethnic group in Singapore, comprising 77 per cent of the total population, their pursuit of cultural identity is guarded. Three factors account for this: (1) the heterogeneous character of the Chinese community, (2) the strength of the Singapore state in its role of social engineer, and (3) the issue of multi-ethnic identity. The Singapore state is particularly notable for engineering the development of a Singapore identity that encompasses multiple ethnicities within an acceptable socio-political framework. Calls for lower-level cultural identity during the early years were closely linked to elements of cultural chauvinism and were actively discouraged by the Singapore state. Today, there is a gradual acceptance of the need to develop respective cultural identities by the major ethnic communities.

Creating a Chinese Community in Colonial Singapore

The history of the Chinese who immigrated from the two southern provinces of Guangdong and Fujian to Southeast Asia from the nineteenth through the second half of the twentieth century has been well documented. A later wave of migration, short and intense, occurred in the 1950s and 1960s following the Communist rise to power in Mainland China. Until the 1960s, many Mainland Chinese continued to move out to Southeast Asia, but since then the new nation-states have imposed entry restrictions, which have made it difficult for would-be migrants to enter. There have also been ethnic tensions and racial riots in Indonesia, Malaysia and Singapore that have made these places less attractive. In addition, effective control on emigration imposed by the Communist regime in China after the Cultural Revolution made it even more difficult for Mainland Chinese to emigrate out of China.

In Singapore, as elsewhere, the migrants were mostly from Fujian and Guangdong. Today, the Fujianese-speaking Chinese form the majority within the Chinese community.

There have been three categories of migrants to Singapore. The first, who constituted the majority, arrived under the ticket-credit system where the migrants worked as a contract labour for a period of time until the passage loan was paid off; the second were sponsored by previously-arrived kinsmen; and the third were independent migrants who arrived with little money and few direct kinship connections, but with some knowledge of *Nanyang* (roughly, Southeast Asia) and with the knowledge that they could draw upon the existing social networks that previous migrants had established.

The early migrants were predominantly able-bodied men, who ranged in age from 20 to 50. They were largely from the peasantry and were armed with few skills, but they had a determination to survive, as well as intelligence and a willingness to perform hard labour. It was only in the early twentieth century that women began to arrive. Their arrival helped to create permanent Chinese settlements.

Wang has categorized these early migrants into four categories: traders, coolies, sojourners and re-migrants (Wang, 1991: 3–21). These four groups were represented in early Singapore society, but it was the peasant-turned-trader and the coolie-turned-trader groups that became the pillars of the economic strength of early Singapore. By 1947 the Chinese population in Singapore stood at 730,133, 75 per cent of the total population of 940,824. Singapore thus became a 'Chinese community' amidst a Malay majority in the geopolitics of the region during these early years. This is still the case today.

These early Chinese migrants were differentiated according to lineage, territorial and linguistic background. Eight distinguishable Chinese languages, dialects or sub-dialects were spoken by the migrants—the three major ones were, and still are, Fujianese (福建), Chaozhouese (潮州) and Cantonese (广州). In 1947, Fujianese-speaking Chinese constituted about 40 per cent of the total Chinese population; Chaozhouese speakers comprised 21.5 per cent and Cantonese speakers were 21.6 per cent. The other minority Chinese languages or dialects were Kejia (Hakka) (客家), Hainanese (海南), Xinghua (Hinghoa, 兴化), Fuqing (Hockhchia, 福清) and Fuzhou (Hokchiu, 福州) (Freedman, 1957: 12).

The main areas from which these Chinese came included various districts in Guangdong, from in and around the port city of Guangzhou (Canton), as well as from Siyi (Sze Yap, 四邑), Meixian (Mei Hsien, 梅县) and Putian (莆田). Fujian migrants came from the port city of Xiamen (厦门) and its environs, and from Quanzhou (泉州), Zhangzhou (漳州), Tongan (同安), Longmen (龙门), Nanan (南安) and Anxi (安溪). These emigrant districts are today the *qiaoxiang* (侨乡)—the ancestral villages of the emigrants and their descendants. Since the 1978 reform in China, these *qiaoxiang* have experienced rapid social and economic transformation as a result of the flow of capital into the region and the increase in their relations with overseas Chinese, and have become important growth nodes and cultural centres in South China.

A sizeable group of immigrants have come from the numerous villages in Anxi County in Fujian. These numbered over 40,000 during the first half of the twentieth century, and the immediate post-war years, 1945–50, witnessed some 20,000 more. Today, the total number of Chinese from Anxi and their Singapore-born descendents is estimated at 185,309, about 10 per cent of the total Chinese population of Singapore (*Anxi Xianzhi*, 1994, vol. 2: 854).

During the nineteenth and early twentieth centuries very few women emigrated from China because of the political restrictions on the part of the Qing, Nationalist rule, and British colonial government policies and also because it was ideologically incorrect for women of good family background to emigrate. The resulting imbalance created a bachelor society of a transient nature, characterized by a sojourner's mentality, in Singapore and at other migrant destinations. However, from the 1920s onwards, a changed British colonial policy involving a relaxation of immigration law encouraged more Chinese women to emigrate. Since then women had arrived in greater number. By 1947, the Chinese male-to-female ratio in Singapore had reached a near-balance, with 387,883 males to 342,250 females (Freedman, 1957: 25). This change coincided with an increasing political instability in China that pushed women out of the country, with a substantial number of women immigrating to Singapore to join their husbands or to marry. Also, a group of independent women emerged in Singapore who had immigrated to take advantage of opportunities made possible as a result of expanding trade and mercantile activity. This small group of women had bun up their hair, i.e., who had decided not to marry and were known as the self-bun maidens, *zishunu* (自梳女).

The coming of women signalled the formation of conjugal families with children and the creation of domestic hearths which, combined with economic opportunities, contributed to a more stable social structure. At the same time, extended kinship structures, clans, and lineage and dialect associations all created an environment that encouraged permanent settlement within the emerging post-colonial Singapore society, and signalled the passing away of the sojourner's transient community and mentality.

The social institutions established by the migrants during the early phases of migration now took on extended roles as the utilitarian institutions that had catered to the needs of bachelors gave way to institutions concerned with families and lineages. Dialect associations became routinely involved in socio-cultural events. These and other Chinese social institutions in Singapore became increasingly involved in reproducing elements of culture concerned with daily social routines, social interaction, domesticity, religion, ancestor worship and customary practices, as the Chinese Singaporeans established permanent homes for themselves overseas. Thus, from the second half of the twentieth century onwards, *luodi shenggen* (落地生根),[1] planting one's roots in the adopted home, became the norm rather than the exception.

The Migrants' Social Experience

Chinese intending to reside permanently in Singapore have been confronted with a variety of rapidly changing political structures and experiences. First, there was the colonial structure. During the nineteenth and the first half of the twentieth century, Chinese migrants had little interaction with the British colonial administrators except through their headmen, or *Kapitans China*. Scholars have argued that the British policies of indirect rule resulted in the establishment of an *imperium in imperio* or city-within-a-city phenomenon, in which the Chinese were left alone to create their own socio-political structures, perpetuating their own lifestyles and their own rule. Right up to the eve of decolonization, the migrants were cushioned from the British administration by their tightly-knit social institutions, which interlocked to form an institutional web impenetrable to outsiders. These social institutions included clan associations, dialect organizations, secret societies and temples. While each of these had their own distinct identity and function, they were nevertheless interlocked in social networks (*shehui wangluo*, 社会网络) involving *guanxi* (关系) within which they shared the same leaders, and so jointly organized social and cultural activities that represented both their own particular subgroups and the wider Chinese community.

It was not unknown, during the early years, for the secret societies to constitute the political arm of the Chinese community, as their leaders held numerous positions in other social institutions. The roles of the secret societies have been well recorded and their legitimacy in the eyes of the early migrants was unquestioned. However, their official role, after the Secret Societies Ordinance of 1867, was marginalized, as they became associated with the criminal aspects of society. Increasingly, their legitimacy within the Chinese community became more of a liability than an asset, and as a result, from 1869 onwards, association with the secret societies could no longer bring social status, and ordinary people avoided joining them. A separation of leadership, between secret societies and other social organizations, occurred, and leaders of clan, dialect and temple organizations distanced themselves from the secret societies, although they might still play marginal roles within them. Thus the delegitimization of secret societies led to an increase in the strength of other social institutions, although in reality some interlocking membership continued right down to the eve of decolonization.

As mentioned, in the early days the clan, dialect and temple organizations were also important in galvanizing the Chinese together and giving them an identity. Each of these organizations provided a network from which its members drew economic, social and emotional support when in need. During the nineteenth century, these institutions helped Chinese bachelors locate jobs, and provided them with shelter and food. They also organized communal, social and religious activities that provided much needed breaks in the otherwise mundane routine life of the coolies. The familiar cultural practices that were reproduced in the alien colonial environment helped many to cope with the monotonous working life, loneliness and homesickness that came along with an isolated migrant lifestyle.

At a later date, after the increased establishment of women and families, the clan and dialect associations financed schools for the children.

A good education had always been considered a privilege of the literati class, and in the colonial environment an English education provided by the colonial administration was restricted to a select few favoured by the British colonialists. These were primarily the 'Straits Chinese', who formed a privileged group, whose English education eventually allowed them to hold positions within the colonial administration. In the aftermath of decolonization, English-educated Straits Chinese filled the civil bureaucracy of the new nation-state. Previously, for the majority of the migrants, education had been a lofty ideal, although for the few wealthy, home tuition (sishu,私塾) had been the only option for their children.

All this changed with the increasing establishment of families and the consequent introduction of Chinese vernacular education, which was provided by the clan and dialect organizations from the 1920s through 1960s. For the first time in Singapore, a modified form of mass education became a reality. Children of Chinese migrants were sent to schools that followed the curriculum offered in Mainland China. Girls were also encouraged to study in schools, although boys continued to be given preference by their parents. As clan and dialect associations funded the education, expenses for the individual family were kept to a minimum, and those who could not afford it could ask for assistance from the associations.

The evolution of clan- and dialect-based education from the 1920s onward was attributed to the foresight of the clan and dialect leaders, together with that of several of the lesser scholars who had immigrated to Singapore. An example of the former was Tan Kah Kee, who was an important proponent of education and who spent much of his wealth on educational projects both in the Nanyang region and in China. Other leaders of education included Lee Kong Chian and Tan Lark See. The availability of a Chinese education constituted the foundation for an emerging Chinese-educated elite group who would become the champions of the Chinese community within the multi-ethnic polity of post-colonial Singapore (Yong, 1968).

From Peasants to Family Business Firms

Chinese social structures, which permitted the Chinese to become self-sufficient within their self-created world, assisted greatly in the development of family business firms. The indirect British rule had left much of the conduct of Chinese affairs to Chinese leaders, and the Chinese also had very little interaction with other ethnic groups: the indigenous Malays and the Indian migrants co-existed with the Chinese, but each group participated only in its own activities. Ethnic interaction among groups was nominal and occurred mainly in the marketplace, the common gathering ground for all ethnic groups, where a small amount of social interaction accompanied economic interaction (Furnivall, 1980) and where some cross-cultural diffusion occurred through the common language of Bazaar Malay, which most Chinese traders and workers managed to speak some form of.

Thus, for the most part, the Chinese were cushioned against an unfamiliar political structure and a multi-ethnic population through their own cultural apparatus and institutions. Many Chinese who started off as coolies took advantage of Chinese social networks and established family business firms. A credit rotation system helped to provide initial capital for the start-up of these small businesses, and other capital was raised from loans from kinsmen and other business people on the basis of trust (*xinyong,* 信用). Self-help and trust were thus instrumental in developing a whole generation of small family businesses and helped with the generation and accumulation of wealth within the Chinese community.

The credit rotation system mentioned above is an informal financial system. In most cases, a person in need of money gathers a group of kin, friends or business associates, usually 10 to 12 or 15, for a credit cycle. The leader is known as the credit rotation head (*huitou,* 汇头), who sets the monthly credit limit. During the early years in Singapore, such a limit might have been $10 or less; today, monthly credit limits might range from $1,000 to $10,000. Each month, the participants pay a stated amount minus the interest that the bidder is willing to pay for the bid. The credit rotation head is usually given the first bid. Usually the bidder agrees to pay an interest of 5 to 10 per cent, depending on competition for the bid for the month. The last person in the group does not need to bid and pay an interest. He or she gets the full amount from each member, thereby concluding a credit rotation cycle.

In the urban environment of Singapore, Chinese peasant migrants learned rapidly and adapted to an economic structure very different from that which they had been used to. Their quickness in learning the commercial ethos of the entrepôt trade, as well as their willingness to do wage labour, enabled them rapidly to shake off their peasant backgrounds.

From the 1920s, the majority of Chinese migrants were coolies and workers in various trades. As some advanced from doing heavy menial labour in the dockyards to become clerical workers and administrators in trading firms, they exuded a sense of hard work, diligence, trustworthiness and perseverance. They also acquired the knowledge of trade and business, and took advantage of whatever opportunities arose to start family businesses. This transition of Singapore Chinese society from a peasantry to a commercial class was completed with the emergence of a new breed of entrepreneurs and businessmen, who relied on hard work and business acumen to make use of little capital to build sizeable businesses during the early years. Some of these businesses have since undergone various stages of expansion and have now developed into modern conglomerates.

This move from peasant to coolie and eventually to trader or entrepreneur is a deeply emotional story in itself. The economic success of many family businesses was made possible by the existence of social networks (*guanxi wang*, 关系网) supplemented by the sworn brotherhoods (*yixiongdi*, 义兄弟) of the secret societies, both of which operated to bring kin and non-kin together, and allow migrants to tap into important sources of business skills and financial support. This *guanxi wang* bonded together clan and lineage (surname) associations, dialect associations, trade guilds and Chinese chambers of commerce. The relationships among traders and these institutions were both formal and informal, but were never legalistic—most of these social institutions did not operate strictly according to the rule of law.

Through the credit rotation system, Chinese small traders could handle their own financial needs instead of relying on formal banking and financial institutions, and continued to promote the rapid rise of small family businesses throughout Singapore during the two decades following independence.

Although, in the agrarian society of village China, the dream was to own a plot of land, in the commercial society of Singapore, where trading was the lifeline of the population, the Chinese migrants shifted their priorities to owning a family business.

Among 40 Singapore Chinese families of Anxi interviewed, 75 per cent had some kind of family business, and the other 25 per cent were workers, some of whom worked for these family firms. Most of these firms are small, ranging from engineering construction to the wholesale and/or retail of hardware, textiles, fruit and tea. Among these 40 families, only 4 per cent had professional qualifications, and these were in the legal and accounting professions. In most cases the sons, and in some cases the daughters, were helping with the family businesses. In 2009, many of the second generation have taken over the business of their parents. With some members of the first generation have passed away, the baton is now forwarded to the second and third generation.

About 90 per cent of first-generation migrants today have only the equivalent of a primary education. However, among second and third generations, over 60 per cent have secondary education, and 13 per cent have tertiary education. The rest have some form of technical and vocational training.

Citizenry and Identity in Post-colonial Singapore

As the Chinese became economically and socially established in Singapore, they gradually came to regard Singapore as their home. However, although all were Singapore citizens, their sense of citizenship and identity came under scrutiny in the newly independent nation-state.

After the end of World War II, as part of the global dismantling of empires, the process of decolonization was completed in the Malay Peninsula, with British withdrawal and exit from the Malay Federation. The political tumults of the 1950s and 1960s affected the social and economic well-being of the region, one result being that Singapore established her self-government in 1965.

After independence, the ruling People's Action Party (PAP) under Lee Kuan Yew had several tasks to consider. One was post-independence economic reconstruction, and the transformation of Singapore from predominantly an entrepôt into one of the most modern and successful economic powerhouses of Asia. The party implemented strict political, but liberal economic, policies, a main consideration being to make Singapore a politically stable place in order to attract foreign investments. Much of Singapore's early economic success had been built upon foreign capital, and now multinational and transnational corporations continue to dominate its economy. The high level of political stability, complemented by an efficient and non-corrupt civil bureaucracy, has resulted in many multinational and transnational corporations making Singapore their regional headquarters.

However, the ruling PAP intrudes deeply into the lives of its citizenry. Scholars and critics of Singapore government have alluded to the authoritarian nature of the government and their strict control over the citizenry. Most citizens, on the other hand, have looked at the PAP as benign and paternalistic, and have accepted the strict controls, which range from campaigns to stop people from protests to those encouraging specific personal values. This behaviour has been largely accepted as a trade-off for a stable, disciplined and economically successful society. Life in the new polity has improved, with better housing, better education and a higher standard of living.

Ideologically, the state has successfully encouraged the gradual transformation of a migrant mentality into identification with Singapore; socially, Singaporeans have become the envy of Southeast Asia; economically, they have carved a niche for themselves as competent businesspeople, entrepreneurs and professionals, and as skilful workers.

In independent Singapore, the Chinese migrants first had to confront the issue of citizenship and choose between becoming citizens of the newly independent Singapore nation-state or retaining the citizenship of their 'home' country. They also had a third option of choosing permanent residence status in Singapore while reforming their original citizenship. However, for the majority, the choice was clear: they opted to become Singapore citizens, and the attaining of the pink identity cards became a symbol of the new citizenship status of these migrants. Those who did not opt for citizenship came to regret it years later.

Two factors account for the decision of the migrants to make Singapore their permanent home. The first, 'pull' factor, consists of the economic opportunity and generally high standard of living in Singapore. There was general consensus at that time that the commercial structure of the Singapore city-state provided better opportunities for them and their children than the agrarian structure of their former villages. There was also great optimism over the political leadership and its ability to rule Singapore. The other, 'push' factor, is the Communist victory in 1949 and the tumultuous years that followed, which convinced many that returning to China could be disastrous not only for themselves but also for their families. By the mid-1960s the Cultural Revolution in China provided further impetus to those who had been indecisive and they finally took up Singapore citizenship.

The difficulty of life for the majority during the early years of independence eased as the encouragement of foreign investors and the setting-up of factories provided employment. Male family heads with wives and children began to see themselves as part of the social fabric of the new nation-state rather than as bachelor-sojourners, and initial motives to return home with fortunes gave way to the better prospect of establishing comfortable homes in Singapore.

In Singapore, the Chinese have learned to operate within a new political structure, an unfamiliar system based on universal suffrage. Together with members of other ethnic communities, they have had to learn the meaning of concepts of election, citizenship, national identity and nationhood which are alien and contradictory to their understanding of Chinese identity and of China; and they have had to wrestle with the policies implemented by the state concerning multi-ethnicity, religious plurality, state-run education, housing, reproduction and health.

Not all Chinese with overseas connections wanted, or managed, to leave their home villages in China, of course. Many experienced poverty and suffered during the Cultural Revolution. Today, with the passing of some of the first generation, many of them continue to have patrilineal and matrilineal kin, or affines in Singapore.

The Ethnicity Question

The Chinese in Singapore have had to confront the nature of ethnicity, and have had to re-evaluate their own ethnic and cultural identities in relation to those of the other ethnic groups. The Malays, Indians and the Europeans are visibly different from the Chinese in phenotype, cultural practice and language, and these factors have been important in the establishment of ethnic enclaves.

British town planning law, which consigned each ethnic group to a specific location, encouraged ethnic segregation during the colonial years. The Jackson Plan of 1827 cut up downtown Singapore into several precincts and slotted the ethnic populations into their respective positions, maintaining ethnic segregation. The dense, institutionalized Chinese social web encouraged self-containment within the Chinese community, while the barriers erected between 'us' and 'the others' made each group inward-looking. Mistrust and unfamiliarity with other cultures became a great psychological barrier preventing group members from venturing out to befriend others.

In post-independence Singapore under the PAP government, the ethnic issue has been a priority. A policy of multiculturalism, implemented to bridge gaps between ethnic groups, together with an integrated education system, has brought about a higher level of interaction and dialogue among the ethnic groups. At a more intimate level, however, Chinese continue to socialize with 'their own kind'.

The contest for identities is thus a complex one. At one level, the Singapore state has consciously and actively shaped the Singapore identity, moulding its citizenry as Singaporeans. Today, all Singapore citizens identify as such. This national identity emphasizes nationalistic and patriotic feelings towards the Singapore nation-state. Citizens are asked to imagine themselves as one people and one nation.

The state-constructed ethnic framework, commonly known as the CMIO (Chinese, Malay, Indians and Others) model, was the guiding *modus operandi* for ethnic relations within Singapore society. Within it, 'Chinese' is a standardized ethnic category. Contrary to this state-projected image of a homogenized ethnic Chinese group, however, it is recognized that the Chinese community is, in fact, heterogeneous.

The Chinese of Singapore can be categorized in various ways. At one level, it is possible to speak of a Chinese-*tangren* (唐人) group and a Straits Chinese group. Chinese-*tangren* are the migrants and their descendants by union with other Chinese. Straits Chinese, also known as Baba-Chinese or Peranakan, are all locally born and are descended from unions between Chinese migrant men and Malay women.

Straits Chinese differ from Chinese-*tangren* not only in their ancestral backgrounds but also in linguistic preference, professional skills and cultural practices. Many speak Malay as well as a Chinese dialect, which is often Fujianese. As mentioned, during colonial times many were English-educated and held high positions within the civil bureaucracy and in the private sector. During the early years Straits Chinese women, known as *nonya*,[2] dressed in *sarong kebaya* and developed their hybrid cuisine, which is closer to Malay than to Chinese cuisine. However, they only dress in sarong kebaya on special occasions these days.

Within the wider Chinese community, including among the Chinese-*tangren*, there are sub-communities differentiated by dialect, region of origin and surname grouping. Thus there are dialect associations (*fangyan gonghui*, 方言公会), clan or surname associations (*xingshi gonghui*, 姓氏公会) and territorial-based associations (*tongxianghui*, 同乡会). However, at one level, the Chinese, like other ethnic groups, are trying to maintain an overall cultural identity. As many of their current cultural practices are mixtures of migrant culture with new additions from their local environment, the question 'What form should this cultural identity take?' arises. From where can we draw inspiration? Should this identity be based on the historically short experience of Chinese in Singapore or should we delve into the pre-migration historical past and traditions for inspiration?

There is an increasing desire among Singapore Chinese to explore parochial cultural identities through dialect affiliation, ancestry, immediate lineage and other kinship networks. Although the persons actively involved in this search represent only a small subgroup of Singapore Chinese, they are influential in re-orienting the direction of the recreation of a Chinese cultural tradition and identity (华人文化传统认同). They are not content with knowing themselves only as ethnic Chinese, or even as Fujian or Chaozhou Chinese; they also search for their ancestral roots, to provide themselves with more specific identities. We are thus witnessing the continuing growth and production of a multiplicity of identities in resistance to the homogenizing influence of the Singapore state, which attempts to turn Singapore Chinese into a uniform Chinese community with Mandarin as its lingua franca.

Thus, Singapore Chinese identity remains composite. Singapore Chinese see ethnic Chinese identity as comprising several layers, and there is a constant demand for them to establish allegiances to the various groups to which they belong. The first identity is the Singapore Chinese (*Xinjiapo huaren*, 新加坡华人) identity, which binds all Singapore Chinese together. This is the preferred identity of the Singapore state, which seeks constantly to promote it. The second identity comes from association with a particular dialect. Here, the commonly used identity terms are Singapore Fujian, Singapore Chaozhou and Singapore Cantonese people. The third identity comes from associations with ancestral homes in China—thus, Singapore Chinese see themselves as Singapore Anxi, Tongan or Meixian Chinese.

These parochial regional identities have become significant, as they represent a renewed sense of confidence in the cultural identity of these Chinese. During the 1960s and 1970s the Singapore government exercised great caution over representations of such identities, for fear of creating ethnic unrest, as Chinese ethnicity was then associated with Chinese nationalism and chauvinism. Today, a more mature citizenry has permitted a more relaxed attitude towards ethnic cultures and ethnic cultural representations; in the 1980s, some government ministers had called for a better understanding of the historical origins of ethnic cultures. The earlier state policy of creating a homogeneous ethnic identity within the CMIO framework has given way to a policy of intra-ethnic diversity. A better understanding of their own cultures is thus helping Singapore Chinese to reproduce and reinvent Chinese cultural elements within the Singapore polity, a process which inevitably takes them back to their ancestral villages in rural China. An understanding of the emergence of cultural identity within the Singapore Chinese community will thus have to take into consideration two processes: the first being one that operates on the level of the Chinese dialect groups and the second that operates between the Singapore Chinese and their ancestral villages.

Reproducing Culture: A Model

Cultural reproduction is seen as both spontaneous and selective. Cultural elements and rituals are produced through time to fulfil the needs of the group of people concerned, with no systematic planning of what elements to include; through time, these elements and rituals establish themselves as a cultural orthodoxy. In the case of Singapore Chinese, cultural orthodoxy is derived primarily from the former migrants' understandings of what they had been taught in village China. It can be said that the strength of Chinese culture comes from the diversity and regional differences among Chinese as, underlying these diversities, the cultural elements continue to be broadly identified as uniquely Chinese. Thus, at the macro-level, it is possible to speak of a Chinese cultural orthodoxy, while, at the micro-level, each Chinese group has practices that are context-specific. Within Singapore, certain of these cultural elements are selectively reproduced and incorporated for specific purposes, both by the members of the Chinese population themselves, acting autonomously, and by the Singapore state. In the case of the state, the attempt is to encourage the creation of a 'made in Singapore' elite version of a standardized Chinese culture.

It is possible to periodize cultural reproduction within the Chinese community. The first period started with the arrival of the first group of migrants from the early nineteenth century. This stage was characterized by spontaneity: each individual, family, lineage or dialect group practised and reproduced the cultural elements with which they were familiar from village China. These especially included folk religious practices that, although geared to an agrarian economy, were yet reproduced in urban, commercial Singapore. This constituted direct cultural reproduction. In time, however, a second stage of cultural adaptation and cultural incorporation, which lasted into the 1950s, involved the gradual discarding of certain cultural elements and the giving of prominence to others. In this stage the repertory of cultural elements continued to be selected from the village culturescape, in addition to those adopted from the involvement in urban commerce, and those from British rule, including the English language, Western-style clothing, Western mannerism especially their cuisine, and for the Baba, elements from the Malay population.

The third stage occurred in post-independent Singapore and involved a conscious attempt at reproducing selected cultural elements that were 'representative' of the wider Chinese community, under which individual interests and regional differences were subsumed. Here, the differences among the dialect and/or lineage groups were streamlined to produce a standardized Chinese culture. The attempt to do this was a response to the demands placed upon Singapore Chinese by the state in its desire to project a unified and homogeneous image of Chineseness in relation to the images of the other ethnic groups.[3] This stage may be called cultural representation.

The fourth stage was an attempt to elevate peasant culture into high culture in a manner in line with the modern Singapore image. The idea was that Chinese culture, like other cultures, must have interpretative and modernizing power. It must also be rational in its ritual content and provide a place for each cultural element within the history of Chinese culture. In this attempt, Singapore Chinese had to confront the issue of cultural representation: Which items should be included as culture and which should be excluded? Nothing was more appropriate than Chinese religious practices, as there was at the time a push towards doctrinal religion. This fourth stage may be called the stage of cultural reinvention.

Finally, there has been a move towards cultural diversity within the Chinese community. In recent years, the state has acknowledged the significance of cultural diversity among sub-ethnic and dialect groups, an acknowledgement that remits in a raised culturescape within the Chinese community. This fifth stage may be called cultural reintegration.

Cultural Dilution

Moving through the different phases of cultural reproduction to cultural reintegration, Chinese culture has witnessed many changes, yet has retained its core elements that define Chinese cultural orthodoxy. However, this orthodoxy is subject to intense competition from modern cultural forms, such as those of popular culture, which have assumed greater significance and popularity among the younger Chinese. The result has been a decline in interest in the 'orthodox' Chinese culture and Chinese social institutions.

Chinese cultural identity largely revolves around activities organized by various Chinese social institutions, with participation on a collective basis. These social institutions include families, lineages, clan groupings, dialect associations, Chinese temples and cultural organizations, where activities are often of a socio-religious kind and the languages used are dialects. Some younger Singapore Chinese choose to become 'less Chinese' or 'modern Chinese' and do not participate in such social and cultural activities. Some move away from Chinese religious practices and adopt Christianity; others choose to speak English.

One indicator of interest in traditional social and cultural activities is participation in activities organized by clan, dialect and other kinship-based associations. Through the years there has been a steep drop in membership in all of these: a look into the composition of such memberships suggests that over 80 per cent of the members of surname and dialect associations are first-generation Chinese. Thus participation in activities organized by these associations has been largely by the elderly; hence, they are often known as clubs for 'old folks'. The types of activities found in these associations reflect the elderly members' interests, such as mah-jong and conversation. Young Chinese are unlikely to participate in such activities, and few young members visit the associations. This has been a worrying trend for the associations and the elders, and how to encourage the younger Chinese to become members has become a critical concern for these associations. Some have provided venues for modern forms of entertainment, such as karaoke facilities and rooms, to attract the young. In recent years they have also organized free-tuition classes for the children of their members and have allowed their premises to be used for other educational purposes, thereby encouraging the young to visit and participate in the cultural activities.

Traditionally, the activities organized by the clan associations were predominantly religious, such as worship of the guardian god, the Jade Emperor of Heaven, Yuwang dadi (玉王大帝), also commonly called *tiangong* (天公), and ancestors, and the celebration of the hungry ghosts at the Zhong Yuan Festival (中元节) (Lunar Seventh Month). Elaborate rituals and food offerings, together with communal feasts, are still common sights at such celebrations. Surprisingly, although mainly elderly men and women attend these religious activities, young male adults also attended during the last decade, partly on behalf of elderly parents, but also to advance emerging social-cum-business networks among themselves. Since the mid-1980s, increasing numbers of daughters and daughters-in-law have been seen accompanying their parents to such activities, reflecting the changing status of women in contemporary Singapore and perhaps a greater recognition of the role of married and unmarried daughter in Singapore and the village.

Among locally-born Chinese, there are increasing trends both towards Christianity and away from any religious affiliation. Those following the latter call themselves 'free thinkers'. Among the non-proselytizing Chinese religions, however, there is no need for individuals to declare their religious beliefs: all individuals within the general community are also assumed to be part of it in religious terms. Communal religious worship thus is separated from personal belief. Singapore Chinese see these religious practices as part of Chinese tradition and culture, and many are passive participants in their religion, leaving most of the worshipping to their parents and other elderly family members. It is therefore common to see many young Chinese observing, but not participating, in acts of worship. Older Chinese sees this lack of active interest on the part of the young as a trend towards cultural dilution.

Another area of concern is the hiatus in family and kinship structures. The extended kinship system has largely broken down as a result of emigration, and there are many cases of immediate family members having been separated, resulting in a dilution of kinship ties within the immediate family. Today, what we find among the Chinese is a truncated kinship structure.

Among Singapore-born Chinese, the main concern is with the immediate family. The shift from extended family structure to nuclear family has progressively changed the kinship structure. Distant kin are no longer seen as important and are paid little attention. This is true both for village kin in China and for Singapore kin, many of whom no longer have clear ideas of who their village kin are and find it hard to categorize their relatives according to the Chinese classificatory kinship system. Many have informed me that they only know a small number of kin who share the same surname.

However, 'sharing the same surname' now has a different meaning for younger Singapore Chinese than for their parents. To the elders, a person with the same surname is a blood relative, despite any social and/or kinship distance between them; thus, during the migration years, migrants were given assistance by 'kinsmen'. The knowledge that a migrant was 'one of us' (*zijiren*, 自己人) was a sufficient incentive for previously arrived Chinese migrants to extend a helping hand. Such was the personalization of assistance to the early migrants. Today, however, Singapore-born Chinese attach little sentiment to the fact of a shared surname, and do not necessarily consider it to be evidence of any kinship tie. They therefore do not feel obligated to assist people with the same surname. Here, we see the ideological conflict between migrant parents and their children, among whom the recognition of kinship relations is now restricted to immediate kin. To the older Chinese, the locally-born Chinese have become socially distant from their cultural upbringing.

In Singapore, among the first generation, kinship relations continue to play an important role in daily life, and there is interaction among kin, who talk with one another over the telephone or over tea, visit one another and do things together. This is less the case among the younger Chinese, whose kinship ties may stretch to second or even third cousins, but no farther, although there is a general acknowledgement of the existence of a greater kin community. A common lament among parents is that after their deaths, kinship relation (*qinqing,* 亲情) will be lost if no attempts are made to preserve it. For the time being, only contacts among the first generation bring the younger generations together for various purposes, albeit obliquely.

However, due to the twists of fortune, the family business firm has now indirectly brought locally-born Singapore kin together, as the kinship ties that helped parents to start family business firms during the early years play different roles today. It is the sons who will inherit family businesses, and occupational specialization during the early years meant that many of those within the same lineage engaged in similar trades, thereby effectively facilitating the continuation of social and kinship relations among younger Chinese.

Most Anxi Chinese in Singapore started in the rags business, collecting and selling second-hand goods. Later, they branched out into hardware. Today, those involved in hardware have broadened their scope to deal not only in metalwork but also in machinery, construction, sanitary wares and building materials. Many of these firms started as small retail businesses catering to local needs, while others were wholesale importers and exporters. Presently, most are also involved in manufacturing. They have branched into other fields and expanded to become medium-sized firms or even large corporate groups, and one group of Anxi Singapore Chinese are involved in finance and banking.

Being in the same trades has provided opportunities for younger Singapore Chinese to interact with kin more intensively both in business and socially, and has helped to maintain kinship relations among kin of second and third generations. This is a reversal of the situation that the coolie migrants first experienced—i.e., one in which kinship ties led the way to business ties. The integration of social networks, *guanxi wang* and economic networks (*jingjiwang,* 经济网), has now become an asset in attempts at business globalization, and in particular for gaining access to the China market. This also leads to a 'discovery' of one's cultural identity. Among the younger generation, some see the kinship in a more instrumental manner as outlined above.

Another factor promoting an overall Chinese cultural identity is the state-sponsored idea that Mandarin (Putonghua) is the lingua franca of the Chinese that will bind all Chinese dialect groups together. This attempt at standardizing Chinese language use in Singapore has led schools to discourage students from using dialects in school. Many Singapore-born parents also encourage their children to use Mandarin at home, seeing this as providing them with a head start in their education. This has reduced the proficiency in the dialects among some of the third and fourth-generation Chinese, thus 'diluting' specific group identities under the umbrella of general Chineseness.

The introduction of English education in schools has meant a bilingualism that places emphasis only on English and Mandarin. The Singapore state promotes English as a tool for economic success, while Mandarin is seen as an important cultural idiom to bind all Singapore Chinese together. However, familiarity with Chinese dialects continues to be viewed as important for the continuation of territorial-based Chinese cultural identity by older Chinese, especially first-generation migrants from the late 1990s. Singapore has begun to relax its official policy on Mandarin, and dialect phrases have begun to appear on the government-controlled broadcasting channels.

Towards the Future

As we move towards the twenty-first century, a confident Chinese community is now re-evaluating its status in Singapore. Its members, citizens of Singapore, are becoming more aware of the complexities of their identities. 'Being Chinese' is only a broad identity, which has to be situated within a social context in order for its meanings to become clear, to self or others. Other identities—Singapore Chinese, Singaporean, Fujian Chinese, Singapore Anxi Chinese, etc.—reflect identification with the nation, with particular ethnicities, with particular dialect groups, and with places of origin. The identities of others have become important local points of comparison, both between groups of Singapore Chinese and between them and other, non-Chinese groups.

First-generation Chinese feel their children and grandchildren have gradually lost interest in Chinese social institutions and have very little knowledge of Chinese cultural practices. As a result of the changing role of the clan associations in Singapore, some second and younger Singapore generation Chinese are now joining some of the activities and especially business tours in Mainland China (see Kuah-Pearce, 2006d). The declining emphasis on family and lineage has meant that elderly persons are sometimes seen more as a burden than as seniors rich in wisdom,[4] while Singapore-born Chinese are seen as having little interest in, or knowledge of, their ancestors and their ancestral homes. First-generation Chinese have begun to refer to the younger Chinese as 'babaized' (*fan, huang* [H] 番)—i.e., uncivilized and 'detribalized' (i.e., separated from the lineage and the Chinese as a people). However, this trend towards 'babaization' is considered reversible through the reintroduction of the younger Chinese to 'Chinese culture' and the re-establishment of 'their' cultural identity.

The task is thus to reproduce Chinese culture and to re-establish the traditional moral order that will result in the re-discovery of a particular cultural identity. For the proponents of cultural reproduction, such a process can only be successful if the young Singapore Chinese are introduced to their 'sources'—meaning their roots in their ancestral villages. These proponents believe that, as the Confucian saying goes, 'when drinking water, think of its source' (*yinshui siyuan*, 饮水思源). This is the key to 'becoming Chinese' (*huarenhua*, 华人化), and undoing the 'non-Chineseness' of 'Chinese' people.

For the older, especially the China-born Chinese, it is a moral obligation to prevent the decline of cultural identity and to prevent the younger generations from becoming 'uncivilized persons', *fanren* (番人). As one elder commented: 'We have to lead the young ones in the search for an identity. They would not be able to find the way. So it is up to us with the seniors to lead the way to our roots [and cultural identity].' This can be done by introducing young Chinese to their ancestral villages and ancestral houses. They thus encourage and lead their children and grandchildren back to visit their ancestral villages and encourage them to participate in village ancestor worship and religious activities, as well as to get involved in village reconstruction.

The Quest for Kinship and Lineage Continuity

The search for ancestral identity is coterminous with a quest for lineage continuity. One informant commented: 'Our link with the Anxi relatives is like a very thin thread. Once broken, it is very difficult to mend.' This is how Singapore Chinese elders see their link with their ancestral villages: to them, the tie is tenuous and needs to be strengthened in order that kinship and lineage continuity can be maintained. The only way they know is to encourage their descendants to explore this source of lineage identity and to kindle in them the sentiments for their ancestral home villages which they, the elders, carry.

Today, this quest for identification with the lineage is an extremely emotional affair. Although some China-born Singapore Chinese are in their forties, many are now in their sixties, seventies and eighties. They regard the preservation of kinship ties with their village counterparts as a matter of great urgency. In the Confucian tradition, the failure to bring together two branches of a lineage and to rekindle kinship relations constitutes an unfilial act, and those who thus fail are held responsible for the destruction of the lineage and the kinship ties.

Left alone, the Singapore and Anxi branches of a lineage would face ultimate separation when the older generations pass away. There would be no incentive for younger generations to revive such ties: younger Singapore Chinese today already perceive it to be disadvantageous to maintain them. Maintaining kinship ties with kin whom one has never met is an extremely difficult task. This lack in Singapore-born Chinese of sentimental attachment to their ancestral villages has driven their parents and other forebears to visit their ancestral villages and to help with village reconstruction. For the younger, however, the different socio-political environment and a set of negative collective memories that they have been brought up with have tarnished the images of the ancestral village and of unknown village kin. They do not have first-hand experience of village life as their forebears did, and only some, in recent years, have visited their ancestral villages. They have only heard of underdevelopment, regional poverty, greed, and the lack of consideration of village kin, and so harbour strong negative sentiments of their ancestral homes and distant relatives. Thus, the challenge for older generations is obvious. One elder said, 'although we have been naturalized in another country, we should not forget our origin. In fact, we should know more of our origin. This is important for our children. They [children and grandchildren] should know more about their ancestors and their achievement. It is important to encourage them to visit Anxi and let them understand their ancestral village and the existence of their village kin. We have the responsibility to introduce the ancestral village to them. But what happens after that depends on themselves.' Another said, 'I will encourage my children and grandchildren to return home for a visit. Whether they want to go or not is their choice. But I will definitely encourage them to do so.' A third said, 'the young ones should know Anxi because it is their roots. They should at least know of this. If we do not have a lineage and culture, then other people will not respect us. We would be like a pack of loose sand without a centrifugal force to bind us together.'

Some first-generation elders feel that one way to encourage the younger Chinese to take an interest in the ancestral village is to become very active in village life themselves. One said, 'it is important to maintain contacts in

Anxi. That is why we visit and participate in the activities there. We also invest in village reconstruction. This is one way to arouse their interest in the ancestral village.' Another felt that 'to arouse their interests, we should show them photos and videotapes of the village so that they have an idea of what the village is like'. Another agreed: 'I have taken many photos and collected information for my children, including maps and videos. It is very important for my children and grandchildren to know their home village. This is because their global outlook has led them to become more preoccupied with the outside world than with their home village. I have also brought them back to the village and will encourage them to go again. But I will not force them. It is pointless to coerce them to go. Rather, persuasion will be a more effective method.' The urgency of showing the ancestral village is encapsulated in this comment: 'It is important for the young ones to know their home village and their ancestors. But if they do not want to go back, we could not possibly force them to go. But we need to encourage them as often as possible. To arouse their interests, we should bring them back to Anxi and see their reaction. If they come back with some interest, then there is hope that they might maintain some contacts with the ancestral village in the future. Otherwise, it is finished. When we die, it will end with us. It will have to be a go-slow approach. We will first encourage them to go back and have a look. The second step will be to encourage them to participate in the activities there. Gradually, they might develop some sentiments towards the village and their village kin.'

While it is easy to lead their grown-up adult sons, daughters, and grandchildren back to the village, it requires more effort to get them interested in village activities and to help with village reconstruction. The elders can only hope that their enthusiasm and interest will become an influencing factor in helping younger Chinese to look at their ancestral village in a more positive manner, rather than relying on the negative memories and sentiments they have heard of the earlier years. This is a difficult task. Some Singapore-born Chinese have expressed some interest and have participated in village activities, and their elders feel that such participation has ignited, to a certain degree, the kinship flame among them, which will allow for lineage continuity. One said, 'very few Singapore-born Chinese recognize their ancestral home. Most of them are English-educated. It takes patience to arouse their interests. But we are gradually getting round and a few have shown some interests.' But the frustration continues; another said, 'I have encouraged them to go and have tried to tell them about their home village. But they are not very enthusiastic. It is very hard to force them to go if they do not want to.'

Some feel that another way to encourage younger generations to become interested in the ancestral village is to participate in various activities organized by the lineage and clan associations in Singapore. Another informant suggested that the Singapore Anxi Association should organize more activities both in Singapore and in Anxi, and that locally-born Chinese be encouraged to join in the activities. Another informant said, 'to arouse their interests, let them explore the genealogy. Explain to them their ancestors and their origin. Then, bring them back to the village for a visit. The genealogy will help them to understand their origin and will serve as a stepping stone to their participation in the cultural and religious activities. It might also encourage them to join Anxi Association.' Locating the self-identity of Anxi Chinese within Singapore is also important. One informant commented that 'they [younger generations] need to know their ancestral village. This is their root. It is important that they are able to answer who their ancestors are when asked by outsiders. If they do not know, then they will be telling the rest of the world that they have forgotten their ancestors and signal broken ties with their relatives. It will also tell the world that they have lost their focus. Under such circumstance, they will not be able to locate their identity. It will be embarrassing for them and for us as parents. It also means that we have failed in our duties as parents.' Furthermore, 'the need to know one's identity is especially important in Singapore. One only needs to look at the history of race relations in this part of the world to tell us that if we do not recognize our own identity, then we would be subsumed by other ethnic groups. Our geopolitical racial relationship is very complex. There is social comfort and security in knowing the importance of being Chinese.'

The attitude of Singapore-born Chinese towards Anxi is exemplified in their comments. One said, 'I was born in Singapore and do not have a clear picture and understanding of Anxi. I do not expect much from my children. I know of Anxi from my parents and have made several visits to the village. If my children want to know about Anxi, I will tell them. I do not actively tell them about Anxi nor do I encourage them to participate actively in the activities. But I am not opposed to their wanting to know more about or visiting Anxi. It all depends on my children. If they are interested in Anxi, we will give them all the support. Otherwise, I will not bother.' Another echoes a more negative view: 'For those born in Singapore, like myself, a third-generation "baba", we should not and would not push for such recognition. It will be very hard to interest us about Anxi. Personally, I feel that those with a Chinese education might think more of their cultural roots, but for those who are English-educated, including myself, we look more to Singapore as our home.'

As for third and fourth-generation Singapore Chinese, most in their twenties and thirties, a large majority see themselves as having only Singapore Chinese identity. One said, 'I considered myself as a *Xinjiaporen*. Singapore is my permanent home.' Others said, 'We are *Xinjiapo huaren*. We should be more concerned with the activities and future of Singapore and not those of Anxi. Anxi exists only for sentimental reasons.'

However, to some extent, visiting the ancestral home village by Singapore-born Chinese has brought about several consequences. First, it has helped deepen their understanding of rural China and of their ancestral homes in particular. They have come to understand the relative poverty and the lack of economic and material goods in the village. Some have developed a measure of sympathy that they previously lacked for their village kin, as they have become aware of the physical locality and the social kinship network embedded within the locality and ancestral village social structure. Secondly, their contact has led them to re-evaluate their identities and to be more conscious of the fact that their ancestry is rooted in rural China.

Thirdly, this contact has made them aware of both the similarities and the great divide between their village kin and themselves. Such differences mark the boundary between insiders and outsiders. Singapore-born Chinese feel that they are both insiders and outsiders in their ancestral home villages. As insiders, they are part of the kinship and lineage network, and are expected to discharge moral duties and ritual obligations as insiders; as outsiders, they differ greatly from their village counterparts in appearance, eating habits, attitudes, actions, linguistic skills and ideology. Through this contrast and comparison with their village kin, they contribute to the construction of more complex cultural identities.

The cultural identity of these younger Singapore-born Anxi Chinese is thus a composite one, with elements of Chineseness from their ancestral home and others that are similarly localized, but within the Singapore Chinese community, and specifically within the Singapore Anxi community. Their identity is also under the overarching influence of the nation-state and of the wider society of Singapore. The final product is a Singapore Chinese identity with specific cultural orientations characteristic of the Anxi Chinese community. It is this composite which makes the Singapore Anxi Chinese different from their village counterparts.

Emerging Local Singapore Chinese Root: *Luodi shenggen* (落地生根)

Irrespective of whether they are first-generation migrants or locally-born Singaporeans, about 90 per cent of the forty persons interviewed told us that they would not consider returning to Anxi after their retirement. Of the first generation, some told us that upon retirement they might travel between

Singapore and Anxi and stay for an extended period of two to three months in Anxi; however, they foresaw several difficulties of relocating in Anxi, and felt they would have to start a new lifestyle to readapt to village life. While this was a romantic idea, they had no illusions about the difficulties, given the relatively underdeveloped nature of the village. Moreover, their immediate families—spouses, siblings, children and grandchildren—were in Singapore and it would be hard to leave them behind. Furthermore, their prevailing social networks of relatives and friends had sustained them through four to five decades of difficulties and agonizing moments, during which they experienced and endured poverty and hardship before achieving eventual success, and they would find it hard to move away from their social networks. A fourth factor concerned the Singapore nation, which they had come to regard as their home. They felt that Singapore had treated them well and they could not just pack and go, as they had developed great emotional attachments to Singapore.

Singapore Anxi Chinese identity is complex. It involves an understanding of nationhood and citizenry, and of the political responsibilities associated with being a citizen of Singapore. These spell out their present status, which they are proud of: being a Singapore citizen indicates social prestige, wealth, progress, urbanity and sophistication—a coveted status out of the reach of their village kin. Yet they claim that 'since our ancestors are from Anxi, we are therefore Anxi *huaren*'. To them, it is only logical and desirable for them to assume both identities. Anxi identity does not contradict their understanding of the political culture of Singapore, while it informs one of one's ancestral origin and cultural affiliation. One informant said, 'we are Chinese but we are Singapore citizens. We need to understand that we are now Singapore citizens as we have already forgone our Chinese citizenship. We should understand this. At the same time, we should not forget our ancestors.' Finally, there is the Singapore Fujian Chinese identity. The fact that Anxi people are all Fujianese-speaking and Fujianese is the most widely spoken dialect in Singapore has placed them in a dominant position within the wider Chinese community. Thus, to the first generation, to claim a Singapore Anxi identity is also to claim a Fujian Chinese identity, which has an established dominant status; whereas to the younger generation, Fujian identity supersedes Anxi identity. Beyond the national polity and ethnic affiliation, Singaporeans increasingly view themselves as part of the global polity and embrace the global cosmopolitan identity.

This group of Chinese assume four identities: Singaporean, Singapore Chinese, Singapore Fujianese speaker and Singapore Anxi Chinese. Others add an additional identity—one of modern global cosmocrat. One informant identified himself: 'I am a *Xinjiaporen*, a Singapore citizen. My ancestry is Anxi. I regard Singapore as my permanent place of residence. I am also a

Singapore Fujian person.' Others also echo this: 'I am Singapore-born and a Singapore *ren* (person). My blood origin is Anxi. I feel that I am half Anxi *ren* and half *Xinjiaporen*.' While they may have multiple identities, they are selective of them and tailor them according to social occasions, depending on whether they are with other Chinese in Singapore or overseas or with non-Chinese. As the full cycle of migration and settlement occurs, migrants and their descendants have come to establish identities that best represent them in various socio-political environments.

3
The Ancestral Village in Anxi County

Having settled permanently in Singapore and assumed Singapore Chinese identity, a group of Singapore Chinese are now searching for their cultural roots in Penglai Zhen in Anxi County. Penglai Zhen officially comprises the market town and 31 administrative villages, but continues to be divided by local inhabitants into several precincts named according to the natural terrain found in the region. For example, the area around the source of the river is commonly known as the creek head (*xitou* or *kway-tau* [H], 溪头); the area around the point where it flows into another river is known as the creek tail (*xiwei* or *kway-ber* [H], 溪尾). A third, forest area is known as 'below the tree' (*xiashuwei* or *ae-chiu-ber* [H], 下树尾). When asked, the majority of the villagers, other than the village cadres, did not have much idea of the official administrative names of the villages in which they lived, and were not concerned with them. Most would say they were from Penglai, and if pushed further, would answer with the local hamlet name. As the district name, Penglai, was commonly known to the villagers and the Singapore Chinese alike, this will be the name used throughout this work. This region was also historically known as *kuitou*, *kui-tau* [H] (魁头) and some of the elders know of this name but the majority of the younger villagers only know it by the common name of *xitou*, *kway-tau* [H]. Both terms sound similar in the Fujianese dialect. However, this is not to be mistaken for the neighbouring Kuidou Zhen (魁斗镇); within it is a village called Kuidou Cun (魁斗村). There are thus two branches of the Ke lineage, one located in Penglai and we will call them the Penglai Ke. The other, the Kuidou Ke, is located in Kuidou Zhen. Our key focus here is on the Penglai Ke, also called *Kway-tau* Ke.

Within Penglai, there are nine surname groups. All villages are of a mixed surname composition although in most precincts, it is usually the case that one surname group will dominate. Many villagers are connected to one another by surname and marriage.

The knowledge of their ancestral villages among the Singapore Anxi Chinese varies greatly among the generations, the first generation having clear concepts and subsequent generations only hazy ones. First-generation migrants are able to name the village precincts where they came from, while subsequent generations commonly only say that they are from Anxi County, although some can now say they are from Penglai Zhen. Few are able to name and locate their specific ancestral village.

Anxi County is one of the poorest in China. This chapter will explore the reasons for this, and the measures taken by the central, provincial and

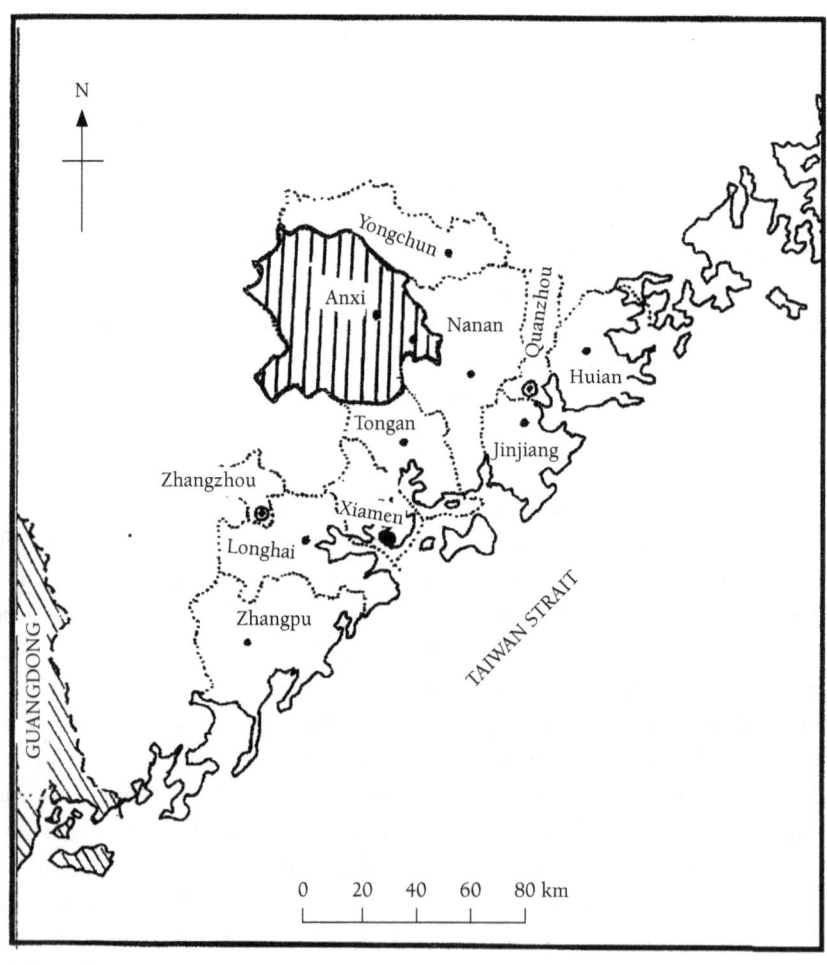

Map 1:   Location of Anxi County in Fujian Province

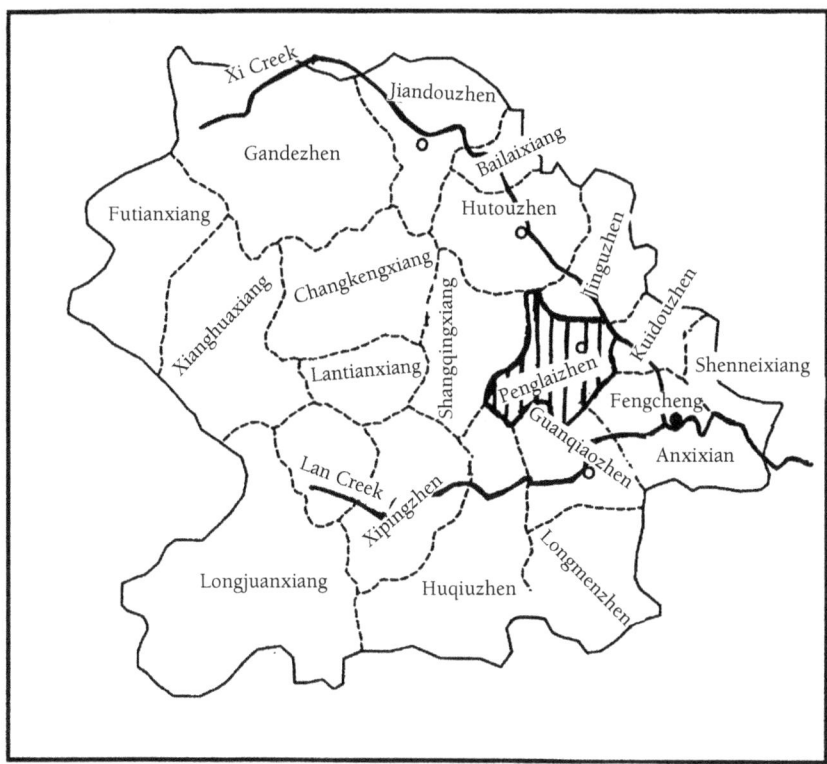

Map 2: Administrative units of Anxi County, Fujian

county governments to eradicate poverty, and their success. As *qiaoxiang*, with overseas Chinese capital, are considered by the government to be potential growth nodes that could bring about development in the county, the chapter will examine how the Singapore Chinese, in part through encouragement of government officials, have provided material and financial resources to help eradicate poverty and to make the *qiaoxiang* prosperous.

Location of Anxi County

Anxi district is located in the southeast region of Fujian, covering longitude 117 degrees 36' to 118 degrees 17' east and latitude 24 degrees 50' to 25 degrees 26' north. It has an area of 3057.28 square metres. In 2009, it had 13 towns (*zhen*, 镇), of which Penglai Zhen was one, and 11 townships (*xiang*, 乡). In 1990, it contained 186,215 households and a total population of 916,204 people, of whom 865,075 were engaged in farming. In 2006, it contained 267,803 households and a total population of 1,066,924 people, of whom 933,685 were engaged in farming (*Anxi Nianjian*, 2005–06: http://www.axdfz.gov.cn/ShowText.asp?ToBook=17008&index=228&, retrieved 30 December 2009). The region is mountainous with numerous ranges rising to 1,600 metres above sea level. It can be divided into inner and outer Anxi. Inner Anxi is more rugged, with an average height of 600–700 metres, and consists mostly of mountainous ranges. It has an average temperature of 17–18 degrees Celsius and an annual rainfall of 1,800 millilitres. Outer Anxi has an undulating landscape of broad plains, valleys and river basins between 300 to 400 metres above sea level, where the average temperature is 19.5–21.3 degrees Celsius and the average annual rainfall is 1,600 millilitres. The climate of Anxi County is subtropical and monsoonal, although the four seasons are easily distinguishable. The region is served by two main rivers, the Xi and the Lan; their tributaries criss-cross the terrain.

Before the 1950s, half of the region was covered with pine forest. However, since the 1950s, with central government policies to conquer and transform wilderness to productive agricultural land, the forested region has declined dramatically. Despite this, only about 10 per cent of the total land area is arable, as the soil is infertile, poor in nutrients and acidic in nature, so that farming is unproductive. Chronic erosion from monsoon rains swell rapid mountain streams (Lyons, 1994: 3–4).

Penglai Town

Penglai Town is situated in the eastern part of Anxi, 25° 7' 48" north, 118° 5' 15" east. It underwent status change since communist victory. It was first established as the Penghai People's Commune in 1958, emerging as Penglai District in 1961. In 1965, it was renamed Penglai Commune and from 1984, its status was changed to a town and today, it is called Penglai Zhen. It occupies an area of 122.38 square kilometres, with 31 administrative villages. In 1992 Penglai Zhen had a residence committee, 30 village committees, 14,438 households with a total population of 67,812. By 2006, the population had increased to 74,042 (*Anxi Nianjian*, 2005–06: http://www.axdfz.gov.cn/ShowText.asp?ToBook=17008&index=228&, retrieved 30 December 2009).

Development in Anxi County

The development in Anxi County can be divided into two main periods. The first began with the Communist Party's assumption of power in 1950 and ran

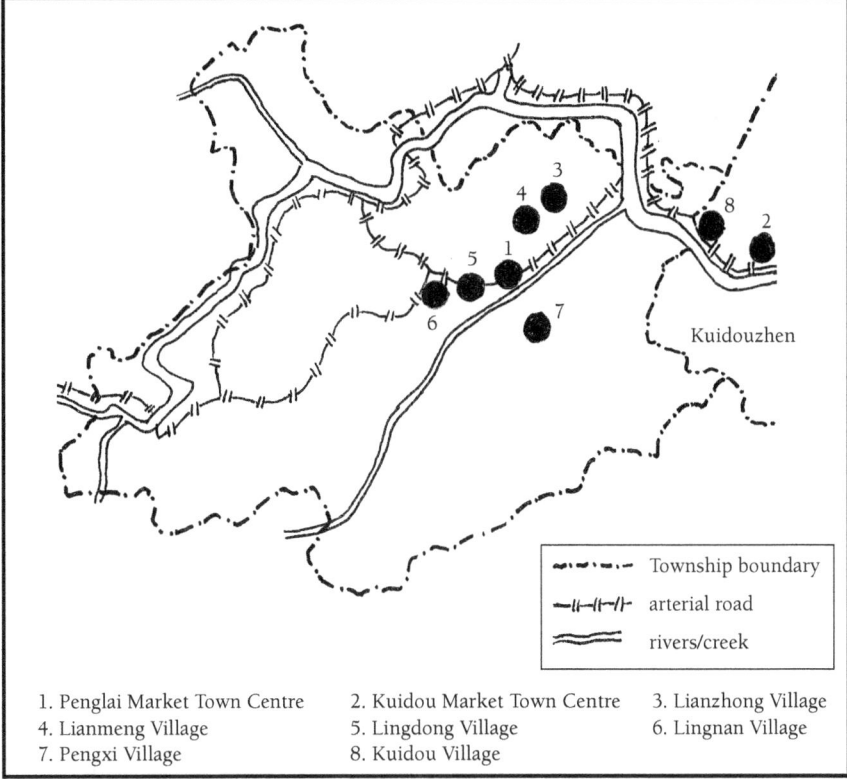

1. Penglai Market Town Centre
2. Kuidou Market Town Centre
3. Lianzhong Village
4. Lianmeng Village
5. Lingdong Village
6. Lingnan Village
7. Pengxi Village
8. Kuidou Village

Map 3: Penglai Zhen, Anxi County

until 1978. The second started with Deng Xiaoping's 1978 reform, when his famous phrase, 'it does not matter whether a cat is black or white, it is a good cat if it catches mice', ushered in a new period of rapid development.

The development of Anxi County from the 1950s to late 1970s was very much influenced by central government policies and the priorities of the Fujian provincial government. Right from the beginning, the rural economy was expected to be self-sufficient, with little or no central funding given for its agricultural development. Furthermore, the region was expected to finance its own basic infrastructure development. During this period, a long-term policy of 'comprehensive harnessing of mountains, rivers, and farmlands' was implemented at the local level, and large numbers of rural labourers were recruited from the collectives to provide labour for the various projects that were essential for increasing agricultural output (Lyons, 1994: 18). By 1984, 14,100 water-control projects had been undertaken, including the construction of 541 reservoirs and 158 pumping stations (Lyons, 1994: 18). This increased the amount of irrigated land by about 55%, to 228,000 *mu*, by 1980. Apart from irrigation, multiple cropping and increased use of fertilizers also increased the production yield. However, yields were also affected by the political climate of the time, as the Great Leap Forward and the Cultural Revolution brought lasting damage to its economy. Prior to collectivization, the county had produced a financial surplus, but from the late 1960s it ran a deficit as a result of remittances to the provincial government, from which it began to receive subsidies.

During this period, Anxi County continued with an essentially agrarian economy under collective farming. Agricultural land was organized into communes in 1958, and as late as 1980 there were still 15 communes, divided into 240 brigades and 2,500 production units (Lyons, 1994: 18). Anxi County continued to have a self-sufficient economy, with a ratio of grain crops (mainly rice, wheat and sweet potatoes) to cash crops (peanuts, sugar cane and tobacco) at 20:1 in terms of sown area. About 91 per cent of the total land area was devoted to the production of grain (Lyons, 1994: 21). Tea and fruit orchards also occupied a small acreage, with 100,000 *mu* devoted to tea plantation and 20,000–30,000 *mu* devoted to fruit orchards (oranges, longans, litchis, plums and persimmons) (Lyons, 1994: 21).

Despite the concentration on grain production for self-sufficiency, Anxi's grain production remained low even by provincial standards; in 1980 it was 9 per cent below the provincial county average or, in terms of yield per *mu*, 5 per cent below. Yields for the major cash crops as well as for tea and fruit were also below average for the province. However, the yields have improved considerably since the 1990s as a result of double cropping, made possible by irrigation.

Apart from agricultural production, Anxi had to cope with basic infrastructure development, with little aid from the central or provincial governments. During this period, basic infrastructure investment—in rail and road construction, education, health and welfare—remained below a pitiful RMB 20 per capita annually until the late 1970s (Lyons, 1994: 15).

During this period, government resources in China were directed towards relatively large water control projects and some hydro-electric power stations, government-owned tea and tree farms and other projects that were deemed essential for the general development of the country (Lyons, 1994: 16). A general neglect of rural development was the result of concentration on building urban industry and securing the welfare of city people (Lyons, 1994: 17). In Fujian, the provincial government's 'inland development strategy' meant directing resources to certain areas where it saw as potential growth corridors. Thus, resources were directed to the area along the railroad running north-south, from Nanping to Longyan in the centre of the province (Lyons, 1994: 17). Cities along the route would benefit from industrialization and development. Anxi, which is off the route, did not.

The second phase of development started with the Deng's economic reform of 1978, which can be seen as a watershed for the transformation of the Chinese economy. The accompanying open door policy permitted the interior region to open up and develop new economic approaches and links with the outside world. There was fundamental change in the agrarian economy in Anxi: instead of encouraging agrarian self-sufficiency, encouragement was given to non-agricultural development and to eradicate poverty. The creation of special economic zones along the coast had great impact on the interior of the country, and the opening of the Xiamen Economic Zone brought about changes in all the counties in Fujian, including Anxi. The 'open door' policy targeted Chinese overseas and encouraged them to invest in China, and in their ancestral villages there.

Following the reform, to encourage non-agricultural development, there was a reduction in governmental control and directives, and external investments in the region were encouraged through various incentives. The Fujian provincial government developed a two-front strategy; one focused on the mountainous interior of the province and the other on the coastal areas. This strategy was to develop specialized districts and production bases according to the resources of the region (Lyons, 1994: 42–43). Following this strategy, production of tea and fruit was encouraged, and priority was given to tea and fruit producing areas for financial assistance to purchase better quality seeds and to expand processing industry, thereby making their tea and fruit competitive in both domestic and international markets.

Prior to the 1978 reform, Anxi County had only 64 industrial enterprises operated by various levels of government or the communes. These industrial enterprises were located primarily in the townships. The labour force working in the industrial sector accounted for only 11 per cent of the total labour force in 1978 (Lyons, 1994: 21). Since the reform, the provincial government has actively pursued overseas Chinese industrial investors and capital through a series of preferential policies. Special regulations to ensure protection of investors' property and legal rights covered Chinese overseas investors, especially the Taiwanese ones, for whom special enterprise zones were established in Haicang and Xinlin investment districts (Lyons, 1994: 45). This resulted in investments from Taiwan, which had set up a total of 1,203 enterprises worth US$1.6 billion in 1991 (Lyons, 1994: 45).

The reform policies thus affected economic restructuring. In the early 1980s, Anxi began to develop small-sized processing plants, and in 1984 received its first foreign investment (Lyons, 1994: 45). In 1985, Anxi County together with 11 other counties such as Jinjiang, Longxi and Xiamen became part of the newly established Minan (Southern Fujian) Open Area. Enterprises in this open area enjoyed preferential treatment, such as tax rebates on import duties for equipment and reduced tax rates on profits of foreign-owned enterprises (Lyons, 1994: 45). In 1987 and 1988, three towns in Anxi County (Hutou, Guanqiao and Jiandou) were designated as key satellite industrial bases by the provincial government for boosting the industrial development of the county and extending economic linkages to bigger industrial bases and to Xiamen City (Lyons, 1994: 48). However, Penglai Zhen was considered too small for economies of scale to occur and so was not designated as a key satellite industrial base.

Another area that the provincial and local governments focused on was the tourist trade. Various areas of Fujian, which were promoted as historic and religious sites, were well received, and the number of tourists jumped from 16,000 in 1987 to 146,000 in 1988, and exceeding 200,000 in each following year (Lyons, 1994: 45). In line with these tourist promotion efforts, Anxi County promoted itself as an important religious site, claiming the Qingshuiyan as its most important temple for Chinese overseas. Since then, there has been a steady stream of visitors to the temple primarily from Taiwan, Singapore and Malaysia. However, the majority of tourists have come to Anxi with the primary aim of visiting their ancestral village and home. In Penglai, 99 per cent of visitors went there to visit their ancestral homes.

The Village Economy

The primary economic activity in Anxi County was, and still is, farming. However, the mountainous terrain makes farming an arduous task, and efforts put into agricultural activities have never been highly productive. Because of the numerous mountain ranges and small amount of flat land, most farming has been carried out on terraces that were cut into steep slopes. In some places, the width of these terraces is no more than a foot, and that makes even walking through the terraced fields hazardous, let alone sowing and harvesting them.

In Anxi County, both subsistence farming and cash cropping are important. Wet rice cultivation is the main subsistence activity. The region produces two crops of rice annually for home consumption, but this production is insufficient for the large and growing population, and rice has to be imported to supplement local production. Since the reform of 1978, farming has been operating under the joint family responsibility system, and the market economy has led to a three to fourfold increase in the price of rice. Despite this, villagers continue to eat rice three times a day as their staple, although in recent years there has been some change in food habits; wheat products, including noodles and buns, have become popular. Vegetable gardening and pig and poultry rearing are also part of the subsistence economy, but vegetables, pork and poultry are now also sold at the busy weekly market. In 1994 a permanent market building was completed, the hawkers who had successfully applied for a license were given a stall to operate and have been able to sell vegetables and other produce on a daily basis. However, the villagers continue to patronize the open weekly market for fresh produce out of habit, as the price is lower. In general, since the late 1980s, there has been a rise in market produce prices, but despite this, a rise in the standard of living has meant that more people than before are able to afford meat and poultry, as most families can afford some form of meat several meals a week.

Since the reform, greater emphasis has been placed on cash cropping for export. In Anxi County in general and in Penglai Zhen in particular, the emphasis now is on tea and fruit growing, as tea and fruit have become the two most important revenue-earning crops, replacing other cash crops. Taking the cue from the provincial government, the local government has placed much emphasis on these two products, as the undulating landscape, subtropical cool temperate climate and sufficient rainfall have made Anxi one of China's important tea-planting districts. In 1990, the total area under tea plantation was 142,270 *mu* and the area actually harvested was 127,490 *mu*. Production of tea-leaves in the same year yielded 7,023 tonnes, giving an average of 55 kg per *mu* (*Anxi Xianzhi*, 1994, vol. 1: 173). In 2006, the total area under tea plantation was 247,562 *mu*. Production of tea-leaves in the same year yielded 26,605 tons, giving an average of 107.5 kg per *mu* (*Anxi Nianjian*, 2005–06, retrieved on 30 December 2009, from http://www.axdfz.gov.cn/ShowText.asp?ToBook=17008&index=122&).

Since the reform, the local government and the people's co-operatives have thus been able to increase the acreage of tea production. Various hybridization programmes have been introduced to produce higher-grade tea. Prior to reform, the main bulk of the tea-leaves produced were sent out to the cities for processing and packaging, but now the Anxi County government is planning to build facilities for processing and packaging of the finished product within Anxi County. In Penglai, there have also been discussions concerning the building of tea processing and packaging factories to solve unemployment problems. For this, officials have courted outside capital—for the most part, Chinese overseas capital—by using their *guanxi* network to activate a moral economy. These efforts worked.

New hybridization techniques and an improved work ethic for crop production have brought improvement in production yields generally. Agricultural production had tripled by 1990 over that of 1978, and was worth RMB 138.17 million. Actual grain production, however, only increased by 14.23 per cent. The pig population during the same period grew to 285,204 pigs. In short, there were major increases in production in forestry, animal husbandry, fishery and grain production, as the average farming household income went from RMB 267 in 1985 to RMB 5,781 in 2006 (*Anxi Xianzhi*, vol. 1: 173; *Anxi Nianjian*, 2005–06: http://www.axdfz.gov.cn/ShowText.asp?ToBook=17008&index=228&, retrieved on 30 December 2009).

However, while production has increased steadily, the amount of land devoted to agriculture has progressively decreased, as a result of land being put to non-agricultural uses such as roads, dykes, houses, shops and factories. Agricultural production has now taken a secondary role, overtaken by commercial and other non-agricultural practices, and this trend has worried both local and central governments. In Penglai, much effort has been used to restructure its economy from an agrarian base to a commercial and retailing one, and the result has been massive conversion of agricultural land for these purposes. The local government often permits the sale of agricultural land to outsiders for commercial uses. Farmland has also simply been converted to commercial use by villagers themselves who have sufficient capital to start up a business. In 1990, the total area under cultivation stood only at 8.64 per cent of the total land area in the vicinity of Penglai. Most paddy cultivation has now been pushed into the mountainous area, and in the 1980s, terrace cultivation constituted 67.15 per cent of all cultivable land (*Anxi Xianzhi*, vol. 1: 174).

Since the late 1980s, Penglai has contained a relatively well-developed town centre surrounded by small plots of agricultural land; some are devoted to rice growing while others are devoted to vegetables. Farming households also rear pigs and poultry for the market as important supplements to rice and vegetables. However, incomes of agricultural households are much lower than those of wage-earning labourers or private enterprises (*siying qiye*, 私营企业), who are engaged in retail trade or other commercial activities.

Although, formerly, both men and women shared in farming, as men moved out of Penglai and Anxi County to the cities in search of employment, an increasing number of plots came to be worked by women.

In 1990, only 28 per cent of the Anxi population were engaged in agricultural production—a total of 175,316 agricultural production household units, with a total farming population of 865,075 (*Anxi Xianzhi*, vol. 1: 75).

Besides pigs and poultry, local animal husbandry includes buffalo and rabbit rearing. However, pig rearing is probably the most important husbandry activity for farm households, as the profit margin on pork is much higher than for other animals, and pig production increased sixfold over the fifty years preceding 1990, when the number of pigs reared totalled 285,204. Water buffaloes are kept for cultivation purposes; cows are kept for their milk, but rarely for their meat. The total number of buffalo and female dairy cattle in

1990 stood at 59,141. The rearing of rabbits for meat and hides has become increasingly important to the farmers, and in recent years the import of a variety of kinds of rabbits from overseas has made this an important practice. Poultry raised in most households as a side activity includes ducks and chickens, raised for both meat and eggs. Total production of poultry stood at 1,756,034 birds in 1990.

As Anxi County is now one of the most important tea-producing regions in China, Anxi tea is associated with well-known labels such as Oolong and Tieguanyin. Tea production is found in both inner and outer Anxi and Penglai. Anxi's 2006 tea acreage of 247,562 *mu* produced 127,490 tonnes; in that year, Penglai had 14,275 *mu* under tea production, for a total of 1,120 tonnes. The average per *mu* in Penglai was 78.5 kg per *mu*, which was below the average of 107.5 kg per *mu* for Anxi County (*Anxi Nianjian,* 2005–06: http://www.axdfz.gov.cn/ShowText.asp?ToBook=17008&index=122&, retrieved on 30 December 2009). Most of the tea-leaves produced were sent to the cities for processing; inferior grades were left behind and processed within the district for local consumption. The number of tea-processing factories in Anxi in 1990 totalled 280, of which 9 were state-operated, 161 were operated by co-operatives, and 110 were privately owned.

Fruit orchards have also become more important in recent years, with fruit being exported. Tangerines and longans are the two most important fruits grown for export: others include bananas, pomelos, sugar cane, peaches, plums and pears. In 1990, total acreage devoted to fruit orchards in Anxi was 112,447 *mu*; total production was 4566.7 tonnes. In Penglai, the total area under fruit production was 3,517 *mu* and total production was 423.4 tonnes. In 2004, total acreage devoted to fruit orchards in Anxi was 156,155,523 *mu*; total production was 25,900 tonnes. In Penglai, the total area under fruit production was 13,550 *mu* and total production was, 1,435 tonnes (*Anxi Nianjian,* 2005–06: http://www.axdfz.gov.cn/ShowText.asp?ToBook=17008&index=109&, retrieved on 30 December 2009).

The average farm size per person in 1990 stood at 1.42 *mu*; farms classified as 'wealthy' averaged 1.6 *mu*, with those 'wealthy' farmers who were partial landowners owning an average of 1.68 *mu*. The 'average' farmers owned 1.54 *mu* each, while poor farmers owned 1.35 *mu*. Those who employed workers to work on their farms had an average farm size of 1.53 *mu*. Tenanted farms were the largest, with an average farm size of 2 *mu* (*Anxi Xianzhi*, vol. 1: 180).

The average income of RMB 546 per person for Anxi in 1990 represented a substantial improvement over RMB 23.9 per person in 1960. However, private traders and truck operators' earnings totalled RMB 2,000–3,000 or more a month in 1990. Since 1996 however, average incomes had increased to RMB 2181.88 per month.[1] This can partially be attributed to a shift from grain production to market gardening, rearing of pigs and poultry, and other cash crop production. More importantly, perhaps, it reflects a shift of economic activities of household members to some form of industrial production or enterprise, such as retail and the service industries.

Eradicating Poverty

One goal of the 1978 reform was to eradicate poverty and raise the standard of living of the peasants in the whole of China. The central government launched an anti-poverty campaign in 1985 to solve the problems of basic subsistence of people living in poverty. It hoped that by 1990, the conditions of 90 per cent of those below the poverty line would be alleviated, and they would attain a decent standard of living. Three hundred counties were designated as national poverty areas. In Fujian province, 14 counties, including Anxi, were so designated (Lyons, 1994: 49). One important strategy in this campaign was the provisions of low-interest loans to these counties, from a national allocation budget of RMB 1 billion. These counties were given grain allocations and other commodities as pay for workers on infrastructure projects in lieu of money. These grain and other allocations were also used by provincial and lower-level governments to exchange for raw materials for infrastructure projects (Lyons, 1994: 49).

As part of its campaign, the Fujian provincial government, in addition to its nationally-designated 14 poverty counties, designated 3 other counties and 200 poverty townships as poor. A provincial anti-poverty bureaucracy was set up and was involved in policy promulgation, implementation and on-site inspection. This bureaucracy was also expected to provide technical expertise, to train villagers in the desired skills and to set up linkages among the poor districts to facilitate the campaign. The province implemented a '3/5/8' strategy; that is, to solve the basic needs of the majority of the poor households within three years (1986–88); to solve the problems of local budget deficits within five years; and to encourage rapid growth in poor areas and turn deficit into surplus to contribute to the provincial treasury within eight years (Lyons, 1994: 49–50). It employed four tactics. First was investment in human capital—to eradicate illiteracy and boost technical skills for the farming households. Second was to encourage commercialization and commodity production, with farming households being encouraged to diversify production, especially to include cash cropping and involvement in the market economy. Thirdly, the provincial government attempted to restructure the local economy by dealing with farming problems such as land degradation and erosion on the one hand and by introducing value-added industry to better harness local resources and produce on the other. Finally, it strove for infrastructure development and promotion of those sectors that were cost-effective and that brought in rapid and high returns to stimulate further demands and production (Lyons, 1994: 50).

In Anxi, the local government implemented three policies to eradicate poverty. The first was to provide capital, technical and commercial knowledge to poverty-stricken households. The second was to provide preferential treatment to mountain districts to promote growth by harnessing local forest resources. The third was to open the county to trade and investment (Lyons, 1994: 52).

In 1987, the county's strategy of 'taking grain as the foundation and forests as the base, using teas for escaping poverty, and fruits for becoming prosperous' resulted in massive destruction of the forested area and the creation environmental problems (Lyons, 1994: 52). This did nothing to solve the problem of surplus labour.

In the early 1990s, the slogan was simplified to a 'strategy for escaping from poverty and for overall development' (Lyons, 1994: 52). In the agricultural sector, local officials were organized to assist farmers with new techniques of farming, while farmers were provided with fertilizers and other farming essentials to help raise yields. At the same time, training classes were organized for farmers to learn the new techniques and methods, and farmers were encouraged to improve irrigation and to use mechanical plows and fertilizers for cultivation (Lyons, 1994: 59–62). The result was that, from 1980 to 1992, grain production increased by 13 per cent (Lyons, 1994: 62).

To encourage diversification and commercialization, the local government adopted a strategy called 'one product per village, one industry per township', with the aim of making local products cash crops and using local resources in industry that could become commercially viable export industry. Each village was thus encouraged to focus on the production of one leading local product, such as one kind of fruit or tea.

For the county as a whole, tea production was highly encouraged. Existing tea production was upgraded with the introduction of more varieties and higher-grade seeds. The Oolong Tea Research Institute and the Oolong Quality Control Centre were set up to improve and standardize the quality of tea produced in the county, and an aggressive promotion campaign to promote Anxi tea around China and in overseas markets was launched. During the 1950s and 1960s, tea had been mainly processed in the designated state-run tea factory, and such factories continued to be important tea processing plants. However, in 1987, village-run plants were permitted, and in that year 50 such plants took advantage of the relaxed policies and began operation. By the 1990s, several hundred village-run plants had been established (Lyons, 1994: 63).

Fruit production was also encouraged. The county government designated that each village should devote 100 *mu* to a collective orchard and that each household should maintain a private orchard of 1 *mu*. Those who complied with this demand were given preferential treatment, and large plots of hilly land were leased to individuals and partnerships for long-term fruit orchards. The result was that by 1992, about 82,200 *mu* of land was devoted to fruit orchards that grew for export (Lyons, 1994: 64).

The result of this was that, in Anxi County in 1992, cash crop production accounted for RMB 19.22 million. By 1996, agricultural production had increased spectacularly to RMB 83.08 million.

There was also encouragement to develop township and village enterprises, and they developed rapidly. Most of these were privately owned, rather than being state- or county-operated. Many were involved in small production, from processing agricultural products to producing building materials, chemicals and consumer goods such as shoes and garments. By the 1990s, the number of township and village enterprises had grown to over 1,000, but all were operated on a very small-scale basis, with an average of about five workers and an average annual income not exceeding RMB 26,000 (Lyons, 1994: 65). In Penglai, each village enterprise employed somewhere between 10 to 20 workers, with annual revenue between RMB 50,000 to RMB 100,000 per enterprise in 1995.

The county government also encouraged foreign investment, and instituted a series of ten preferential policies for foreign and joint-venture investments. It particularly appealed to Chinese overseas to invest in their ancestral villages, especially encouraging basic infrastructure development, export-oriented industries and general agricultural development (Lyons, 1994: 68). Although in 1990, there were only 7 foreign-invested township and village enterprises in operation in Penglai, by 1991 there was a total of 38 foreign-invested enterprises in Anxi County, of which 14 were garment industries. Others included enterprises producing umbrellas, silk flowers, rattan products, chemical products, recording tapes and shampoo. Twenty-five consumer goods enterprises were equity joint ventures, two were co-operative ventures and eleven were wholly foreign-owned. Most of these were located in the county seat of Fengcheng and other large towns such as Hutou, Penglai, Kuidou, Xiping, Jingu and Shangqing (Lyons, 1994: 69–70). The average investment capital for these enterprises was US$280,000; only a handful had investment capital over US$1 million. Foreign investors were primarily from Taiwan and Hong Kong (Lyons, 1994: 70). By 1990, these enterprises were employing over 10,000 workers (Lyons, 1994: 71).

In 1990, Penglai had 11 joint venture enterprises involved in plastics, garments and tea processing. These joint ventures were set up with capital from the Chinese overseas. To encourage further investment into the region, the contributions of these Chinese overseas were publicly honoured (Lyons, 1994: 73), and the local government allied closely with Chinese overseas social institutions—namely, the territorial-based home village associations (*tongxianghui*), like the Anxi Association—to promote further investment.

In 1992, industrial production for Anxi County accounted for RMB 23.3 million and enterprise activities accounted for RMB 38.52 million. By 1996, industrial production and enterprise activities had increased several fold, to RMB 146.18 million and RMB 210.46 million, respectively.[2] In 2006, industrial production for Anxi County accounted for RMB 21.8 billion (*Anxi Nianjian*, 2005–06: http://www.axdfz.gov.cn/ShowText. asp?ToBook=17008&index=228&, retrieved on 30 December 2009).

Concerning basic infrastructure, a railway from Zhangping to Quangzhou run through Anxi for 115 km was completed in 1998. Highways, telecommunication and power plants were also in the pipeline (Lyons 1994: 74). Apart from these major state-sponsored projects, many feeder roads, bridges and power plants were built with money from Chinese overseas. In Penglai, numerous local roads were constructed. From 1992 to 1996, a total of 36.3 km of sealed surface road was constructed, costing about RMB 5.3 million.[3]

These measures, together with substantial money flowed in from the Singapore Chinese, have made the town and villages in Penglai some of the wealthiest town in the Anxi County.

Opting out of an Agrarian Economy

While agricultural activity is important in this landlocked and mountainous region, many of the peasants opt out of it whenever there is an opportunity, as the work is hard and the income from it is low. This negative attitude towards agriculture has been further reinforced by the devaluation of agricultural pursuits, both in the eyes of central, provincial and local governments and in those of their Singapore kin, who are biased towards commerce and trading. The fact is that there is simply insufficient land to feed the growing population.

Subsistence farming brings little or no wealth to a family, and local farmers have traditionally found it hard to provide sufficiently for their families from their meagre incomes. Even with the market reform and the freedom to decide what crops to grow, agricultural incomes continue to lag behind those of other occupations. The most lucrative form of agriculture is market gardening, and fresh vegetables and produce are now sold daily in the marketplace; however, although prices of such produce are now governed by demand, incomes remain lower than those earned from businesses. It is thus not surprising that many young villagers are deserting farming for other kinds of jobs. To them, farming is a dead-end job, with farmers confined to the village, with no prospect of social mobility and no possibility for wealth accumulation. This attitude is shared by their Singapore kin, many of whom have discouraged their kin from going into farming or have persuaded them to give up market gardening in favour of the trading and service industries. Given this disdain for agriculture, Singapore Chinese have not contributed significantly to improving agriculture.

Thus, today, many villagers with Singapore connections have opted out of agricultural production. Those with farmland have several choices: some lease their land to other farmers; others engage farm labourers to work it for them; and a third group trades their land to the district government for sums of money which are then used to buy shophouses in Penglai Zhen, in which case the land, especially that near the town centre, is put to commercial use. Yet others have built modern-style houses for themselves on agricultural land with money provided by their Singapore kin.

The impact of the shrinking agricultural areas has been felt in recent years. Anxi County and Penglai must now import more of its daily needs, and this has resulted in price inflation for all products; the prices of basic essentials like rice, oil, and vegetables have gone up four to fivefold since the early 1990s.

Luxury items like cigarettes and beer have also suffered a price hike, as a result of increased consumption. Villagers have complained loudly about this inflation but have been helpless to stop it. They have blamed it on the reform, on massive consumption by Singapore Chinese when they visit, and on the increasing number of wealthy Anxi villagers with ostentatious lifestyles.

To a certain extent, those with wealthy Singapore kin have been cushioned from the rising cost of living, while those without overseas connections have felt that life has become tougher. Irrespective of this, however, many feel that the changes have been good, having brought wealth to some and opportunities to others. The very poor without overseas connections now have the opportunity to become tenant farmers and earn a reasonable living. Sometimes the wealthier households with farmland but no one to work on it even lease the land to the landless farmers without charge, allowing them to move beyond subsistence farming and earn income from surplus production.

At any rate, the reform and rekindling of kinship ties with their Singapore kin have enabled Anxi villagers to have bigger dreams and to turn them into reality. Many now have had opportunities to move out of the villages and live in Fengcheng, or in cities such as Xiamen. For a long time, they had kept their heads down and had gone on with a life that was dictated to them, with little to dream about and no vision beyond the village boundary, fighting only to survive unscathed. Now, situations have improved, and in dreaming of life beyond the village, their life energies once again flow, making them ready to face new challenges.

4

Negotiating Collective Memories and Social Experiences

Since the nineteenth century, emigrants have moved out of Fujian to Nanyang and elsewhere in search of better economic opportunities, and a large number moved to Malaya and Singapore and settled there. After World War II, another 20,000 Anxi villagers immigrated to Singapore. Today, the number of emigrants from Anxi to Singapore and their descendants totals 185,309, or about 10 per cent of the Chinese Singaporean population. Of these, 41,075 came from Penglai (*Anxi Xianzhi,* vol. 2: 854). The primary reason for this early emigration trend was extreme poverty.

From the late 1970s through the 1990s, it was this poverty in Anxi that lured the same Singapore Anxi Chinese to visit their ancestral villages and assist with the rebuilding of their ancestral homes. Several factors accounted for this. Some remembered their ancestral village, having experienced the poverty and later witnessed its continuation when they first returned for visits in the late 1960s and early 1970s. Many felt simultaneously fortunate and guilty about their relatively comfortable status in Singapore and their helplessness to assist during the 1960s and 1970s. After the 1978 reform, the changing political climates in both China and Singapore have enabled them to re-evaluate their situation and their relationship with their Anxi kin. They are now in a position to assist, and feel the compelling need to provide assistance to their village kin and to the villages in general.

This chapter will explore how collective memories serve as an important power and moral capital that constantly nags the Singapore Anxi Chinese and tugs at their conscience. These memories do not go away, but challenge their emotions and sentiments until they have done something for their respective ancestral villages. However, the same set of passed-on collective memories also serve to discourage their Singapore-born descendants from visiting the villages, and the result has been an inter-generational tension between the China-born and the Singapore-born Chinese. This is also the case between the Singapore Anxi Chinese and their village kin.

The Flow of Collective Memories

For the Singapore Chinese, the collective memories of their ancestral homes are selective ones. In reconstructing past events, many recount the great difficulties and poverty that they faced, their fear of the unknown when they set sail for Singapore, and their eventual success, however modest, in Singapore. They also remember the early years of struggle for survival in the villages. It is these memories that they have kept alive and that they choose to pass on to their descendants.

Poverty and great difficulties not only pushed these migrants out of their villages but also pushed them to work hard and overcome difficulties of their early years in Singapore. This contributed to the 'refugee mentality' and the spirit of survival. Today, even after attaining success and wealth, some of these Singapore Chinese continue to work hard. And memory has guided the migrants in providing assistance and involving themselves in constructing and reconstructing their ancestral villages and to help to eradicate poverty among their kin. Projects which began with the aim of helping immediate family members and lineage kin have gradually shifted towards helping the wider community. In making this shift, the migrants have attempted, with their contributions, to make clear distinctions between private needs and public demands.

The migrants' memories and strong sense of belonging allow them to locate themselves within a known and manageable social framework grounded in kinship ties, and facilitate the revival of relationships. This in turn involves taking a measure of their self-worth and fulfilling moral duties, which include providing a bridge to link the younger Singapore Chinese to their ancestral homes. Through routine conversation, they have had some success in making the younger Singapore Chinese aware of the plight of their ancestral villages.

In keeping alive the memories of their home villages the Singapore Chinese are reminded of ritual obligations and of their initial failures to carry them out, either in Singapore or in their ancestral villages, during times when the Communist regime even prevented the villagers from carrying out religious rituals and ancestor worship. Now that political pressure has eased, the Singaporeans hope to revive and reproduce these rituals.

Maintaining Links from 1960 to 1978

The last major wave of migration to Singapore began in the 1950s, when many young men and women in their teens, twenties and thirties emigrated and joined families already in Singapore. During this period, the established nature of the Singaporean Chinese community, with its numerous social networks, enabled the newcomers to adapt to the new environment with relative ease. Independent migrants, too, could tap into existing networks. This was a period when wives and daughters joined husbands and fathers, a period of great reunion for immediate families.

However, family life was difficult in the 1950s and 1960s. Most new guests, sinkhehs[H] (*xinke*, 新客) gained employment as workers where wages were low and lived in crammed housing with sparse amenities. It was common for several households, usually of kin, to share one house.[1] While the men were at work, often for ten hours or more a day, the women were left to cope with a limited budget, a shared kitchen, a growing family and very limited physical space. Most households then lived in a single room of a house, but there was mutual assistance among them. Women informants have told me that the lack of money forced women to help each other with food and cash.

From the 1970s onwards, livelihood among the migrants have improved substantially and some have moved into private housing while others into subsidized housing built by the government. From 1960 to 1978, many families maintained links with their village kin, often sending money, parcels and letters to Anxi regularly. My mother, for example, would go through our wardrobe, selectively pick out some of our old clothing and, together with some new clothing, fabrics, food and medicated oil, bundle it into a parcel, which would then be sent to our village, either by post or via returning relatives. Though some were on very tight budgets and often did not have enough for their immediate families, many continued to send small remittances, motivated by their knowledge of the great poverty in Anxi. The letters helped us to create images of village life during the early period. The letters written by the villagers emphasized the difficulties of making ends meet—those of scarce resources such as food, clothing and medicine, and of large families, bad weather, and poor harvests, during the collective years in China. Most households were then barely subsisting, and many letters sent to Singapore kin asked for various forms of supplies. The most frequently-requested items included foodstuffs, clothing and medicine; large items included bicycles and sewing machines.

Maintaining contacts between Singapore and Anxi was not an easy task. Those left behind in the village were often semi-literate or illiterate, and most letters were written by village letter-writers who charged a fee for their services. Thus most of these letters were identical in style, with limited variation in contents. Most villagers did not write regularly, generally only two or three letters a year, receiving the same number in return. Additional letters were dispatched to Singapore only when there were important matters to report, such as the death or impending marriage of close kin. Letters from Anxi villagers included inquiries concerning health and family well-being, as well as accounts of their own difficulties. Special needs were generally implied rather than stated openly, and readers were expected to infer what these were from suggestions, and to act accordingly.

For the Singapore Chinese, sending a letter was not a straightforward affair, as it was expected that a remittance, and occasionally gifts, would be included. The norm was that letters were sent during Lunar New Year to help with the festivities of the occasion.

Receiving a Singapore letter in Anxi was an exciting affair, because of the gifts—money, clothing, medicine, foodstuffs, bicycles, sewing machines and so forth, and it became increasingly difficult for the Singaporeans merely to send a letter of inquiry without accompanying gifts. The majority had therefore reduced the incidence of communication with their Anxi relatives. Thus, receiving a 'China letter' (*tangshanxin*, 唐山信) created a plethora of imagery, and of wants that the Singaporeans found hard to satisfy at times, and there was very little joy in receiving *tangshanxin*. A common attitude towards receiving a China letter came to be: 'It is expected, they will ask for things. Why bother to receive them?' Another informant commented: 'Here it comes again, they are asking for money again.' After a time, some simply stopped responding to such letters, and this led to mutual ill feelings. One villager Kim commented: 'What is the use of having overseas Chinese kin, *qiaoqing* (侨亲)? They don't even bother to maintain contacts with us. We have received no benefits from them. They don't send us anything. It is better not to have them as *qiaoqing*.'

Correspondence and gift-giving were more difficult during the Cultural Revolution and the immediate years that followed. The fear of persecution by those with capitalist *qiaoqing* connections meant that few letters were sent by villagers to their Singapore kin; likewise, there was a drop in the number of letters and gifts from Singapore. Although parcels of old clothing were sent to those in dire need, almost no new clothing was sent. A few stashed pieces of new clothing might be sent in bundles of old ones. Or, the new clothes were deliberately made to look like worn ones; one common method was to patch them with small pieces of old linen. Such small parcels were sent, but many people were not confident that the parcels would reach their village kin intact, as there was much suspicion that part of the gifts was pilfered or confiscated by people in authority.

Many Singapore Chinese, as well as villagers, remembered this as a very difficult period for their village kin. There was great political upheaval and uncertainty in the villages, and overseas connections were politically suspect. Most Singapore Chinese did not know how to respond to the changes that were occurring. Since even very limited correspondence or contact could jeopardize village kin, many stopped writing. For those who continued, letter writing became an art of allusion, with few words: letters of this period contained only a few sentences, or at most a paragraph, most contained only words of greeting and inquiry of health and general well-being, and were otherwise devoid of sentiment or emotion. Such precautionary measures were necessary, as it was common for letters to be opened and read by postal officials before being sent on to Singapore or forwarded to the villagers. The general attitude, then, was that no news was good news, although receiving any letter was a sign that village kin continued to survive. After a while, everyone in Singapore knew of the harshness of life in the villages, and people became very adept at reading into the absence of letters. The Singapore Chinese could understand the broad picture, although it remained impossible for them to reconstruct the details.

During the course of this research, I was told that many letters sent by Singapore Chinese to their village kin had been destroyed, although more recent ones were kept. However, I managed to acquire a sizeable collection of letters from villagers to Singapore kin. Only after the 1970s did more sentiment and emotion appear in the letters as, after the reform, things returned to normal and steady communication was once again the norm, when, two or three times a year, each side would write. By the 1980s, face-to-face contact had become more common, and as more *qiaoqing* visited Anxi, communication by letter was reduced to a secondary importance.

Today, long-distance telephone conversations have taken the place of letters. As late as the mid-1980s, telephone calls were made at the village post office. Households which can afford them now have had long-distance telephone lines installed to facilitate communication with their Singapore *qiaoqing*. But while Singapore Chinese had begun to rely substantially on telephone communication with their village kin in the event of matters needing immediate attention, this was not the case for the villagers, for whom the cost of making a long-distance call was still huge in the 1990s. Instead, they continued to send letters two to three times annually. It was fortunate for my research that, apart from being more economical, letters, being tangible, continued to be regarded as important testimonies of communication between the two groups. By 2000, almost all villagers called long-distance and the younger ones have mobile phones. Long-distance calls were also cheaper and more affordable to many; regular contacts were done for those with closer ties. Now, they also have computers and correspond via email, MSN, QQ and

Skype, which enable the two groups of kin to communicate without having to worry about the cost.

Trips to Ancestral Villages in the 1960s and 1970s

A second method to maintain ties is to visit the ancestral village in person. This was extremely difficult before 1978, but some people did manage to do so. The main reasons for the difficulty were political, as in both Singapore and China the Cold War was still raging. The Singapore government imposed severe restrictions on communications and travel to and from China, and those below the age of 45 were not given exit permits to visit China. Likewise, getting a Chinese visa to visit China was also subjected to various restrictions.

However, from the 1950s through the 1970s, despite the difficulties, a small number of Anxi Chinese managed to visit their home villages. Those who travelled by air had to transit in Hong Kong and then make their way by sea to Shantou (Swatow, 汕头), and then travel over land. Others made the journey to Shantou or Xiamen (Amoy, 厦门) by sea.

During these early years, only a few travel agencies specialized in trips to China. The agencies would arrange for exit permits, visas to China, ticketing and all other related matters, including the handling of crates of personal effects when travelling by sea. Passenger ships plied from Singapore to Shantou, Xiamen and Quanzhou (Chuanchiu, 泉州) on a regular basis, usually once a month. Many visitors travelled by sea, not on an individual basis but in small groups of ten or more related kin, one of whom would initiate the journey and then invite others to join it. Each passenger was allowed a crate of personal effects—hence the attraction of sea travel, as airlines permitted only 20 kg of baggage.

During these years, more women than men travelled to their home villages, partly because of the lengthy time period required for the trip. The journey by sea would take several days, and usually two to three weeks would be required for the visit, such that the whole journey often lasted a month. It was difficult for working men to travel for such extended periods, and those men who did so travelled by air and were usually in the village for only one or two weeks. Many male travellers were retired elderly men who had more time to spend. During this period, majority of the women were housewives, looking after a usually big family. Some could spare the time for the trip when their children were grown-ups.

In Singapore, the women did most preparation for such journeys. Most travellers would prepare one or two wooden crates of goods to be distributed, and there would be much agonizing over the items to be included, as it was extremely difficult to know the exact needs of village kin. Some knowledge of conditions in the villages might be provided by a few who had visited earlier. Although decisions as to what to take were mostly made by women, they 'discussed and informed' their husbands of their decisions so that they would be given money to purchase the items. During these years there was very little surplus money within the household, and in many cases it was the men who controlled the purse, although women had some 'private room money', *sifangqian* (私房钱), consisting of money given by husbands to satisfy personal needs plus savings from their marketing expenses. This money was also used to purchase gifts for the journeys.

In addition to the clothing, fabrics, bicycles and sewing machines, the foodstuffs taken included biscuits, cooking oil and dried meat; medicines included medicated oil, various types of vitamin pills, cod liver oil pills, Western medicine for headaches, flu and cold, and Chinese medicine, including ginseng. Although there were occasionally a motor-scooter or other more expensive items packed into the crate, the Singapore Chinese were cautious not to take too many such luxury items out of fear that they might be taken away by customs officers when the crates were opened for inspection at Shantou or other ports of disembarkation. Singapore informants told me that the villagers had very little clothing, some with only one or two new sets of clothes a year, and hardly had enough to keep them warm during the winter months. Medicine and vitamins were non-existent in the villages. Cod liver oil was considered a very good health supplement and was much sought after by the village kin. During this period, Chinese-style pharmaceutical houses sold them in big packages to be taken to China. Singapore-produced medicated balms such as Tiger Balm, or Hubiaoyou, Hor Piaw Yew [H] (虎标油), and White Flower Oil, or Baihuayou, Pae Hway Yew [H] (白花油), were most sought after, and visitors would generally take several dozen of them to distribute to their relatives. Traditional Chinese medicines such as ginseng, herbal roots, and animal extracts and products were expensive and would be purchased in smaller quantities for immediate family members. These would be packed in hand luggage. A limited amount of gold jewellery was also taken as gifts, including rings, earrings and gold chains, some of which were worn as personal items to avoid customs declaration. Inexpensive watches were taken for the men. Most people would also carry a limited amount of cash, but this was to be distributed to more distant kin, as it was general knowledge that cash was less important than material goods at this time. One villager said, 'during the early years, it was pointless to have money because there was nothing one could buy with it. All material things were rationed to us. So, it was better for our relatives to bring us material goods.'

Although these Singapore travellers packed as much as they could into the crates, somehow there was never enough, for everyone wanted a share of the goods. During this time, somewhat mysteriously, the kinship circle expanded: everyone who came to visit the guests from Singapore in the village claimed that they knew, or were related to, someone in the immediate family, and it became very difficult to reject these distant relatives and neighbours who came, and so each would be treated to a meal and a small amount of cash (about RMB 5).

In 1974, my mother made her first trip back to her home village, 24 years after she had sailed for Singapore. She was very excited, and this was contagious among the children. Two weeks prior to her departure, my father had instructed his company workers to assemble a wooden crate about one cubic metre in volume. Inside the crate, my mother packed new and old clothes, fabrics, and large tins of cooking oil, biscuits, grains, shoes, medical products, a sewing machine and a bicycle. My siblings and I took turns to flatten the fabrics to create extra space to pile in more things. My mother also took small jewellery items, such as gold rings and earrings, for the women, and inexpensive watches for the men.

Although my mother only packed one crate, some of our Singapore female relatives prepared two or three. Together they journeyed by sea, and endured a week of sea-sickness and extreme discomfort. They disembarked at Shantou, met their relatives and travelled, with their crates to Xiamen, then to Anxi and finally reached the village. Altogether, it was an arduous journey. Although conditions on board had improved compared to those encountered during their maiden trip to Singapore in the early 1950s, they were not ideal; the food was poor, and overcrowdedness was the norm. Later, they travelled to Xiamen which shortened their land travel.

In the village, my mother stayed with my father's elder sister and her family. She had thought that, after the crate was opened, she would be able to distribute small amounts of the contents to each household related to her. As my father had only two elder sisters (one deceased in the early 1970s) and my mother had two elder brothers and one younger sister, in her mind there were only five households closest to her with which she considered herself to have true ties, and a large share of the goods would go to them. Ties to others were more distant, and they would be given an item each, while those who visited her, but with whom she had no blood or other close ties, would be treated to a meal. However, she was soon awakened to reality when her understanding of the order of kinship relations proved to have little bearing on events. When her crate was opened, there was a mad rush for all the goods which my mother had brought back. Despite the fullness of the crate, there was hardly enough to be distributed to all, and those who were more daring simply grabbed more.

Although my mother tried to stop them, it was a futile exercise: the goods were too much of a temptation for civil behaviour. My mother had underestimated the boldness of some relatives, or maybe she had underestimated the extent of the material poverty and deprivation of the village kin. She could not stop her nephews and nieces from taking things from the crate. The result was that the goods that she had painstakingly planned and placed in the crate for the various kin were taken away from her. The kinship order had collapsed in front of her. She was disappointed and disillusioned. When this event happened in the household of her husband's elder sister's family, the helplessness which she felt must have been hard for her to bear. The oppression of being a junior member within the extended family structure dictated that she hold her tongue and swallow the bitterness and frustration emerging from within, as there was nothing she could do. It was a painful and pitiful sight to see the looting of her treasure, yet be helpless to do anything about it. In her words:

> My relatives met me at the port of Amoy. My husband had earlier written and informed them of my trip. So my brothers, one sister-in-law [the other deceased] and nephews waited at the port for me. Then they hired a van that brought us to our village. We had to stay for a day in Amoy to unload the cargo. Once we had the crate, we set off for the village. It took us a full day from Amoy to reach Anxi.
>
> I was taken to my sister-in-law's home. The condition of the house was not very good. They had not yet renovated the house as they awaited my husband to send them money to help with the rebuilding. At that time, although there was a guesthouse for overseas Chinese, it was not appropriate for us, especially women, to stay there on our own. All of us stayed with our relatives. I was no exception. Further, the main idea behind the trip was to rekindle our relationship with our relatives. Staying elsewhere would not have been the right thing to do.
>
> When we arrived at the home, even before I could have a little rest, my nephews started opening the crate. They did not ask for my permission, nor did they ask whom the goods were intended for. They assumed that it belonged to them. When the crate was opened, they took out everything and those they wanted, leaving very little behind. I was not consulted over whether the goods were for them or not. At that time, as I was still suffering from motion sickness and fatigue, I did not have the energy to tell them not to take all the goods that were in the crate. So, they had the lion share of it. My siblings had very little. Fortunately, I had also placed some clothing and medicines in my personal suitcase and they had no

access to this. It was locked and I did not let them open it. I was able to control the distribution of the little I was left with.

Suddenly everyone in the village became related to you. They told me that they knew my parents and grandparents. It was difficult to ignore them. I would give a small amount of cash. At that time, I would give RMB 5 to each person. I tried not to give them the clothing and goods that I brought back for my close relatives. But it was very hard to ignore some, especially the very old ones. They came and asked for an extra shirt to keep them warm. But most would come asking for medicine. There was nothing in the village and they would say, 'Could you please give me a bottle of Hor Piaw Yew ? I often feel dizzy and I feel good after inhaling this medicine.' Others would say, 'Could I have some ginseng from you? My health is bad and ginseng would provide the tonic that my body needs.' It was hard. How could I reject them? Many a time, I found myself dividing these into small portions and giving to them. But, no matter how much I brought back, there would never be enough to give to everyone.

When my mother returned to Singapore after a month's visit, she was exhausted and disappointed. She tried to be empathetic, and talked much about poverty in the village. But there was little doubt of the disappointment she had experienced with some of her kin, and it would be another ten years before she set foot in her home village again.

Dividing the goods to be distributed thus proved to be a more difficult task than expected for the Singaporeans. What was supposed to be a straightforward distribution was complicated by the need to display a sense of diplomacy, generosity, compassion, good kinship and neighbourly ties. As the kinship circle had inevitably widened, it was not possible to include all, yet one had no choice but to take into consideration all these 'extra people' who appeared on one's doorstep in order not to be branded with the phrase *buhui zuoren* (不会做人), i.e., one who does not know how 'to be a person' and behave with propriety, in this case, a miser or mean person.

My mother's experience was not a unique one. Throughout our kinship circle, both women and men had been trading their experiences visiting their home village. The stories were of poverty, great difficulties, fear, sadness, greed and resignation. The picture, by all accounts, was not cheerful. However, another informant Kay considered herself more fortunate:

I was met by my husband's brother's family in Amoy and stayed with them for a whole month. His family members had better upbringing. When we arrived at their place, they asked me to have a wash and a little rest. They served me some tea and food.

> The crate that I brought was left in the house. But no one opened it as other relatives of mine had experienced. They were polite and inquired about my journey and my family. It was only on the second day, after I had rested, that I asked my brother-in-law to open the crate. When the crate was opened, none of his children rushed and asked for things, although they were in the house. My brother-in-law and sister-in-law helped me to unpack the goods from the crate. I was able to control the situation and told them of my distribution plan. They did not ask for anything more than what I had given them. It made the task a lot more pleasant. Because they did not ask for anything, I felt that I had to give them more. Anyway, if you stayed at someone's place, it was expected that they would receive more from you although they did not say it. Also, they were our closest relatives and they were so polite. So, I did not mind giving them more than the others.

The negative views which the Singapore Chinese returnees held were reinforced by the lack of amenities and the difficulties that they faced in the home villages. Poor housing, inadequate heating during the winter months, poor food and unhygienic sanitary conditions made their visits unpleasant. Living in orderly and stable Singapore for two to three decades had made village life seem exceptionally harsh to them, and for some the culture shock was more than they could handle; others adjusted with difficulty, even though they only stayed for short periods. Informant Bee retraced her encounters with the reality of village life:

> I knew that the conditions in the village would be very bad. But I did not expect it to be so primitive. The house was old but it was liveable. What I did not expect was the toilet facilities. It was very bad. They had to go to the communal latrine (*maowu*, 茅屋) which was basically a hut made of dried leaves. The *maowu* had several holes dug out to contain the human dung. The smell was very bad even when one walked past it. I did not know how they could use it. But I just could not. This was the worst shock I had when I visited the village. Fortunately for us, we had our own latrine outside the house. So, at least, I did not need to go to the communal latrine.
>
> The village was even worse than the *kampong* in Singapore during the early years. It was dirty and smelly. The smell from the poultry and pigs was unbearable most of the time. But there was nothing one could do. Also, the place was very dusty and it was difficult to feel clean.

> The food was also very bad. The villagers did not know how to cook good food and it was tasteless. Fortunately, I brought some chilli sauce so that I could flavour the food with it. I would prefer to cook my own food but it was difficult for me to venture into the kitchen. The women kin would not allow me to do so. But I went into the kitchen several times and taught them how to cook with spices so that the food would taste better.
>
> The stay was not very easy although I tried my best to adapt to the place and not complain about it. But conditions have improved substantially today compared to the first trip I made in 1974.

Negative Representations

The behaviour of the village kin was often seen as uncivil and barbaric, and there was little that the returnees saw that they liked. However, these women attributed it to the great hardship and poverty that their village kin had undergone under Communist rule. Life had been hard and there was great material poverty. The villagers simply had nothing and they lived in poor condition, mostly in broken sheds and huts. There was insufficient food and clothing, and children were given only basic education. It was this impression that brought them some sympathy and sadness, and that pushed them to want to further assist their village kin in whatever small ways they could.

However, it was the set of negative representations which they brought home to Singapore and which became commonly known among the Singapore Anxi Chinese. They exchanged information and provided advice to other intending travellers. In this way, their experiences and understandings were told and retold, and the stories became an important part of the repertoire of memory and representation of their ancestral villages, which was passed down to their descendants, remaining in circulation today. Elderly Siu explained,

> These village people were very greedy. They were like bandits and demanded everything of you. They wanted not only the goods that you brought with you, but also the clothing, jewellery and money that you had with you. When they came to visit you, you were expected to play host. You were expected to cook and feed them and if you were a man, you would be expected to throw a feast for all villagers. So, the household that you were staying with would be very busy. They had to cook continuously and served those who came to pay you a visit. Besides, you would also be expected to give them something before they left for their home. Some might

ask you for specific items especially the medicinal products. Others would just talk and talk with you until you gave them a small amount of money.

This imagery became a standard way of portraying the villagers in Anxi. They became stereotyped as 'greedy', 'bandit-like', 'demanding', 'inconsiderate' and other negative phrases. A whole generation of Singapore Chinese was brought up with these images, through trips to home villages where their village kin made insatiable demands. Affection for their village kin and ancestral home soon turned into disappointment, frustration and resentment. What the Singapore Chinese envisaged before their return trips turned into stressful and unpleasant experiences, and this led to tension between them and their village kin. However, despite this negative impression, they continued to visit their ancestral homes in later years.

Thus, for Singapore-born Chinese, the archetypal village kinsperson is utilitarian: his or her friendliness is measured by the amount of gifts and money given to him or her. He or she is demanding and greedy, and thinks that the *qiaoqing* owes him or her a living. He or she may be subtle or outright in demanding material goods and money from the *qiaoqing*. As will be discussed, he or she may be lazy and not bother to work for a living, but sits around and does nothing except talk with other villagers, drink tea and smoke.

The archetypal village was one with an undeveloped road system and limited accessibility. There were little or no modern amenities, such as piped water, air conditioning, or electricity. There was also no proper sanitation. The village was very undeveloped, with few schools, bridges, roads, or hospitals to cater for the local needs. There were no entertainment facilities—no cinemas, karaoke bars and skating rinks. There was also a lack of non-agricultural employment.

It is often the case that habit dies hard, and perception and attitudes are even harder to change. As individuals and groups visited their home villages and brought back similar stories, and as their experiences were told and retold over and over again to their children and grandchildren, the resulting static pictures of village life and village kin came to reflect the conditions of the 1950s and 1960s. In the 1990s, despite some attitudinal changes, this set of negative images continued to influence the outlook of the Singapore-born Chinese, and to shape their relationship with their village kin. It was these stories of our ancestral village, and of China in general, that we, the children, were brought up with—yet we were supposed to feel a sense of sympathy for these village kin. While the first-generation Singapore Anxi Chinese, despite their harassment and disappointment, had developed a sense of empathy, some members of the younger generation developed strong feelings of resentment, and it was not surprising that some chose not to be part of this kinship matrix, but to become outsiders. This resentment was a powerful and irrational force that served to turn many away from visiting their ancestral home. Although sympathy later drew others back to the village and some, seeing the underdeveloped conditions and material poverty that surrounded the households, willingly provided assistance to village redevelopment, their early memories had already marred their sentiments, and they therefore depersonalized their contributions—instead of providing assistance to immediate kin, they engaged in charitable and philanthropic activities, contributed to public projects and helped with general village reconstruction of roads, schools, hospitals, and temples that benefited the community as a whole rather than selected kin. This action could be attributed to the need to 'save face' and at the same time, avoiding intimacy with people who would make demands on them. Many villagers, especially those who had gained little from their Singapore kin, found it hard to understand the logic of this, and among them there was much ill-feeling. Such Singapore kin, often seen as 'outsiders' by their village kin, were 'overseas comrades' (*qiaobao*, 侨胞) to the official cadres, who had sought to attract Chinese overseas capital.

Renegotiating Kinship Sentiments since the 1978 Open Door Reform

A new era—the Open Door Era initiated by Deng Xiaoping in 1978—marked a new watershed in Chinese history, and a new beginning in the history of *qiaoxiang* relations. The reforms affected the socio-cultural and economic life of the villages, and especially of the emigrant villages, where changes have been dramatic. In Anxi, the policy changes were greeted with excitement and renewed energy, and led to renewed efforts to encourage Chinese overseas to help with national construction and reconstruction in China. Two new official policy initiatives towards the Chinese overseas were made. The first was to lure Chinese overseas capital for investment purposes; the second was to encourage Chinese overseas to help with village reconstruction in rural areas, especially in the emigrant districts.

These new Chinese policies coincided with attempts by the Singapore government to encourage the globalization of local firms, and thus the Open Door Policy was looked upon by the Singapore government as a great opportunity for both the Singapore state and the Singapore Chinese to expand their economic interests in China. China represented a vast untapped market, and the Singapore Chinese were, and are, considered to be in a good position to embark on economic expansionism because of social and economic networks already in existence. There was a normalization of diplomatic ties with China and an increase in the number of Singapore Chinese travelling there for both social and economic purposes. It is not surprising that both the Chinese and Singapore governments, each with its own agenda, encouraged, and continue to encourage, Chinese Singaporeans to become involved in China.

The 1980s witnessed a change in the kinship matrix between the Singapore Chinese and their ancestral villages, as is evident among the Singapore Anxi Chinese, including those born in Singapore. The rise in the standard of living and increased wealth resulted in a more confident Chinese community in Singapore. This has led to a re-evaluation of the Singapore Anxi Chinese relationship with their ancestral villages. Also, the warming of the political relationship between China and Singapore meant fewer travel restrictions for those who wanted to travel to China—as well as for those Anxi Chinese who wanted to travel to Singapore. The result has been an increasing flow of visits and an intensification of social links between Singapore Anxi Chinese and the Anxi villagers from this period onwards.

Since the 1980s, an increasing number of elderly China-born men and women, together with their Singapore-born children, have taken advantage of these policy changes and made visits to their ancestral homes (*zujia*, 祖家). This is the case with the Singapore Anxi Chinese. Because of their recent migration history, many of the families have a generation depth of only three to four generations. A substantial number of the Singapore-born second and third generations have now accompanied their parents on visits to their ancestral homes. Many had to be coaxed into making the trip. However, while most made their initial trips reluctantly, they nevertheless developed some sentiments towards their respective villages after their visits.

How did these Singapore Anxi Chinese view their ancestral villages and kin? To what extent did they feel for them? We found that all Singapore Anxi Chinese interviewed were aware of their ancestral origins in Anxi, and 60 per cent said that they had some positive sentiments towards the place. Here is one of their responses:

> Anxi has some meaning for me because I know I am from there. It is where my roots (*genyuan*, 根源) are. It is a place where our ancestors and parents were from; I went back to search for my roots. There are sentimental and lineage ties and kindred spirit (*qinqing*, 亲情).

However, about 27 per cent stated that although they knew of their ancestral home, they did not have any sentiment towards it or the village. One of them responded in this way:

> I myself do not understand China (Anxi), so how can I feel for it? Anxi has not much meaning as I do not have any impression of the place and therefore, I treat it as another place like America or Britain.

A third group, or 13.3 percent, had weak sentiments towards Anxi. One responded in the following manner:

> I don't have much sentiment compared with my father. But I still care a little about our home village and our relatives there, but I have maintained some distance and reservation. It is not very good to become too close and attached to the place.

The survey showed that those in the higher age groups (the majority of them were first-generation, but with a small number of the second-generation group) had stronger emotional attachment to their ancestral villages. Most Singapore-born descendants, on the other hand, felt that they needed to know something of their ancestral village but did not have the strong sentiments that their elders had. Many had more negative feelings towards Anxi as a result of the negative representations with which they had been brought up, with no personal autobiographical experiences to counteract them, such as the first-generation immigrants had. Furthermore, the experience of ancestral visits made it less likely for them to like the place, but most made their initial trips reluctantly and they nevertheless developed some sentiments towards their respective villages after their visits, even though most of these sentiments were negative. However, the youngest age group had ambivalent but positive feelings, as will be discussed.

It is possible to chart the level of emotional attachment and sentiment through an analysis of intergenerational differences. If the above reactions are placed in a three-generation framework, we can better understand why the different generations responded differently to their ancestral home village.

The first factor concerns the search for roots. For the first-generation, China-born migrants, Anxi is their birthplace and is part of their personal biographies. Hence, they have strong emotional ties to it, and they seek to recreate these cultural roots and identity for their children and grandchildren. The second generation, on the other hand, has been brought up with many negative images and memories, which they find hard to ignore. While there have been attempts at creating positive images of home village and village kin, these were yet to become fully accepted even in the late 1990s. In time, after many more trips to the village, they may lose these negative feelings and images that have been deeply etched in their memories. Third and fourth generations have been brought up with more information, and have witnessed the active participation of their grandparents in village activities in Anxi. They do not know much about their ancestral villages, and therefore do not harbour as much alienation as their parents do.

It is possible to chart feelings and emotions for the Anxi home village in relation to knowledge of the place (strongest among the migrant generation) and the extent to which persons are influenced by parents and grandparents. Those for whom Anxi evokes some sentiments, including negative ones, have some knowledge of the place and of village kin, and their visits to the ancestral village in recent years have given them a clearer image of village life. Most have expressed sympathy with the plight of their village kin and a willingness to assist in the improvement of the village.

Among those who have strong positive sentiments, over half (55 per cent) have a reasonable knowledge of their village kin and are aware of close living relatives in the village. They can spell out the relationships between these relatives and their own families and are able to classify their kin according to the Chinese classificatory kinship system.[2] Others can only manage to classify the village kin as paternal or maternal uncles or aunts or cousins.

Table 1: Strength of sentiments in relation to knowledge of kinship

Knowledge of Anxi Kin	Strong sentiments	No sentiments	Weak sentiments
Intimate knowledge	10	4	3
Some knowledge	7	3	1
Little/no knowledge	1	1	0
TOTAL N=30	18	8	4

Thus, those with a degree of understanding of the ancestral village are more likely to attach a relatively strong sentiment to the place, while those with less knowledge feel less sentimental attachment. This is especially the case among those who have made several visits to their ancestral village and who are able to deconstruct the negative representations of village life and their village kin.

The Singapore-born Anxi Chinese interviewed in my survey were aware that their parents and/or grandparents had sent remittances and had helped their village kin in various ways. Among second-generation members, some had given money and helped their village kin. These second-generation Anxi Chinese expressed their awareness of contributions. One said:

> I know that my father and uncles have sent money to Anxi but I did not ask my father in person about this. Personally, I think if they can afford to send some money to the village kin, why not? This is especially needed if the relatives in Anxi are really poor. This was

especially so in the 1950s. My father had also sent foodstuffs, e.g., flour, cooking oil and others to the ancestral village. But if they are wealthy and comfortable, then there is no need.

Another said:

> My parents send money home because it is a tradition and a virtue and out of brotherly love and concern.

While there were thus those who were supportive of their parents' provision of some form of monetary and material aid to their village kin, there were others who disapproved of their parents and Singapore kin sending money. They argued that such assistance would breed laziness and dependence. One informant expressed the following:

> There are two effects of sending money home. One is the negative aspect and the other is the positive side. During my first trip home, some were really poor, so it was good that we helped them a little. On the other hand, it created a sense of laziness and dependence. They think that if they do not have money, their Singapore relatives will send them more. Although it is understandable that there is little job opportunity in Anxi, sending them money will only lead to less incentive to create jobs for themselves. So, it is better to establish cottage industries and create employment opportunities for them instead of giving them money.

The money that their migrant parents sent to their village kin varied quite significantly, in both amount and regularity. From the 1950s to the 1990s, only a very small number of Singapore kin sent remittances on a monthly basis; the majority remitted two to three times a year, usually on special occasions such as the Spring and Qingming festivals. In the 1960s and 1970s, the amount remitted was usually small, ranging from S$100 to $200.

Voices of Anxi Villagers

After 20 to 30 or more years of not meeting their siblings, parents or other immediate Singapore kin, there was great expectation when Anxi villagers heard news of a home visit of siblings, parents and other blood relatives. The wait had been long and there was great excitement. In the words of one: 'They [brothers by blood] went away when we were all young and unmarried. Now we are all middle-aged, with children and even grandchildren of our own. It is good to see them again. Our children have not met them before. It will be good for them to meet their uncles and their families. After all, we are still a family.'

In Penglai, most villagers knew of their Singapore kin. Most of the younger generation of Anxi villagers, in fact, were better versed than their Singapore counterparts on their kinship ties and could accurately classify their Singapore kin. They had been conscientiously told by their parents and grandparents of them and expressed great excitement when meeting their uncles, aunts, cousins and other Singapore kin when the latter visited the village.

There was, in fact, a range of emotions and attitudes held by the villagers towards their Singapore kin. One comment by Villager Ting was:

> We have a close relationship with our Singapore relatives. Our relatives in Singapore include our father's brothers, their three sons and their family. They have visited us regularly, especially after the reform. Contacts are normally through letters and oral messages. We also talk regularly on the phone. They often send us gift parcels through visiting relatives.

The second attitude was a negative one:

> We have three uncles in Singapore. We used to write letters to them. But only one uncle replied. He only wrote once a year and sent us S$50 each time. After the death of our uncles, their children did not write at all. Two years ago, two of our cousins came and visited our village. They stayed at the overseas Chinese guesthouse in the village. They did not attempt to contact us. We knew of their coming and so we went to visit them. They were very distant. They gave us S$100 and that was all. They did not even bother to come and visit our place or offer any assistance to us. Instead, they were contributing large sums of money to schools and for road works. And they got on very well with the village cadres and the officials of the provincial government. I think they are very snobbish. They look to people with power and look down upon us relatives because we are poor. It is an embarrassment to have this kind of relatives. Sometimes, it is better not to have than to have them. It makes me very sad knowing that they are not willing to acknowledge their kin.

Another example:

> The Singapore kin did not contribute sufficiently, materially and financially, to help improve our social situation. Our Singapore

relatives were wealthy but 'heartless'. They were barbaric and detribalized (*fan, huang* [H]), arrogant, self-centred, mean and miserly. The Singapore women were too lady-like and waited to be served.

Thus some of the villagers, too, had negative representations and generalizations of the Singapore Chinese. To them, they were uncivilized, arrogant, mean and reluctant to help out, and Singapore women were seen as women of leisure, 'too lady-like'.

Many villagers, however, were very generous with their praise of their Singapore kin—those who had been very pleased with the generosity of their kin for providing assistance for their immediate family needs, ranging from construction of their old houses and education of their children, to expenses for marriages and purchase of electronic goods for the household. Others expressed gratitude for the enormous contributions which some Singaporeans had made to build village schools, roads, temples, hospitals and other infrastructure developments. Contributions by some individuals amounted to over S$100,000.

At one end of the spectrum, some villagers had very close and intimate relationships and enjoyed being in contact with their Singapore kin; at the other end, some had little or no contact with their kin and no special feelings for them. Most fell between these extremes, and they tended to be those with some contact with their Singapore kin, who had received some remittances and assistance for their various needs. They were generally satisfied with the relationship and other material benefits they got from their kin. They used the phrase 'we can't compare to the wealthy ones above us, but we are more than adequate compared to the poorer ones below us' (*bishang buzu, bixia youyu*, 比上不足，比下有余) to indicate that they were generally content with the modest improvement in their daily life after receiving some help from their kin.

However, maintaining contact with their relatives in Singapore was of central importance to the villagers, since they might receive material and financial assistance from them. One informant described how he and his relatives were corresponding in the 1990s: 'Usually they sent messages through visiting relatives, inquiring about us or entrusting us to perform various tasks on their behalf. If there was something urgent, they might telephone us and we would phone them too. Letter writing was very troublesome. We usually had to ask people to write for us.' Another informant said, 'my mother and eleven brothers and sisters are in Singapore. We have regular contacts and a normal relationship. But I rarely write because I am illiterate and all my brothers and sisters are English-educated and do not read Chinese.'

All in all, most villagers considered relationships between themselves and their Singapore kin to be reasonably good. However, some felt that their relations had weakened progressively over the years and between generations, saying that, after the death of the first-generation migrants, contact with the Singapore-born generation decreased to a minimum, as the Singapore-born Chinese rarely wrote or sent money anymore. One said, 'I was an adopted child of the family. When my father was alive, there were contacts through letters and oral messages from visiting relatives. He would also send gift parcels for me and my family. After his death, there were no contacts between my Singapore relatives and me.' Another said, 'I have three elder brothers in Singapore. When our mother was alive, there were regular contacts and they would send money to support us. Now that she is dead, there is very little contact.'

Some felt that the Singapore Chinese were more concerned about their immediate families and life in Singapore and had less concern for their village kin. One informant said, 'there is still a little contact; it is not broken yet,' although 'even if you write, they can't even be bothered to reply.' Some villagers who had visited Singapore told me that 'the Singapore Chinese are very whimsical about us'. They said that some of the Singaporeans had much regard for them and were very happy when they received Anxi letters, but others were not. Some would 'not bother to read our letters and would throw them into the bin without opening them. Since last year, I stopped writing. The previous year, I wrote but there was no reply. So I think, they must have thrown my letter away without reading it. Why should I write if this is the case?' Another informant had this to say:

> My husband's younger brother and his family live in Singapore. But there is very little contact between us. It is very hard for us to send letters to them because we do not know their addresses and names. We have to ask our relatives to take the letters to them. But they seldom reply. We rarely receive phone calls and gift parcels.

Yet another explained the difficulties in maintaining the relationship:

> My Singapore kin include my father's three brothers and their families, my father's second wife and their children, my half-brothers and half-sisters. Previously, there were some contacts. At the moment, only the elder brother maintains contact with us. Most of my half-brothers and half-sisters do not want to have any contact with us. They do not even want to recognize us. Even when our village relatives visited Singapore, they did not wholeheartedly receive them. Originally, my elder half-brother said that he would

sponsor me for a visit to Singapore in 1993. When 1993 arrived and I asked him again, he did not reply to my letter. I continue to write to him occasionally. In recent years, I have received no reply, so I stopped writing.

As some Singaporeans had made it known publicly that they were no longer interested in maintaining ties with their village kin and wanted to have nothing to do with the ancestral village, they neither wrote nor communicated in other forms, nor would they provide financial assistance to their village kin. Such an attitude, to the villagers, was both un-Chinese and unfilial. This is why such Singaporeans were said to have become 'uncivilized'.

Communication implies two-way traffic. In most cases, contact is reciprocal between villagers and Singaporeans, normal communication being two to three letters a year in each direction. However, some villagers were losing interest in continuing to write without receiving replies, as they faced being snubbed by their better-off Singapore relatives, and some of whom looked down upon them. It is this negative attitude that Anxi villagers resented most.

Visiting Singapore

Since the 1978 reform, an increasing number of Anxi villagers have visited Singapore; of villager-informants who visited, over 30 per cent of them did so from the mid-1980s onwards.

The easiest way for a villager to visit Singapore was to ask a Singapore kinsperson to sponsor the visit. Such visits were most common when close relatives visited the village. Such requests often began in the following manner: 'I am already so old and have not been out of the country. It would be very nice to go overseas and see the world. I have heard so much about Singapore. It would be good to see what it is like. Would you sponsor me to visit Singapore?' Some relatives responded by saying, 'I will see what I can do,' while others gave no indication of their decision. Villagers often had to suggest this to their Singapore kin several times before gaining a positive response, perhaps a few months later. They then would apply for a passport and exit visa from the immigration authority in the county town of Fengcheng and wait several months before receiving them, upon which they would inform their Singapore kin. From the Singapore end, the relative would then arrange for the necessary documentation, buy an air ticket and entrust a visiting relative to take it to the village. Alternatively, he or she might avail himself or herself of the services of one of the travel agencies in Singapore that prepared such documentation and arranged for the tickets to be sent. The Singaporeans then notified them when they had to arrive at Xiamen airport and arranged to meet them at the airport in Singapore. Singapore relatives might also send motion-sickness pills, with instructions to take them prior to boarding the flight.

When villagers visited Singapore, many would try to impress their Singapore kin by bringing local produce to Singapore, most commonly Chinese tea. Many would bring several kilograms, to be distributed to numerous kin; wealthier villagers would buy export quality pre-packaged tea.

It became a norm for the Singapore Chinese to sponsor their middle-aged and elderly village relatives for at least one visit. These relatives would normally stay for the maximum period of the visa, usually two or three months. Some have visited more than once.

During the first few years when social visits by the villagers first became possible, the Singaporeans made great efforts to ensure that their village kin got the best treatment and enjoyed their stays. They were eager to ensure that the villagers returned home with good impressions of them and of the Singaporean way of life. At that time, 'China guests' (*tangshanke*, 唐山客) were a novelty, especially for the younger generations, so when a visitor or visitors arrived, members of the lineage were informed, and the visitors' immediate families housed them and treated them as honoured guests, taking them sightseeing and so forth. Other Singapore relatives would also take them out for meals, sightseeing and shopping, and would present them with gifts, or give them *hongbao* (红包), i.e., customary red packets of money (common sums were S$50 or S$100). Anxi relatives would also visit the homes of various kin and, during this initial period, Singapore kin were obliging and drove the villagers to visit all the relatives they wished to see. It was all in good spirits, and everyone was enthusiastic about the visits of their *tangshanke*. Villagers might then return home with much money, gold jewellery, expensive watches, electronic goods, clothing and other items, not uncommonly amounting to a value of several thousand Singapore dollars or more, in cash and in kind.

As time went by, however, such enthusiasm began to wane, as more and more visitors were able to come to Singapore. It began to look like a time-consuming affair to pick up the guests from the airport, entertain them, and take them sightseeing and shopping. It also became a very expensive affair for some, as they had to finance the trips as well as to give substantial sums for various purposes. Finally, it became an embarrassment to have the visitors go on a circuit of house-calling when it was obvious that their primary motive was to collect *hongbao*. A matter of too much in too short a period, '*tangshanke* fatigue' set in sooner than expected: what had been exciting and welcoming became tedious, and the *tangshanke* turned into a source of embarrassment.

Since the 1990s, although the *tangshanke* have continued to arrive in substantial numbers, they become more house-bound and are not taken to all their relatives. Indeed, many Singapore sponsors no longer see the need to inform their other relatives of the arrival of these visitors. Although they are taken for some sightseeing, meals and shopping, most of their time is spent with their immediate relatives. Despite requests to visit other relatives, Singaporeans now exercise tighter control over who they visit, the visitors usually being taken to the homes of their closest relatives but not to those of others. Some of the visitors are not very happy about this restriction and have complained that they do not meet all the relatives they know, thus defeating their purpose in visiting Singapore. Others, confined to the home as they are, with nothing much to do, get bored.

On the whole, most visitors have been proud to have made a trip to Singapore. They are pleased to have met their Singapore kin and to have 'seen the world', *kanshijie* (看世界). Many like the orderliness, efficiency and modernity of Singapore. Such a visit had been a dream that became reality: even setting foot out of the village had been a difficult affair for some, let alone making an overseas visit. Making such a visit was also a reflection of their social status within the village and lineage structure and stepped up their link with Chinese overseas—a formidable force in China today.

Visits to Singapore have not only been made by elderly villagers. Today, an increasing number of young villagers are searching for ways to visit Singapore. For those in their twenties, thirties and forties, a visit to Singapore is a lucrative adventure. However, the chance of these young villagers being sponsored by their Singapore kin has been less than that of their elderly parents since, among Singapore Chinese, there is greater sympathy for the older villagers. Few are willing to sponsor the younger ones.

Those who want to visit Singapore on their own generally apply to travel as tourists, but approval is given readily if arranged by a travel agency. As for sponsored applicants, it often takes two to three months or longer for their applications to be approved by both the Singapore and the county immigration departments. They generally have to borrow money for air tickets and the expenses incurred in applying for exit permits. While making these arrangements, they inform their Singapore relatives of the intended visit and the tentative date of arrival. When everything is finalized, they phone their closest relative of their impending arrival, expecting that they will be picked up from the airport and provided with accommodation. For this group of visitors, the primary motive has been to find a job in Singapore. In the beginning, many failed to understand that visitor's visas do not entitle them to work. On arrival, they expected their Singapore kin to recommend them to employers. Later, they continued to go to Singapore in search of temporary jobs, expecting their uncles and other relatives to provide them; if jobs were not arranged for them, they sometimes tried to work in an illegal capacity.

This created much dissatisfaction and annoyance for their Singapore kin, and it has become a standard practice for those with family businesses to give 'employment' to their village kin and according to businessman Keng, 'to occupy them so that they do not go out and work illegally'. They have thus often been given odd jobs to do in the family business and have been paid an 'allowance' for the duration of the period they stay in Singapore. In the words of a Singaporean relative, 'at least they need not go and work illegally and get into trouble with the authority. Also, they will earn more than enough to cover the expenses that they have incurred for the trip. They will also learn that the work ethos here is different from that in Anxi and that they cannot expect free things in life. They also will not go back empty-handed.' Singapore kin who do not own a business will try to arrange for some kind of temporary employment with the firms of relatives or friends, as some of the Singapore-born feel a sense of obligation to their Anxi kin and are resigned to the fact that, once they arrive in Singapore, there is nothing they can do but to help them at least to recuperate the expenses that they have incurred in making the trip.

The imposition on the Anxi Singaporeans and the expectation of a job has created much tension between the two groups. Singaporean relatives feel the visitors have unreasonable expectations, as they do not understand Singapore labour law. It is especially annoying that they have begun to come on their own, that there is no means of stopping them, and that they have to provide them with accommodation, whether they like it or not, as they simply cannot let them sleep on the streets.

To the Anxi villagers, a visit to Singapore is expected to provide them with a window of opportunity to earn enough to start a small business or build a house for themselves and their family in their village. However, they find that the trip has not lived up to their expectations. Some do not earn as much as they have expected, especially as they cannot stay beyond the visa limit. The unwillingness of their kin to extend their visas adds to their frustrations, and as a result, some feel their kin are not so friendly, but rather mean and selfish. As Hong said, 'they only take care of themselves and their family but not the village kin.' Some feel they are not well treated as, unlike earlier visitors, they are not plied with as much money or as many gifts and are not treated to banquets and much sightseeing. Being young and literate, the Singapore kin expect them to be able to make their own way round the island and not being chauffeured around. Many of these expectations have arisen from information they received from other, previous visitors who have been pampered with gifts and shown around Singapore. Thus, not being showered with gifts and shown around implies that they are not being welcomed by the Singapore relatives.

Towards a Compromise

Contacts between the two groups of kin have thus brought about fulfilment for some and burdens for others. Among the Singaporeans, fulfilment has gradually given way to burden and fatigue. By the late 1990s, the increased contacts between the groups had, at times, brought simmering tensions to the surface, resulting in much loss of face for both parties. One reason for the increased tension had to do with the stereotyped images and expectations of each other held by both Singaporeans and villagers. One said, 'they [nephews and nieces] are very polite and will greet me. One or two might have a little conversation with me. But most will not. They talk among themselves in Mandarin or English. They hardly speak in Fujian dialect.' Another lamented, 'the grandchildren could not even communicate with me in the Fujian dialect. All these young ones are so good in English, but they can't speak our own language. What do you think? They have become *huang* [H], *fan* [uncivilized].'

Of the younger generation of Singapore Chinese who have visited Anxi, some returned to Singapore more convinced than ever that their village kin are a group of lazy villagers. One said, 'they spend all their time sipping tea, talking and smoking. It is OK if the old ones do this. But look at the young ones, they are all the same.' Another commented, 'it is not that we do not understand that there is not much opportunity for them. But they have to be willing to go and look for opportunities. You cannot just sit and sip tea and expect opportunity to knock on your door.' A third said, 'they just refuse to think for themselves and expect us to do everything for them.' Yet another commented, 'they do not take initiative on their own. If we tell them to do something, they will do it. Otherwise, they would just sit and wait. This is why it is very difficult to entrust them to do something for us. Many times they would not even do the task well.'

However, attempts were soon underway to eliminate the negative images that each party had of the other. For the Singapore Chinese, one important reason for sponsoring their village kin to Singapore was, as one said, 'to let them see and understand that we have to work very hard for what we have and that life is not as easy as what they think it is.' Another said, 'it is important for them to understand that we too have our family here to look after. It is not possible for us to look after every single relative in Anxi.' A third said, 'even though we care for our Anxi relatives, it is not possible for us to cater to every demand that they have asked for. Besides, they will also have to understand that they cannot expect charity all the time. They have to work for it. By bringing them here, they can see how hard we all work.' After visiting Singapore, in fact, some villagers returned to the village with a new perspective of what their Singapore kin were like. Some told me that life was not easy in

Singapore. One said, 'they have to go out early in the morning, 7 or 8 a.m., and only return at 6 or 7 p.m. It is also a hard life for them.' Another said, 'although they earn so much money, the cost of living is also very high in Singapore. They need a lot of money to maintain their house, their family, to buy food, etc. After all these, they are left with very little money. Although they seem to have all the material things in life—television, videocassette recorder, nice flat, nice clothing—they also have to work very hard for them.'

The younger villagers, of course, resented being labelled 'lazy' and 'dependent' and argued that this was unfair. They felt that there was much misunderstanding between them and their Singapore relatives, and that their Singapore kin failed to see the differences between a peasant and a commercial economy. They worked very hard as farmers, especially during the sowing, transplanting and harvesting seasons. At other times of the year, they reared poultry and pigs, and some also performed odd jobs during the off-season. Despite this, many continued to live in poverty. Thus, to label them 'lazy' was unjust. Contrary to what their Singapore relatives said, they claimed that, although they were poor, they did *not* ask anything from their Singapore relatives and depended on themselves, so how could they be called 'demanding' and 'greedy'? Finally, they felt that, although there was a small group of villagers who had been untrustworthy with money and responsibility and had simply taken money and failed to perform work properly, thus earning a bad name for all villagers, their Singapore relatives should not use one label for all.

Most villagers felt that the only way to erase the negative labels that Singaporeans placed on them was to demonstrate their diligence and their trustworthiness in the various socio-religious and economic tasks entrusted to them by their Singapore kin. They also felt that their younger Singapore kin should be educated about the difficulties which they, the villagers, faced, so that they could better understand village life; and that regular communication between the two groups would bring about better mutual understanding. Besides better mutual communication, the villagers were confident that the economic reforms would help to transform the relationship from one of dependence to one of mutual co-operation.

The desire of the villagers to eradicate the negative image of themselves was complemented by attempts by the Singaporeans to find positive images among the Anxi villagers. Their increased contacts with their village kin and some understanding of the village structure later made some Singapore Chinese become more aware of the restrictions of village life and village economy, and they began to see the social realities and complexities that surrounded village life instead of being influenced by the collective memories of the 1950s and 1960s. The imagery of the villagers as being 'lazy', 'demanding' and 'greedy' gradually gave way to positive images of 'hardworking' and 'resourceful' villagers. The numbers of young villagers who have engaged in private enterprises have also helped transform the old image.

The 1980s and 1990s witnessed rapid changes in village life, with the emergence of a new generation of villagers whose attitude differed from those of their parents and grandparents. Today, the changing environment and the economic dynamism in Anxi County are accompanied by the rise of a group of modern-minded village individuals whose modern approach to businesses and social activities has helped to deconstruct the negative image previously held by their Singapore kin.

However, the Singapore Chinese have also come to realize the limited opportunities of a village economic structure. There are few job opportunities and insufficient resources for development. In the 1990s, they began to understand the political economy of the region and the failure of both the regional and central governments to develop Anxi, and gradually began to accept the proposals of district and local cadres, who sought Chinese overseas capital for village development.

The poverty of the 1950s to 1970s did, in fact, give way to new opportunities as a result of the opening to the outside and the relaxation of internal restrictions, and the villagers were no longer confined to their traditional economic and social roles, but were able to take on more active roles without awaiting instructions from the provincial or central government. An increasing number of private businesses and an emergence of rudimentary enterprises could be found in the villages. A number of small traders and businesspeople had begun to permanently commercialize an originally peasant region. This meant that villagers were able to move out of their established social roles. This was a transformation that resulted in renewed confidence about the villagers in the eyes of others and the confidence of the villagers about themselves.

For the Singaporeans, coming into contact with the villagers and visiting Anxi thus affected the way they looked at their village kin, who were no longer strangers. Singaporeans began to understand that their village kin could be pleasant socially, could be trained to perform skilled work, and were not ideologically dogmatic, and that the villagers too wanted to excel, become successful and attain material comfort. Some worked hard to achieve this when opportunity arose; some were prepared to move out of Anxi to Xiamen, Singapore, Hong Kong or other places to work. They were prepared to take risks, quit the iron rice bowl job of state employment and become businesspeople. In short, the villagers could become dynamic people when the political situation allowed them to do so and when they had the opportunities to excel themselves in the economic ventures. Given this re-evaluation of their village kin, the Singapore Chinese became more prepared to assist in village development.

The role of Singaporean relatives in the transformation of village life and economy cannot be underestimated. Much Chinese overseas capital was injected into these emigrant villages, making possible recent rapid changes. The capital used for infrastructure development and individual businesses has turned once-quiet villages into prosperous *qiaoxiang*. In Fujian, it was the extreme poverty of these villages that had pushed so many villagers to emigrate for a better livelihood in a foreign environment. Today, these same villages are again in the limelight in China. This time, it is their material wealth and cultural richness that have attracted attention and have become the envy of the region. This has been made possible because of their *guanxi* network of continuous ties with the Chinese communities in Singapore and elsewhere.

5
The Moral Economy of Rebuilding the Ancestral Village

The *qiaoxiang* villages of Fujian and Guangdong have been the recipients of wealth and assistance from their Chinese overseas relatives since the 1978 reform. It has been a policy of the central government to encourage not only remittances but also contributions from Chinese overseas for village infrastructure and economic development.

As mentioned, there has been a revival of interest among Singapore Chinese in their ancestral villages. The Singapore government has also been instrumental in encouraging Singapore Chinese to invest in China. However, this has had very little effect on their decision to invest or contribute to their ancestral villages' development—reasons other than those of economic rationality that affected these Chinese to contribute to develop their ancestral villages. This chapter will explore the extent to which the Singapore Chinese are locked into a set of social relationships within a moral economy that constantly pushes them to assist with village development, including the rebuilding of ancestral houses.

The 1978 Reform and Village Reconstruction and Development

Ancestral property, new and old houses

As discussed, after the 1978 reform, the more liberal political climate of relations between China and Singapore enabled an increasing number of Singapore Chinese to make regular social visits to their ancestral villages. Their involvement in village development has been primarily in terms of financial assistance, but they have also provided technical support in four main areas of basic infrastructure development: (1) construction of roads, bridges and power plants; (2) development of educational facilities; (3) assistance to hospitals and medicine; and (4) the establishment and promotion of petty trading and retailing.

However, the operation of the moral economy that has led to such assistance has had much to do with the reconstruction of their ancestral houses.

Remittances and the Rebuilding of Old Homes (Laojia, 老家)

Financial assistance to ancestral villages and lineages by Singapore Chinese began with early emigrants' regular remittances to their families in their home villages. Today, the number of Singapore Chinese visiting their ancestral villages and financing the rebuilding of their *laojia* has led to a boom in the construction industry.

It is estimated that remittances to all of Fujian, from all of the former Straits Settlements, during the 1930s, amounted to the equivalent of today's RMB 500 to 700 million annually. Remittances to the interior regions of Fujian (including Yongchun 永春, Huian 惠安, Anxi 安溪, Longan 龙安, and Tongan 同安) at the time amounted to more than RMB 10 million annually. Most of these remittances were sent through the ports of Xiamen and Fuzhou (Foochow) (Hicks, 1993: 152).[1] It is estimated that all overseas Chinese remittances to Anxi in 1938 amounted to slightly over RMB 3.6 million (Hicks, 1993: 265). Most of these remittances (a total of RMB 265,386) were sent by post rather than through the ports mentioned above, although small amounts were carried back by returning Chinese in 1938 (Hicks, 1993: 273).

However, greater total remittances to China were probably made during the 1930s than during any other period; after that time there was a gradual decline. From Singapore alone, remittances amounted to only RMB 1.5 million in 1954; by 1960 they had dropped to just over RMB 1 million. However, the years before and after the 1978 reform saw a jump in remittances to Anxi from Singapore: in 1976 they totalled RMB 3.53 million, and the amount continued to increase steadily for the next few years, reaching a new high of RMB 7 million in 1983. Later, however, remittances declined substantially. In 1984 the amount was still over RMB 5.4 million but by 1990 it fell to RMB 2.1 million (Chen, 1994: 97).[2]

Most remittances sent to the home villages from the late 1970s through the first half of the 1980s were for personal uses, primarily to rebuild old family houses (*laojia*, 老家) or to build second, modern homes (*xinjia*, 新家).[3]

This modernized the essentially rural landscape, in which stone and brick homes replaced mud or wooden ones. In addition to the traditional housing style with its central courtyard, we now have three- to four-storey buildings surrounded by paddy fields.

In my survey, I found that most villagers had received some form of monetary assistance to help rebuild and renovate their old houses. Of 203 respondents, 152, or 75 per cent, said that they or their parents had received financial assistance from their overseas kin to help rebuild or renovate the house or construct a new one. In the 1980s, several millions RMB were remitted from Singapore for this purpose, usually at the written request of the villagers to Singapore relatives. Sometimes, rebuilding might take a few years, with bits and pieces added on to an old house. The amount sent would range from several thousands to several tens or hundreds of thousands of RMB.

To persuade their relatives to contribute, visiting kin would be brought to witness the condition of the *laojia*. However, for this they would approach only those older and immediate family members who had more empathy and greater sentiment for the ancestral village. One villager said, 'it would have been easier for us to open our mouths and ask our parents or brothers or sisters to help us. But we found it embarrassing asking our grandparents, grand-uncles, grand-aunts or uncles as they are either too old or not so close to us.' Apart from this, another one told me, 'we realize that some of our Singapore kin are not very wealthy. They are not fat kin [*feiqiao*, 肥侨] but thin kin [*shouqiao*, 瘦侨]. So, to lessen their financial burden and to ensure that the *laojia* is being rebuilt, we ask for a smaller sum each time, over a period of time. We found it easier to open our mouths this way.'

But why is the *laojia* so important and why does it need to be rebuilt?

Most villagers consider the *laojia* as the house of their ancestors, primogenitor, and that it should not be allowed to collapse. The Singapore Chinese also feel that the *laojia* provides them with a physical space that grounds their cultural roots and allows them to recollect their nostalgic feelings of village life, although they may be harsh ones. Rebuilding the house is a matter of filial piety towards their ancestors and allows them to remember their origins or 'source' (*yinshui shiyuan*, 饮水思源, 'When drinking from the fountain, one remembers its source'). It also allows them to glorify their lineage and ancestors (*guangzong yaozu*, 光宗耀祖).

Rebuilding also involves 'face'. One villager said, 'we encouraged our Singapore kin to renovate the old house. I told him that it would cost RMB 500,000. My grandmother here brought up their father and their grandfather originally built this house. This is their original source [*genyuan*, 根源], and if they let the house go into disrepair, they would also lose much face in the village and in Singapore, if our kin knew that they had deliberately allowed the *laojia* to collapse. It would also be very bad for their, and our, descendants, as the collapse of the *laojia* will bring about bad *fengshui* to all the living.'

Many *qiaoqing* had lived in their ancestral houses as children and so feel sentimental about it; thus rebuilding them is a matter of sentiment and nostalgia for village life. Yet, in many instances, when the Singapore Chinese returned to visit their ancestral village, the comment that 'there is a road that leads to no home' (*youlu wuwu*, 有路无屋) was made especially for those who did not have an ancestral home to return to.

Some Singapore kin gave only minimal assistance, and some villagers were less than happy about this. One village woman said, 'he [paternal brother] contributed about 1,000 Singapore dollars towards the building of the house some seven to eight years ago. There is no possibility that they will help us with the house, although we hoped they would. They have been in Singapore for too long and have turned into *fanren*.' Others, however, were more understanding and forgiving of their Singapore kin.

Those who did not receive any assistance for building the house expressed their dissatisfaction, sadness and at times disillusionment towards their Singapore kin. One farmer with paternal uncles and cousins in Singapore, with whom he had had little contact, said, '[they] did not help build the house. They should have helped us but did not bother. All of them are now Singapore citizens. We do not know their addresses. They have left the home village for too long. Even those in their fifties did not even come back once.'

Concerning new houses, younger villagers felt that it was very difficult to ask their Singapore uncles or cousins to help them build one, or to purchase a modern apartment, partly because most of their Singapore kin had already helped their parents with a house; thus many, although they hoped for help, felt embarrassed to ask for more. One 35-year-old housewife said, 'they [Singapore relatives] have helped the elders to build houses. I hoped that they would help us to build ours. But they have contributed only very little.'

Most *laojia* that have been repaired or rebuilt or have had new wings added reflect both the new and the old. This blending of the new and old makes for an interesting village landscape. Several *laojia* were pulled down entirely and new ones built on the site, and these are referred to by the seemingly contradictory term *xin laojia* (新老家), or 'new old house'. In this case, the term *laojia* is more of a social concept referring to the house of a particular household; its involvement with a specific location stretches back unbroken to an earlier generation. The location is thus the 'original source' of a particular family, whose ancestors are important. The *laojia*, whether 'new' or 'old', thus remains an important physical element in the landscape, reminding individuals of their immediate family background and constituting their ancestral home.

Today, there are many renovated *laojia*, although many of them are left vacant, or have few people living in them. This is because many have moved to new, more modern houses. In general, most of the occupiers of *laojia* are elderly people who have lived in the house for several decades and do not want to move out. They attach great sentiment to the house, and also prefer its style, with a spacious central courtyard, where they can sit and relax with other elderly people.

Wealthy households, apart from renovating or rebuilding the *laojia*, may also build or buy a new house, for which younger villagers often request financial help from their Singapore kin. In the 1990s, there were already a sizeable number of villagers living in relatively luxurious three to four-storey modern houses, equipped with modern amenities. One happy 36-year-old housewife said, 'our Singapore uncle sent us money to build this four-storey building, which cost RMB 400,000–500,000. We are very happy and satisfied with it. This house is very comfortable.' Such construction has modernized the rural landscape, which is now lined with both traditional houses and their central courtyards and modern three to four-storey buildings surrounded by paddy fields.

Four types of housing are distinguishable in the villages. The traditional house with a courtyard in the middle was previously the most sought-after type of housing. Each family once aspired to build a traditional house, although most did not manage to, and it was largely wealthier families that had them. Many of these were the *laojia* of emigrants who had sent remittances to help rebuild them. Within the villages, such traditional houses are scattered about, mostly with elderly people living in them, as the style is now considered old-fashioned by younger villagers, who prefer modern apartments. There have been many efforts made by heads of household to modernize these *laojia*, especially if their Singapore kin choose to reside in them during their stays in Anxi. In these houses, it is common to find that modern mosaic or tile flooring has replaced cement. Modern bathrooms, toilets, piped well-water, air conditioning and a modern kitchen together with gas cookers are considered by both Singapore visitors and younger villagers to be essential. Most of these homes now have electricity, although power limitations often led to inadequate lighting in the 1990s and various domestic tasks could not be performed simultaneously. However, after the 1990s, another power station was built and such problems became less acute. Because of the relatively high cost of electricity, villagers have continued to use other forms of power though, as electricity costs much more than firewood and charcoal.

The openness of the traditional courtyard house makes it very difficult to keep dust out, and because of this it is often regarded as 'dirty' or 'unclean' by the Singapore Chinese. The open central courtyard in the middle provides ample ventilation, but there are no doors and windows to keep dust out; household members therefore close their room doors, but let the living area remain open. Furthermore, as female members of most households rear poultry for eggs and meat, and chickens are left to roam around the gardens and, often, into the house as well, the stench makes many Singapore Chinese feel reluctant to stay there when they visit.

However, anthropologically speaking, the traditional family house is a 'friendly' type of housing for extended family, as the central courtyard serves as a common place for interaction, while bedrooms provide privacy for couples and their children. It is more spacious than modern apartments.

Previously, extended family members occupied the *laojia*, and it was not uncommon for members of several *fang* of extended families to reside there. Today, however, although households may include elderly parents, grown children and young grandchildren, it has become more common for young couples to live as nuclear families if they have the means, and so an increasing (albeit still small) number of young married couples live on their own. When the family can afford it, or when their *qiaoqing* help them acquire a modern shophouse apartment, young couples move out. This arrangement has become fashionable and reflects on the wealth and social status of a particular household. Most, however, cannot afford this luxury.

Since the late 1980s, modern three- to four-storey housing blocks with modern plumbing and facilities have been constructed by *qiaoqing* for their relatives; many also come with air conditioning. This is a variation of the Singapore apartment type of living of the 1960s and 1970s, before high-rise and high-density living became the norm in Singapore, where the scarcity of land has made such buildings a necessity. In Anxi, however, villagers can still afford lower-density housing. However, such three- and four-storey buildings are now seen as synonymous with modernity, and every villager wants to own and live in one. It is now common to find such buildings in the middle of agricultural fields, next to *laojia*. In most cases, one such houses an extended family, with each son and his family usually occupying a floor, if there is sufficient space; if not, two sons and their families may occupy a single floor.

The third type of housing is the two-to-four-storey modern shophouse; the ground floor is occupied by a retail shop and the upper levels are used as residences. These are very popular in Penglai Zhen, and are found mainly in Penglai Zhen. A majority of these retail shops sell clothing, shoes, small electronic goods, sundries, toiletries and/or dried foodstuffs. Usually, the upper levels are occupied by nuclear families.

The last type is the mud and wooden houses, in which those with no overseas relatives and without financial means continue to reside. These houses once constituted the most common form of housing for a large number of poorer villagers, and today a small number of villagers continue to live in them. Most are found in the hilly regions in the outskirts of Penglai Zhen and are now a rare sight.

In the village environment, having a good house is more than just for comfortable living. It is also a testimony of the social status, wealth and material comforts of the household. It spells out to other villagers the connection of the occupiers with their wealthy Singapore kin, and is an important asset for marriage considerations, particularly for grown sons seeking suitable brides.

The house is still considered the single most important asset that an individual household possesses. In the villages where the paddy fields and shops are communal properties of the extended household, the house remains solely 'individualistic', and is regarded as the ultimate place for immediate family members to conduct individual and private affairs away from communal inspection. Since the reform, villagers have been able to record their names as legal owners of the house they occupy.

Reclaiming one's ancestral land

An issue related to village land is that of ownership of land taken from the Chinese overseas during the collective years. Under the reform system, the Singapore Chinese began to explore the possibility of reclaiming land that originally belonged to them or their forebears. Although many would have liked to reclaim their agricultural land, they were less concerned with this than with their ancestral burial sites, the *fengshuidi* (风水地).

The redistribution of farmland after the 1978 reform became an issue of contention among village households, who were mainly those that had been large landowners prior to collectivization. Many of these villagers had become wealthy through their connections with their Singapore kin. With decollectivization, some of them had hoped that the land formerly owned by their ancestors would be reallocated to them. However, this was not to be the case and there was much lamentation. There was little they could do beyond appealing for a reallocation, with slim chance of success, and many were simply resigned to the outcome.

However, among Anxi households and their Singapore kin, the issue of land ownership is an emotional affair. Land ownership, as Freedman said, is important for both the individual and the lineage in the old society, and so many households continue to express their desires to own a piece of land even though they are no longer engaged in farming. For some, the piece of land they want is specifically their ancestral farmland. Many villagers can point out where it was.

This issue of land ownership is often tied to consideration of the *laojia*, the ancestral burial ground and remembrance of past status, all of which can serve to remind descendants of local family history. During the collectivization years, and especially in the aftermath of the Cultural Revolution, almost all burial grounds were exhumed and turned into agricultural land. With decollectivization and the return of private plots, many villagers and their Singapore kin have attempted to regain former farmlands, and those with connections to local cadres have been able to do so, although others have been less successful. For some Singapore Chinese, the desire is to rebuild the burial sites and the *laojia*, and some of them have been able to establish *guanxi* (connections), through kinship relations, with the village and town cadres to further their claims to their former farmlands. In Penglai where links with emigrant kin remain strong, many original plots of land, with *laojia* and *fengshuidi*, have been returned to the closest kin of the original owners. Larger stretches of farmland, however, were broken into small plots and allocated to other families during decollectivization, and former landowners and their descendants were not able to reclaim their original plot before collectivization.

Although Singapore Chinese were considered overseas compatriots (*qiaobao*) by the official cadres, they were not reallocated their original farmland. Few elderly emigrant men and women were able to point out to me the larger stretches of land originally owned by their grandparents. They came to accept that land ownership in village China was no longer the preserve of private individuals but was subject to the discretion of the Chinese government. Even though they might have established strong social connections with village-level and town-level cadres, their *guanxi* only permitted privileges within the boundary of central policy. Those who were allocated lands surrounding their *laojia* and *fengshuidi* regarded it as privileged treatment, a testimony to their *guanxi* networks with the right officials. However, some were not so fortunate, and could only apply to the officials for the lease of land on which their ancestral graves were to be relocated and new homes were to be built. Still, in order to encourage overseas Chinese to visit, contribute to the village economy and assist with village development, the local government adopted flexibility in processing requests by Singapore Chinese for *fengshuidi*, and granted them different plots of land to rebuild their ancestral graves on numerous occasions. This policy has gained them much goodwill among the Singapore Chinese.

As suggested above, ancestral graves were located not far from agricultural fields. Lin (1947) in his work, *The Golden Wing*, has fully illustrated the significance of the ancestral burial site as a protector of the family. Freedman (1958, 1966) has also pointed out the significance of the ancestral burial ground as a main conduit for the flow of wealth into the family. It is therefore especially important to ensure that such a site is not destroyed. However, Communist Party policy opposed this traditional belief and most of these sites were destroyed, especially during the Cultural Revolution, with the exception of a few tucked away in hilly terrain and hidden by thick bushes.

These burial sites were strategically located to oversee the village, the agricultural field and the family home. Visiting and giving offerings to one's ancestors often entailed climbing up into hilly areas, which were often accessible only on foot and by sedan chair. Most visiting Singapore Chinese attempted to climb up the hills and trudge through the terraces to reach the original or the relocated ancestral tombs. Many of the elderly had to be carried in sedan chairs. Despite the inconvenience, for most of them the trip to Anxi would be incomplete without visiting and praying at their ancestral tombs.

Development

(1) Development of basic infrastructure

The most important infrastructure development has been the construction of roads, bridges and power plants. Despite Anxi County's poverty, funding for basic infrastructure from the central and provincial governments remained miniscule in the early years. In the late 1970s, there were only 700 km of motor-roads, with 2,200 vehicles; there was no rail service, and the two main rivers were navigationally insignificant (Lyons, 1994: 29). Many villages remained inaccessible by motor car. This was the case of Penglai until the late 1970s when Chinese overseas capital poured into the district to help with local road construction.

Roads

During the anti-poverty campaign, state-funded basic capital construction was directed mainly towards transportation and communication systems, electric power stations and transmission lines (Lyons, 1994: 74). The most important project was the construction of the Zhangping–Quanzhou rail line, with 115 km running through Anxi. The western section of this line was completed in 1985. Other projects included construction of the Xianghua–Longjuan highway and the Hutou–Jiandou Highway, also in the 1980s. By 1992, Anxi's road network had increased to 1,485 km and served the main towns. By 2008, Anxi's road network had increased to 3,957 km (Anxi County Government http://www.fjax.gov.cn/pagehtml/2008/04/b83cf92a-0887-4acd-acd4-6495256579d7.html, retrieved on 30 December 2009). In the 1980s, scheduled bus services began to connect Anxi with Xiamen City and other population centres (Lyons, 1994: 75). Public buses from other towns and cities stop at the entrance to Penglai and there was no local bus service plying around Penglai Zhen, so villagers had to take local motor rickshaws to travel around Penglai.

In the 1970s and early 1980s, the main arterial road leading from Xiamen to Anxi was poorly constructed and many visiting Chinese found it difficult to travel to Anxi. Movement of goods and people had been difficult because of the inadequate road system. Although the county government promised money to build roads, the progress remained slow. The lack of governmental funding and corruption were seen as twin factors in the continued delay in road construction. The main road from Xiamen to Anxi was only completed in 1997. Also, only the main roads were constructed with funds from the government; there was little funding for feeder and local roads to villages, and there was a lack of political will to improve them. In the emigrant districts, policies of the central and provincial governments were to encourage Chinese overseas capital to fund such projects, and it is therefore not surprising to see that little or no government money was earmarked for this purpose, despite pressures by the Chinese overseas—in particular from the Singapore Anxi Chinese in Penglai.

One method advocated by Anxi Chinese overseas was to split the cost of construction with the government. The stretch of road leading directly into Penglai was constructed under such a fund-sharing agreement. However, many local roads were constructed wholly from funds from Singapore and Malaysian Chinese. The result was that, from 1979 to 1991, a total of 91.1 km of roads were constructed in Penglai with overseas money (*Anxi Xianzhi,* vol. 1: 361). In 2004, the construction of a section of a highway in Anxi County that links Anxi and Xiamen City began. The total length of this section is 6.86 km and the width is 24.5 m. This section of the highway was funded by the county government and cost RMB 30.89 million. It was completed in 2007. In 2004, the railroad reached Anxi with a length of 96 km and nine stations that transport goods to the region (*Anxi Nianjian,* 2004–05: 207).

More dramatically, in 1995 the Long Men Tunnel was constructed and opened to traffic. The cost of building this tunnel amounted to RMB 2 million, all of which was Singaporean and Malaysian Chinese capital. The tunnel, which burrows through a mountain in Long Men Township, reduces the journey from Xiamen to Penglai from 5 hours to 2 $^{1}/_{2}$ hours.

(b) Bridges

The Anxi County is cut in two by the Anxi River. In Penglai, seven bridges were built with funding from the Chinese overseas (*qiaohui,* 侨汇), totalling

267 m and costing RMB 2.5 million to build. The single longest bridge is 100 m in length and cost RMB 2.25 million to build (*Anxi Xianzhi*, vol. 1: 379). These bridges permit the villagers to travel to different villages with ease and make daily communication and interaction possible.

In our survey, we found that all villagers mentioned that one of the greatest contributions made by Chinese overseas had been the construction of roads and bridges, and that all were aware of this. Many of the respondents' Singapore relatives had contributed varying amounts, and villagers felt that without these contributions the roads and bridges would not have been built, or would have been of poor quality. Without their contributors, the burden would have been heavy on the villagers and all households would have been required by the local government to contribute to the construction costs. Even though the county government had promised financial assistance, money was not forthcoming, and it was only with the contributions from the Singapore Chinese that the arterial road leading to Penglai was finally completed and opened at the end of 1996.

The older villagers were aware of large contributions by several Singapore Chinese. Even during the 1950s, 1960s, and 1980s, three main donors from the Ke lineage in Singapore had contributed to the building of three different bridges, allowing the villagers to cross a tributary of the Xi River with ease. Other contributions came from the Singaporeans from the 1970s until 2000; one had paid the entire cost for constructing two bridges in Penglai district. Some of these bridges have the names of the donors inscribed on them.

In general, there were three types of attitudes adopted by the villagers in regard to such contributions by overseas Chinese. The first was that Chinese overseas had a responsibility to help them with such infrastructure projects. This was the attitude of the majority of the villagers. The second attitude was that it was the responsibility of the county government to build the infrastructure in order that investments could be encouraged into the region. About half of the informants subscribed to this view, including some who also subscribed to the first attitude. The third attitude was that Chinese overseas should contribute if they had the ability to do so but should not be held responsible for such development. Only a handful adopted this attitude.

The Singapore Chinese saw that helping to construct roads and bridges was a way to become involved with their ancestral villages, and an important way to establish *guanxi* with provincial, county and local cadres for the men, as many of them were businessmen, some with businesses in the towns of Anxi and in Xiamen. For many others, who had no business in Fujian Province, giving donations and helping with infrastructure development simply meant goodwill from all sides, including government officials and villagers. With the status and social capital thus gained, they would be in a better position to negotiate with government officials over the staging of numerous socio-religious activities through the years, which often had the support of village and county cadres. Another reason, of course, is that a better road system simply made their trips to their ancestral villages more pleasant and less dangerous, and thereby would encourage more Singaporeans to visit their ancestral villages.

(2) Education and schools

A second area of development concerned the building of schools and the expansion of education. This area of development was supported by almost 90 per cent of the Singapore Anxi Chinese. The main goals were to raise the literacy level of the villagers and to provide a way to develop the agrarian villages into towns, and thus provide an escape from rural poverty. They were especially concerned about village girls, who were then receiving less education than boys.

The provision of education for all the children of the villages in Penglai was an important priority for the Singaporeans. Largely through their efforts, the town was officially labelled a 'cultural district' (*wenhua qu*, 文化区) by the county government because of the number of educational facilities for village children and the relatively high literacy rate of its young population in comparison with other mountainous districts (*shanqu*, 山区). To this day, the town and county cadres have expressed pride in this, and openly attribute the high literacy primarily to the work of the Chinese overseas who began to help with the provision of educational facilities as early as the 1940s. By the 1990s, contributions for education were growing much faster than those for other sectors.

From our survey, we found that almost 25 per cent of the villagers had gone beyond the compulsory years of education. About 37 per cent of the villagers had had some form of primary education; 27.5 per cent had middle school education; 16 per cent had upper secondary education; 5.5 per cent had teacher or technical education; 1.5 per cent had tertiary education and 18.5 per cent had had no formal education. However, taken together, 95.7 per cent of male respondents had received some form of education while only 48.3 per cent of female respondents had formal education. In addition, despite the fact that 140 of the 200 respondents were male, of the 18.5 per cent of those with no education, 15.5 per cent were women. However, this is not surprising as the villagers continued to value sons over daughters.

Table 2: Sex and distribution of education and literacy

	No Education	Primary	Secondary/Post-secondary	Technical	Tertiary	Total
Male	6	53	68	11	2	140
Female	31	19	9	0	1	60
Total	37	72	77	11	3	200
%	18.5	37	43.5	55	1.5	100

By the late 1990s, however, the general attitude among Penglai residents was to provide at least nine years of education for all children, male and female alike. In wealthier households, the desire was to provide as much education as possible for female children if their grades permitted them to go on with their studies. In 1996, several young women in Penglai were attending a teacher's training college or institute (i.e., not a full university) in Quanzhou. Thus, although the villagers in Penglai continued to prefer boys, the attitude was gradually changing, with some families treating their daughters with as much care and attention as were given to boys.

Table 3: Age groups and educational attainment

Age	No Education	Primary	Secondary/Post-secondary	Technical	Tertiary	Total (%)
20–29	2	3	16	0	0	21 (10.5)
30–39	3	10	25	1	0	39 (18.5)
40–49	11	19	15	3	1	49 (24.5)
50–59	15	17	15	4	2	53 (26.5)
> 60	6	23	6	3	0	38 (18.0)
	37	72	77	11	3	N= 200

Table 3 shows the level of education for each age category. The 81.5 per cent with some form of education have been the reason for Penglai being considered a 'cultural district', with supposedly a higher level of literacy than other areas of the county. Sixty-five per cent of those in the 20–29 and 30–39 age groups have attained secondary, post-secondary or technical education, and there was a focus on encouraging younger villagers to pursue higher education. The village schools were competing with one another to produce the best students to send to the best secondary schools and university, and children are encouraged to study and obtain good grades by parents.

Educational improvement was a target of the local cadres, as well as of the Singapore Chinese. There were three main objectives: (i) to expand education in general; (ii) to encourage contributions to education from *qiaoqing*; and (iii) to upgrade teaching skills. The Singapore Chinese had contributed substantially to numerous education projects. Since 1978, an expansion of educational facilities has included new buildings for primary and secondary schools and new staff quarters for the teachers. The latter attracted better teachers to Penglai, and this in turn resulted in better grades for the children. Formerly, students had to travel to the county town for upper secondary education; today, primary, and both lower and upper secondary education can all be acquired within the town. The local No. 8 Secondary School in Penglai started offering upper secondary education in 1992 and has rapidly acquired a reputation for producing good students. In China, secondary schools are divided into five bands. Band 1 schools are the best and are usually found in cities. To attain a Band 3 status for a village school is an achievement. The No. 8 Secondary School had attained Band 3 status and was aiming for Band 2 status awarded in reference to student success in the national examination system in the late 1990s. To attain Band 2 status was almost unheard of in rural China, so this represented an ambitious goal, for which a lot of assistance and resources from the Chinese overseas was needed.

From 1979 to 1990, the number of primary schools in Anxi County increased from 355 to 424, and the number of students went from 84,557 to 97,387. The number of secondary schools increased from 4 to 17 during this period, while that of upper secondary schools decreased from 15 to 10, as some secondary schools offered both lower and upper secondary education. This same period witnessed an increase in the number of students in post-primary education from 21,750 to 28,518, of which 25,460 were in lower secondary education while 3,508 were in upper secondary education (*Anxi Xianzhi*, vol. 2: 953). By 2006, the number of secondary school was 61 and the student number reached 87,564. The number of primary school was 344 in 2006 and the student number was 94,144 (*Anxi Nianjian*, 2005–06: http://www.axdfz.gov.cn/ShowText.asp?ToBook=17008&index=185&, retrieved on 30 December 2009).

Involvement of overseas Chinese in education in Anxi County began in 1949, when 2 secondary and 17 primary schools were built with funds from Chinese overseas. After the reform, Chinese overseas capital continued to finance educational projects, adding another 10 secondary and 12 primary schools. It is estimated that, from about 1954 to 1994, overseas Chinese contributed over RMB 53 million to education in Anxi (*Anxi Xianzhi*, vol. 2: 974). Such contributions were made, either by single donors or by groups of

Chinese overseas, to particular schools, often to those in particular ancestral villages. *Qiaoxiang* with a large number of wealthy visiting overseas kin benefited greatly since the reform years, while those with few visiting overseas kin had fewer resources and non-*qiaoxiang* remained comparatively poor.

Quite a few schools in Anxi were begun with overseas funding during the early years of Communism, with subsequent funding from members of the same lineages; as a result each school became associated with a particular lineage and surname group. Villagers of the lineage bearing the same surname were strongly encouraged to send their children to these schools, although children of other surnames would also be admitted. Freedman also noticed similar behaviour of lineages in terms of schooling during pre-revolutionary, and even pre-modern, times (Freedman, 1966). In these schools as high as 80 per cent of the students would be of the same surname group—a situation facilitated by the fact that each village tended to be dominated by one surname group, and therefore visiting kin of this group were substantial contributors and had considerable influence in the school administration. Within Penglai, three surname groups have schools affiliated with their lineages.

In Penglai, the Ke lineage dominates Penglai Kuitou precinct, which has both a primary and a secondary school. These two schools carry the name of a late donor of the Ke lineage, and are known as Jinlai Primary and Jinlai Secondary School, respectively.

Ke Jinlai went to Singapore in the 1910s and had made his fortune by the 1930s and 1940s. He returned to his home village and started the first village primary school in the 1930s; in the 1950s, he contributed another sum of money and built the secondary school. Since then, other donors from the same lineage have contributed substantially to improve educational facilities and the teaching environment in Penglai.

Contributions have also been made to the construction of teachers' quarters for Penglai's No. 8 Secondary School; in 1994 the contributions amounted to an estimated RMB 1 million. This was considered a very important project for attracting and retaining good teachers to this interior town with few modern amenities and recreational or entertainment facilities. Previous accommodations had been built in the 1950s by the teachers and local people themselves, and were in extremely dilapidated conditions.

Whenever Singapore Chinese visited Penglai, they would be taken to visit No. 8 Secondary School, various rundown buildings would be pointed out and the visitors would be asked to sponsor new projects. In 1994, sufficient funds were collected to enable the school to construct its staff quarters, and at the end of 1995 the first teacher household moved into the new building. Soon the building was fully occupied by teachers, mostly from other districts, and the school was planning to construct a second building for teachers, to replace another old building. The school authorities hoped that Anxi Singaporeans would again help with the financing. In 1996 when I was there, there were talks about asking the Singapore Chinese to help equip the schools with computer facilities.

According to the principal of No. 8 Secondary School, when the school was first built, donor Ke Jinlai suggested that it become an educational project of his Ke lineage. The school administration accepted this proposal and took contributions only from members of Ke lineage. The principal told me that, in excluding members of other lineages from contributing to the school, the school administration hoped that the Ke members would contribute more.

This became a common strategy adopted by various schools and a de facto policy in Penglai—that only members of one surname group or lineage could contribute to each school. Thus the school has become a de facto lineage school, although admission is open to all surname groups.

According to a school principal, the advantage to this practice was that it created an environment in which members of various lineages would compete with one another to build better facilities for their particular 'lineage school'. Here, 'face' was at stake, and members of the dominant lineages wanted to win 'face' for themselves. Thus, understanding the psyche of the Singapore Chinese and promoting inter-lineage rivalry in educational projects became strategies used by local cadres when they attempted to solicit funds from their respective Singapore lineage kin.

The Singapore Chinese, on their own initiative and at times in response to suggestions from local cadres, also established scholarships, awards and bursaries for students of their 'lineage schools'. Students with the best results in a given year were given awards, usually sums of money and memorabilia, for their scholastic excellence. Those who were accepted into universities or other tertiary institutions were given scholarships, and students from poorer households were given financial assistance and grants-in-aid to enable them to complete their studies.

In Penglai, Singapore Chinese had contributed several million dollars to various educational projects such as those mentioned above, and were in the process of raising another million (RMB) for scholarships and bursaries in the late 1990s. To encourage teachers to perform and remain in Kuitou and other villages, it became a common practice to offer additional salary and bonuses, as well as better housing and living conditions to the teachers. This money also came from funds given by Chinese overseas.

(3) Public health and hospitals

The third area of development has been that of public health and medical facilities. Anxi was one of the poorest counties. It was, and still is, somewhat neglected by the central and provincial governments in terms of health services. From the 1950s to the late 1970s, few funds were devoted to providing medical facilities, although there were 'barefoot physicians', some clinics and at least two hospitals. Local people could only be treated at the county city hospital, which was difficult for villagers to reach because of the cost involved. In the 1980s, even though there was an anti-poverty campaign, the health sector continued to be neglected, as energies were being channelled into infrastructure and enterprise development.

In Penglai, the situation was no worse than in other townships. Since the early 1950s, local health and medical provisions have benefited from financial support from Chinese overseas. Today, Penglai Huaqiao Hospital is the only medical institution in the district. The original medical clinic established in 1953 and was expanded in 1956 when five Singapore Chinese joined together to raise funds and helped establish the Penglai Chinese and Western Medical Clinic (Penglai Zhongxi Zhenliaosuo, 蓬莱中西诊疗所). They donated RMB 124,000. The facility was renamed Penglai Huaqiao Hospital in July 1956. In 1972, it was again renamed as Penglai Public Health Institute (Penglai Weishengyuan, 蓬莱卫生院). From 1984 to 1990, the hospital underwent various phases of modernization and extension, financed wholly by Singapore Chinese capital. In 1990 a new four-storey wing was added to the hospital, with three floors for in-patients and the uppermost floor for meetings and for entertaining guests. The contribution for this came from two sons and the daughter of a Singapore family, and the wing was named after their late father, a big contributor to village reconstruction. About the same time, the hospital upgraded its medical equipment with funds contributed by other Singapore Chinese, who also donated medical equipment, as well as blankets, beds, refrigerators, a car, and other items of daily medical necessity. From 1985 to 1992, contributions totalled over a million RMB. Today, there is no charge for medical treatment and a nominal fee is charged for the medicine. The hospital has upgraded its services and is one of the most modern hospitals in the region, and villagers from nearby districts in Kuitou travel to have their medical treatment there.

Apart from Penglai Hospital, there are several medical outposts providing some form of basic treatment to the sick and the injured. However, some villagers, especially those in mountain areas and those without overseas kin, have found it difficult to pay for treatment and medicine and resorted to self-medication. Their only recourse was to travel the distance to Penglai Hospital for better and free medical treatment. They would also be assured that they would be given treatment.

However, like other public institutions, the hospital continued to suffer from insufficient funding from the county and local governments. The staff were poorly paid and the increasing number of patients made for a heavy workload for doctors and other medical staff, most of whom were trained in Chinese medicine, although top administrators-cum-doctors claimed knowledge of Western medicine. While the hospital levied a small charge to cover medicine, this did not cover costs. Doctors informed me that they were often out of pocket in treating patients. The deputy director of the hospital related the following incident to me:

> Last year there was a peasant, a woman, aged 22 years. She was pregnant with twins but had no knowledge of it. Because the family was not well-off, she did not even once visit our hospital or other clinics. Like many peasant women, on the day of her delivery, she went into labour at home alone. For over ten hours, she was trying to give birth, but the babies were in a breech position and she could not deliver. She was bleeding a lot and by the time her husband and other family returned home, she had already lost a lot of blood. She was already in a semi-conscious state. Her husband brought her to our hospital. It was a shocking sight. We had to try to save her life as well as the babies. We operated on her immediately. But it was too late: the babies, two sons, were delivered stillborn. Because of this, the husband was disgusted and refused further medical treatment for her. But we could not just discharge her like this. We hospitalized her and treated her. After she recovered and was discharged, her husband did not and could not afford to pay the bill of over RMB 200. He did not consider it worthwhile, as he had already lost two sons. As for her welfare, he did not show any concern at all. I had to pay the bill out of my own pocket, as the hospital does not have emergency funds to cover non-payment.
>
> Fortunately, after I mentioned this incident to one of the Singapore *qiaobao*, he reimbursed me the amount and suggested that the hospital set aside an emergency fund for such cases. Now, the hospital has decided to ask for contributions from the *qiaobao* to help with this emergency fund. I hope everyone will contribute some to this.

Given their situation, the hospital authority thus found it easier to turn to Chinese overseas for donations than to ask for an increased budget from government agencies, and since the 1980s has engaged in intense lobbying for funds from Singapore and Malaysian Chinese. Funds were needed in all areas. The new wing effectively tripled the hospital's capacity and included a staff quarter, and they solicited funds to purchase medicine so that local villagers could continue to enjoy relatively cheap medical care. In the 1990s a villager needed to pay only several RMB for medicine, but with the trend towards privatization and due to the fact that physicians are now allowed to engage in some sorts of private practice, health costs for villagers are expected to rise. In Penglai physicians employed by the hospital are permitted to charge more in their private practices and still use hospital space. Some of these enterprising physicians charge RMB 10 or more for consultation and medicine, making it extremely difficult for poorer villagers to receive medical treatment. The administration hopes that, with contributions from Chinese overseas, they will be able to continue to provide low-cost medical care for needy villagers while charging wealthier villagers higher fees. Only in the late 1980s and the 1990s was the hospital able to afford certain essential equipment such as X-ray machines, ultra-sound machines and ECG machines, which were then seen as luxuries in village China. Without contributions from the Chinese overseas, such equipment would have been found only in wealthy hospitals in the big cities, used by the privileged class. The relatively high status attained by the hospital has made the Penglai residents feel very proud of the hospital itself, and also of their overseas connections. The hospital has good after-care facilities. Previously, many diagnoses and semi-complicated treatments could only be treated in the county hospital, two to three hours away, but today reasonably good health care can be found locally.

Many villagers refer to the hospital as the Huaqiao Hospital, and feel the name truly reflects the concern of their *qiaobao* for them. These were their responses:

> ... if the *qiaobao* did not provide financial assistance, up till today, we would still be without a hospital. The hospital is clean by village standards and the doctors are good. We can now be treated for various illnesses and even have surgery done locally. We do not need to travel to the county hospital for surgery anymore. Besides, the charges are very reasonable. Everyone needs to pay only a few RMB to see a doctor and more for hospitalization and surgery.
>
> I think it is good that the *huaqiao*, especially the Singapore Chinese, make big contributions to basic infrastructures in the village. It is especially good of them to make donations to the

hospital. I think they should donate more so that we all can benefit from it.

Although dependence on the life-force for healing, commonly known as fate (*mingyun*, 命运), mitigated by the numerous deities, continued for many local people, medical treatment now brought another dimension of hope. However, changing of attitudes remained gradual and many villagers continued to rely on supernatural elements to improve their health, although some did so in addition to accepting modern medical practices. Younger villagers, especially, would go to the hospital for consultation over minor ailments, although the elderly continued with home remedy for ailments such as colds and flu. Although some villagers still found the cost of medicine, even at only RMB 2 to 3, to be an expense that they did not wish to incur unnecessarily, they all agreed that if there was a serious illness, they would consult the doctors at the hospital. However, in serious cases some had to travel to Chuanzhou or even Xiamen for medical treatment.

Many Singapore Chinese expressed disbelief that the central and provincial governments did not provide sufficient funding for such an important service as a hospital. They told me that they began to understand the meaning of 'life is cheap in the villages' and began to realize that the various levels of government had no interest in village life and village affairs. As their forebears were from Penglai, however, they were interested and were willing to provide the help.

(4) Financing small businesses

The fourth area of Singaporean assistance has been to help transform the district from an agrarian to a petty commodity and trading economy. Until today, this strategy has met with little success in Penglai.

The interior location, mountainous terrain and poor transportation are the main deterrent factors for industrialization and commercialization in Anxi. After the 1978 reform and with the anti-poverty campaign on its way, Anxi continued to have very few industries or commercial enterprises. Most of these were cottage industries that made use of local resources and were geared towards local consumption. These included the production of paper, sugar, local alcohol, tea, handicrafts, rattan goods and furniture, and wood products.

As a result of the 1978 reform, there was an increase in industrial production for export, and in forms of secondary and tertiary economic activities. In 1982, there were only 854 enterprises; by 1990, the figure had leaped to 7,069. The main industries included farm machinery production, a power station, tea processing plants and construction; together the various enterprises employed a total of 37,304 workers (*Anxi Xianzhi*, vol. 1: 353). Of the 7,069 enterprises, 194 were operated by towns, 810 by villages, 370 by the Overseas Chinese Bureau and 5,695 by individual households (*Anxi Xianzhi*, vol. 1: 354); 1,072 of them were involved in industrial production, 422 in agricultural production, 24 in construction work, 617 with transportation and roads, 4,285 in commercial and retailing activities, 642 in service industries, and 7 in other activities (*Anzi Xianzhi*, vol. 1: 354). By 2006, Anxi has 74,016 enterprises in total, 15,648 of which are Township and Village enterprises with 158,505 employees (*Anxi Nianjian*, 2005–06, retrieved on 30 December 2009, from http://www.axdfz.gov.cn/ShowText.asp?ToBook=17008&index=134&; http://www.axdfz.gov.cn/ShowText.asp?ToBook=17008&index=228&).

In 1990, however, there were only 114 enterprises in Penglai, employing a total of 2,479 workers. After reform, Penglai had witnessed the emergence of three cottage industries, which produced pottery, rattan goods and furniture, and processed tea. All were geared towards export and used local resources and local expertise. In 1990, the pottery and rattan factories each employed just over 20 workers, and they were women in their late teens and early twenties. The clay pots and vases, made from local clay, were fired in local kilns made by local men. Then they were taken to the factory where the girls wove rattan baskets around them. These pots and vases in baskets were then exported to the big cities of Southeast Asia, including Singapore, and Europe (*Anxi Xianzhi*, vol. 1: 353).

From 1978 onwards, government officials at various levels have intensified their efforts to encourage Chinese overseas to visit and invest in both big cities and ancestral villages. Chinese overseas with close *qiaoxiang* connections were especially encouraged to invest in emigrant villages so that their investment would bring about development in the rural sector. The Overseas Chinese Bureau worked intensely towards encouraging capital investments for infrastructure and enterprise development in the emigrant counties. County and district cadres made regular trips to Singapore to rekindle ties with Singapore kin and to re-establish *guanxi* networks, hoping that through these social networks the Singapore Chinese could be encouraged to visit their ancestral homes and to invest in Anxi in general and in Penglai in particular.

This period coincided with a high growth rate in the Singapore economy and in Singapore's policy towards globalization. The relatively wealthy status of the Singapore Anxi Chinese made them more prepared to deal with their ancestral home village in a generous manner, and when the village and county cadres came to Singapore to ask for financial assistance for infrastructure development, their active participation in village reconstruction and effort in making the emigrant villages prosperous was a way of reflecting their own well-being.

The lifting of restrictions on travel to China by the Singapore government meant that Singapore Chinese no longer needed to apply for exit permits. The potential of the China market and the low labour costs there led many Singapore Chinese to invest in China by setting up factories and various types of businesses in the port cities and special economic zones of Xiamen, Hainan, Shenzhen and Suzhou. However, the Singapore Anxi Chinese also focused on development of their ancestral villages. Although village and county governments were eager to encourage capital investment in industry and manufacturing, the Singapore Anxi Chinese were less interested in this; to them, economic rationalism dictated that they set up factories in port cities and the special economic zones rather than in the villages, where there was little economic infrastructure to support such investments. Yet, they were still interested in assisting their immediate kin to develop small businesses and enable them to move out of agriculture.

Solving Unemployment with Enterprise Development

By encouraging Chinese overseas to invest in local industry rather than to support cultural and religious activities in the villages, local government hoped to solve the unemployment problems of the Anxi region. A rapidly growing population, as a result of the partial failure of family planning and the shrinking of the cultivable land area, has made for a large pool of surplus labour in China. Traditionally, agricultural involution in paddy growing had been insufficient for absorbing surplus labour in coastal areas such as Fujian; emigration was one result of this. The population of Penglai in Anxi County hoped that the market economy would solve the local unemployment problem. In the 1990s the county town was in a transitional stage, and Penglai Town had attempted to transform its economy without much success.

Interviews with the official cadres at the time elicited the following expressions of hope that Singapore Chinese or other groups of Chinese would return and set up factories in Anxi and Penglai:

> It will be good if the Singapore Chinese come and invest here. They should come and set up factories here. We are very short of electricity and they should come and set up a power plant here.

> The county government and the Singapore Chinese have co-operated and set up a power plant. They should now concentrate on industries, such as the garment industry, to help solve our unemployment problems.

> These Singapore Chinese have their priority wrong. They are only interested in the cultural and religious functions and are willing to spend large sums of money on them. When it comes to setting up factories, they are not so willing to do so. Some even reject this suggestion outright.

While industrialization and development of the market economy were the goals of the official district and county cadres, many had only sketchy ideas of how to go about them, as they had very little exposure to, or knowledge of, the operation of a market economy, or of industrial development. Most found it hard to articulate what they expected of industrialization, or the types of factories that were appropriate for Anxi. Many simply expressed that, as long as there were factories, the villagers would be able to work and earn an income, and this would solve the unemployment problems. These were their responses:

> I do not know what types of factories would be good. But any type of factory would do. As long as there are factories, they would be good for our economy and our people.

> I would like to see manufacturing factories. But I have very little idea of what types of manufacturing would be appropriate for Anxi. I guess I would leave the decision to the Singapore investors. They would have better ideas than we do here. After all, they are businessmen.

> I would like to see factories that will absorb many workers. Maybe light industries such as garments, bags, etc., are good for us.

However, several cadres had some knowledge of the operation of a market economy. While they too hoped that the Singapore Chinese would come and invest in the county, they had reservations about their success in encouraging these investments, feeling that the central, county and district governments did not play a sufficient role, pointing to their lack of commitment to develop basic infrastructure. To them, governments at various levels had failed in their promise to build more roads and other transportation facilities, as well as power plants that would provide the necessary energy to run factories. The arterial road from Xiamen City to the county town of Fengcheng and Penglai was delayed for several years due to lack of funding on the one hand and corruption on the other.

Corruption is a widespread phenomenon in China, especially in the rural areas. Bribes and kickbacks line the pockets of officials at different levels, leaving only a small amount for such projects as the construction of basic infrastructure. In the case of the arterial road, the level of corruption, according to the villagers, increased according to the length and quality of road completed. Since the arterial road was to pass through several counties, each county government was required to contribute to the construction of the stretch of road through the county. The county government thus distributed financial responsibilities to its component *xiang* and *zhen* governments. As a result, going through the counties, various stretches were completed while others were not; in the various districts, some stretches were better constructed than others. According to the villagers, in districts with less corruption the roads were in better condition and new roads were built faster than in others. Under pressure from the Chinese overseas and with additional contributions from them, the road was finally completed in 1996, to the relief of all, especially the Chinese overseas.

In an economy in transition, from one based on agriculture to one based on petty commodity trading and cottage industrialization, the issue of employment takes on new meanings. Previously, farm workers had surplus time during off-seasons. With the shrinking of farmland, many farm workers became unemployed. Furthermore, the township now produced many young men and women with ten years of education who had no desire to work on the farm but wanted paid employment. As this was a transitional economy, it was unable to generate sufficient jobs. As such, young people sat around smoking and engaging in idle conversation. It was such scenes that led Singapore Chinese to label them 'lazy'.

Convincing the Singapore Chinese to set up factories in Anxi County was an uphill battle for the county cadres, especially when it concerned Penglai. The Singapore Chinese remained lukewarm in their attitude towards large-scale capital investment there. However, a few lineage members whose ancestral homes were in Penglai financed small-scale garment factories and other enterprises set up by their village kin, in addition to making considerable financial contributions for infrastructure development.

Enterprise Profile in Penglai Zhen

The Singapore Chinese have given small amounts of capital to their immediate relatives to start small manufacturing and retailing businesses in Penglai Zhen. As in many rural counties, Penglai villagers opt to become self-employed and own small businesses if possible. In my late 1980s survey, there were 2 factory-owners, 17 shop-owners, 5 self-employed drivers, 1 photographer, 1 ironsmith, 1 carpenter and 1 artist in Penglai, representing an increasing pool of self-employed individuals who were operating within the limits of the reformed 'socialist market system'. Most of these had small retail businesses geared towards local needs and consumption.

By the 1990s, there were over 100 shops in Penglai; each was privately owned. These shops sold a variety of goods including clothes, personal toiletries, small electrical goods, transistor radios and cameras. A booming tyre business emerged and catered to the car population in the district. There were several ladies' hairdressing salons and two photographic studios. Some shops had pinball machines.

By 2007, Penglai had 23 types of enterprises in total, with RMB 80 million of industrial production worth (retrieved on 30 December 2009, from http://ax.dmw.gov.cn/onews.asp?id=1428). One important type of business was called 'the religious and funerary industry' (*zongjiao sangzang hangye,* 宗教丧葬行业), which catered to emerging religious practices in the villages. Shops emerged to produce religious paraphernalia such as joss-sticks, streamers, candles, joss-papers, house for the dead (*lingwu,* 灵屋) and fire-crackers. The revival of religious activities and ancestor worship helped revive traditional skills and handicrafts that were essential in the making of these religious items. Those who could produce such items were able to make substantial profit. A religious celebration, or a post-death ritual, commonly called *gongde* (功德), could cost RMB 5,000 or more, and an equivalent amount could be spent on purchasing the paraphernalia. To attract more Chinese overseas to visit and stage communal religious fairs in the village, villagers actively encouraged and the village and county cadres tacitly approved large communal religious activities in order to gain Chinese overseas contributions to the local economy.

For the first time since the founding of the People's Republic of China (PRC), there was an emergence of 'the flesh industry', i.e., prostitution, in Kuitou precinct. I was told by several women villagers that a small number of 'immoral and indecent women' (*buzhengjing nuren,* 不正经女人) from other parts of China now lived in the district and catered to out-of-town men who came to Penglai for business and stayed overnight. A few of these women were mistresses of these businessmen. The villagers, especially the women, did not welcome this, and felt that the prostitutes and mistresses had contaminated the town.

Creating a Moral Economy

By contributing substantially in the various ways mentioned above, the Singapore Chinese assisted with village development. The very poor villages of Penglai Zhen were transformed into economically prosperous emigrant villages that were also culturally vibrant. But why did the Singapore Chinese feel obligated to do this?

The moral economy which binds the Singapore Chinese to their ancestral villages rests on two sets of factors. The first set has to do with the attitudes of the Singapore Chinese and their understanding of, identification with, and affinity to their ancestral villages. These are very much shaped by collective memory, a sense of moral duty and moral consciousness. The second set of factors consist of how village leaders and cadres and villagers, through cultural concessions and moral persuasion, further bind them to the moral economy.

Moral Duty and Sentiments of Singapore Chinese

The operation of collective memory among the Singapore Chinese concerning their ancestral villages has been discussed in Chapter 3. A Confucian sense of moral duty continues to govern their relationship with their ancestral village. The Confucian phrase concerning 'remembering the source when one is drinking water' (*yinshui siyuan*) was frequently invoked by my Singaporean informants, and related to their ancestral homes. They did not necessarily have to like them, but they felt they should not forget them, as their parents and/or grandparents were from there. Their feeling of duty was evident: one Singaporean informant said, 'when the elders came to us for contributions for village projects, it was hard for us to turn them down. Somehow, it just did not seem right to say no. We usually gave whatever they asked from us. Generally, we would be asked to contribute S$500 or $1,000. After all, it is our ancestral village.'

Returning to their ancestral villages produced a moral consciousness among the Singaporeans, in that they were confronted with real poverty and an underdeveloped social and economic structure. For the first time, some began to understand what village life and village structure was all about, especially the Singapore-born. One said,

> Before visiting Anxi, I imagined that the villagers were lazy and did not want to work. After visiting Anxi, I begin to understand that it is not because they do not want to work, but rather that there is no work for them to do. Apart from farming, there is little they could do. We also understand that the government has very little interest in helping the region to develop. So, among some of us, we decide to help with setting up a hydro-electric power plant. We also help our relatives to start some small businesses to cater for local needs.

A related reason that the Singapore Chinese give is that of relative wealth and guilt feelings. They told me that 'presently, we are relatively well-off and comfortable. We also do not wish that our village kin would starve and live meagrely. They don't have to live the way we do in Singapore. But at least, we could help them to live comfortably by village standards. After paying visits to the place, we realize that many of them live in very poor conditions and have few material goods. So, we should help a little.'

Finally, there is the desire to maintain continuity between the two groups of Chinese. One informant commented: 'Our relationship is like a thin thread, it should be maintained at all costs, so that our future generations have reference to their ancestors and their source of origin. If it is broken, then the future generations will not be able to search for their ancestral roots and they would become headless.'

Cultural Concession as Cultural Capital

The second set of factors are the actions and attitudes of the Anxi village leaders, cadres and villagers. Two forces, cultural concession and the extraction of social capital, worked in favour of the villagers.

Village leaders and cadres understand the psychological needs of the Singapore Chinese and provide cultural concessions to them. Some village leaders told me that many of the older Singapore Chinese were interested in religious activities when they visited their ancestral village, so they facilitated the reproduction of religious practices. They also provided full support and assistance for the rebuilding of ancestral houses and temples. By permitting and helping the Singapore Chinese to stage large communal ancestor worship and religious celebrations and allowing the rebuilding of ancestral houses and temples, they developed social capital and established good *guanxi* for themselves, and this in turn bound the Singapore Chinese further into the moral economy, so that they could be called upon to contribute and assist with various aspects of village rebuilding. Villagers in Anxi County also actively promoted a series of moral sanctions to publicize Singapore kin who failed to discharge their moral duty. This can be analyzed in terms of patron-client relations, similar to the way James Scott (1985) analyzed passive resistance of the peasantry towards landowners.

Labelling: As mentioned, the villagers openly described those Singapore kin who failed to help as having become *fan* or *huang* [H], i.e., like the natives of Nanyang, whom they perceived as having no sense of propriety and *qinqing* (kin sentiments). It is also used against those who persuade others not to contribute to their ancestral home. The villagers commonly labelled the Singapore-born Chinese *huang* [H] because they were generally less interested and sympathetic to the ancestral village and often tended to distance themselves from it. They also behaved very differently from the older

Singapore Chinese in manners and attitudes. Many of them spoke English and some could not speak the Fujian dialect well. In the eyes of the villagers, such persons, usually of younger generations, had betrayed their ancestral origins.

Moral persuasion: The villagers invoked their kinship relations as moral suasion to entice the Singapore Chinese to help with local development, often invoking phrases like 'we, part of one family'; 'blood relatives' (*xueyuan guanxi*, 血缘关系); 'the leaves returning to their roots' (*luoye guigen*, 落叶归根); 'that they should remember the ancestors'; 'when drinking the water, remember the source'; 'irrespective of wealth, one should not be divorced from the ancestor' (*fugui bulizu*, 富贵不离祖); and 'they are offshoots from this family and this lineage'.

Social and Economic Changes

By engaging in the building or rebuilding of houses, roads, bridges, schools and hospitals, the Singapore Chinese helped to redevelop and alleviate conditions in what had been poverty-stricken Penglai region. This economic development brought about a boom in the construction industry and other related businesses. The filtering-down effect had far-reaching consequences for the village/township economy. During the construction boom, almost 70 per cent of the able-bodied men were engaged in some form of construction work. Others were involved in retailing and service industries. Likewise, the large communal religious fairs and ancestor worship ceremonies led to an increase in the number of people engaged in this trade. As the village moved away from a pure agrarian economy into a mixed economy, the farms became neglected. Many men became involved in some kind of capitalist pursuit or moved to neighbouring towns and cities to work, leaving women to work in the fields. Wealthier households with financial support from Singapore kin no longer worked on the farms at all; they either rented the farms to the poorer villagers or engaged workers to work on them. This created discrepancy among the wealthier and poorer households and often attracted jealousy, resentment and envy from those who were less well-off.

The rebuilding of the old houses and the building of new ones and shophouses impacted on the land use pattern. Substantial farmland was encroached upon for the construction of new buildings. As a result, the amount of arable land has been shrinking. However, the villagers adopted an optimistic outlook in this regard, as many no longer wanted to work on the land anyway, and found such work difficult and without prospect. Under the influence of their Singapore kin, many wanted to move into the towns and cities, and those with wealthy Singapore kin started small businesses there.

Some managed to go overseas, especially to Singapore, for employment, where many of them worked in electronic factories, printing houses and in construction.

Conclusion

The development of ancestral villages and the economic prosperity that these villages experienced was the result of the working of a moral economy based on collective memory and a sense of moral duty on the one hand, and on the ability to extract social capital through cultural concessions given by the village leaders and members on the other hand.

The relationship between the Singapore Chinese and their Anxi ancestral village can be summed up as follows: for the Singapore Chinese, the family (*jia*, 家) continues to be seen as the most important primordial social group, and needs to be held together despite all adversities. The lineage (*zongzu*, 宗族) is an extension of the family, and its primordiality hinges on the interconnectedness of its people through both collective consciousness and social conscience. *Moral* conscience, for the Singaporeans, is embedded in their self-identity, their identity vis-à-vis their village kin and their identity within the Singapore nation-state. It is couched in Confucian terms of loyalty and compassion, which leads them to return to their home villages and help with local development.

The success or failure of ancestral home reconstruction, village development and the transformation of the economy is also dependent on how the Anxi Chinese transform social relations into social capital, which they impose on their Singapore kin, making it extremely uncomfortable for the latter not to provide some form of assistance.

Photo 1   Old and new houses (photo by author)

Photo 2   New homes and renovated traditional home in the foreground (photo by Ke Jianyuan)

Photo 3   Qingshuiyan Bridge in Penglai (photo by Ke Jianyuan)

Photo 4   Pedestrian bridge (photo by Ke Jianyuan)

Photo 5   Tea plantation producing the famed 'Iron Goddess' tea (photo by Ke Jianyuan)

Photo 6   No. 8 Secondary School (photo by author)

Photo 7   Jinlai Secondary School teachers' dormitory (photo by Ke Jianyuan)

Photo 8   Retail shops (photo by Ke Jianyuan)

Photo 9   A new and prosperous Xiancheng (photo by Ke Jianyuan)

6
The Bond of Ancestor Worship

With the coming of the Singapore Chinese after the reform years, the social and cultural life of the villagers became more colourful and exciting. The period from the 1980s to the late 1990s witnessed a revival in both traditional socio-cultural and religious activities. Much cultural life now centres around three types of worship: (i) that of the ancestors, which involves the ancestral house and the performance of meritorious deeds for dead ancestors (such performances are called *gongde,* 功德); (ii) that of the living, which involves religious rites for the flow of descendants (rites called *juanding,* 涓丁); and (iii) that of other deities, such as the celebration of the Buddha's birthday (*fo dan,*佛诞), communal village celebrations, the procession of the county deity (*ying Qingshui zushigong,* 迎清水祖师公), the rebuilding of Qinghui zushigong Temple and its environs, known locally as Qingshui Yan (清水岩), and the reconstruction of small village temples devoted to various local deities, such as Zhouyue Miao (州月庙) and Penglai Si (蓬来寺). These religious activities can be broadly divided into communal and individual.

This chapter and the next will explore religious revivalism in the ancestral villages, *qiaoxiang* of the emigrants and their descendants. I will explore the significance of ancestors within the Chinese cosmology and the revival of ancestor worship of the Ke Lineage in Penglai, and the extent to which ancestor worship and related practices are gradually being reproduced to cater for both the increasing, overt needs of the Singapore Chinese and for those of their village kin. Practices associated with ancestor worship permeated village life by the end of the 1990s and brought together the Singapore Chinese and their village kin ritually to acknowledge their common ancestors, thereby forcing them to acknowledge the kinship ties that exist between them. I will examine the extent to which religious rituals and culture are reproduced in the village environment, the extent to which the revival of ancestor worship is relevant to the contemporary Chinese family, lineage and village, and the extent to which this revival is the result of a request for cultural continuity rather than purely an instrumental act aimed at luring Chinese overseas to the village for financial contributions. Other issues to consider are whether the revival is a reflection of the understanding of ancestor worship by the Singapore Chinese alone, and to what extent the practice of ancestor worship has changed with the interaction, in contemporary time and space, of different sets of social players and social environments.

Bridging the Social Gap: Ancestors and Ancestor Worship

Who are the ancestors? Throughout Chinese history, ancestors, both living and dead, have been an important part of the Chinese family, lineage and community. They are collectively seen as both the source of the lineage and as transmitters of Chinese culture. Records of ancestors, their roles and their significance, are found in numerous writings. One of the earliest works to revere ancestors is the Confucian *Book of Filial Duty* (*Xiaojing*, 孝经), in which Confucius outlined proper behaviour towards elders. Descendants were extolled to treat their living parents with filial-ness (*xiao*, 孝) and their dead ancestors with ritual propriety (*li*, 礼), and it was important to treat both living and dead ancestors with respect and human-ness (*ren*, 仁).

Ancestors occupy a central position in Chinese cosmology. Death is not seen as the ultimate cessation of life (De Groot, 1964, vol. 1: 4), but as the separation of *yin* (阴) and *yang* (阳) energies. After death, the spirit (*hun*, 魂) moves from one realm of existence, that of the human world (*renjian*, 人间), where the physical form is visible to the naked eye, to the netherworld (*yinjian*, 阴间), where the dead assumes a spirit status in a form undetectable to human eyes. Ultimately, the dead aspires to attain a godly status and to reside in the heavenly realm (*yangjian*, 阳间) (Yang, 1961: 150–151). In the after-life, either in the netherworld or in the heavenly kingdom, the dead continues to interact and interface with the living in the human world. The disposal of the newly-dead with proper rituals (*sangli*, 丧礼) and the proper conduct of ancestor worship (*jizu*, 祭祖) were seen as essential,[1] and all descendants, from the emperor downwards, were required to fulfil ritual duties to their ancestors. Among Confucianists, such acts express 'gratitude towards the originators and recalls the beginning' (Yang, 1961: 44). Ancestral halls (*zongtang*, 宗堂) and memorial halls (*citang*, 祠堂) where descendants could perform sacrificial offerings and ancestor worship were found both within palaces and in villages (Freedman, 1958: 81–91).

Ancestor worship thus provides continuity between the living and the dead. Dead ancestors interact with the human world in various ways. They are especially concerned about their immediate kin members and are known to assume a protective role over the welfare of their family. When the burial site of the ancestors is propitiously located, its *fengshui* (风水) harnesses the *yang* energies (*yangqi*, 阳气) of the ancestors to protect and to accrue benefits for the descendants (Freedman, 1966: 118–154). Performing regular ancestor worship and conducting correct rituals are important acts of respect and propitiation to ancestors, both involving offerings and sacrifices that guarantee that ancestors protect rather than harm their descendants. Spiritual attacks by ancestors are, in fact, considered justifiable if descendants neglect them, especially if ancestors have turned into lonely ghosts (*guhun*, 孤魂) or wandering ghosts (*youhun*, 游魂).[2]

Ancestors and ancestor worship are important in bridging the social gap between the Singapore Chinese and Anxi villagers. In Singapore, Chinese households continue to practise ancestor worship, often within individual households, although there is also communal ancestor worship in the memorial halls and in temples. The present trend is towards placing ancestral tablets in such temples, where individuals can now lease space for the purpose and then visit and worship individually. Communal worship and offering can also be conducted by the temples' monks or nuns (Tong, 1982).

In China, the 1978 reform made it possible for ancestor worship to be conducted openly. Before this date, overt communal ancestor worship had been prohibited, even though some individual households worshipped in private (Parish and Whyte, 1978: 283). Since then, there has been a great revival of communal ancestor worship and related rituals, especially in emigrant villages. The performance of meritorious deeds (*gongde*) and the rite of gratification for the flow of descendants (*xiezu juanding*, 谢祖涓丁), as well as the resiting of burial grounds, have all become important ritual activities for these two groups of Chinese. Among the emigrant villages, the building of lineage ancestral houses has become important. All these activities reflect joint effort by Singapore Anxi, who provide financial and emotional support, and local Anxi residents, who provide labour and participate actively. All of these activities have become hallmark functions of a prosperous emigrant village.

Reinventing the Lineage Ancestral House (*zuzhai*, 祖宅; *zucuo, zhorchu* [H] 祖厝)

One of the most important activities of ancestor worship is the construction of the lineage ancestral house, *zuzhai*, also called *zucuo*. A search through the

Ming and Qing Historical Records revealed records of Ke lineage ancestral temples (*zumiao*, 祖庙), lineage temples (*zongmiao*, 宗庙), and lineage ancestral temples (*zongci*, 宗祠), but not of a *zuzhai*. Could there have been one that locally performed the role of such a temple or would it have been a different social institution altogether? The *zuzhai*'s functions were similar to all of the above, and the *zongci* or *citang* are found commonly in Chinese communities overseas, where such halls allow groups of Chinese to commemorate and worship their ancestors. Yet *zuzhai* is more than the above, as it represents the physical location of ancestors, where it allows individuals to engage in dialogue with their forebears and come to terms with the social reality of the past, and to understand and 'feel' the social experiences of the ancestors.

The creation of *citang*, also called *zongci*, translated as memorial hall, is a common feature among the clan associations of Singapore. Clan or lineage members gather in them on specific occasions to worship their ancestors today. Such memorial halls have been erected by Chinese migrants in various parts of the world in order to fulfil their duties of ancestor worship. These socio-religious institutions helped migrants settle into new environments.

Zuzhai, however, can only be located in the original physical space where the ancestors planted themselves in a locality. Elderly Ke lineage members continue to see Anxi as their ancestral home, and have made no attempt to create a separate lineage from that of Anxi. Following the reforms in China, the Ke in Singapore and Anxi were able to obtain approval for the construction of a lineage ancestral house, as this would enable the separate branches of the Ke lineage—in Singapore, Malaysia, Indonesia and Taiwan, as well as Anxi—to come together after five decades of separation. For Ke lineage members, the *zuzhai* would act as a reminder of the existence of their lineage, its history and future.

In Anxi, ancestors are worshipped in several places, but they are jointly worshipped in the *zuzhai*, which is communal property where every member can lay claim to his or her ancestors and where he or she can go to honour his or her ancestors on special occasions marked by communal celebrations. All lineage households within the village belonging to the lineage participate in such activities. Within the *zuzhai*, each member can erect an ancestral altar for his or her immediate ancestors. Some well-to-do families might create an ancestral shrine room for their ancestral tablets and for worshipping their immediate ancestors, simply on a daily basis and more elaborately on special occasions. For some of these, the *laojia* itself may be converted into a private ancestral house, to be used solely for the worship of family ancestors.

Both Singapore and Anxi informants responded positively to the idea of the construction of a *zuzhai*, especially the Singaporean Ke, and a few wealthy lineage members contributed large sums while the majority contributed what they could afford; sums ranged from several hundreds to tens of thousands of Singapore dollars. Several active elders in Singapore acted as leaders of this fundraising exercise as their high social status within their community allowed them to raise the money with relative ease.

The supervision and the actual work of construction were left in the hands of the Anxi Ke lineage members. On several occasions during the construction, the Singaporeans visited the site. The Anxi team took great care in ensuring that the project stayed within the budget and was completed in time, and that the house was well constructed. They told me that the Singaporeans expected them to be efficient and corruption-free; in fact, the Singaporeans had feared that corruption would hinder the completion and quality of the project.

As a memorial building, the present *zuzhai* is in traditional Chinese architectural style, with a curved tile roof. The building comprises a large shrine hall and an uncovered front courtyard. The shrine hall is divided into three main sections: in the middle, there are built-in shelves reserved for the ancestral tablets; to the left, an altar is reserved for a guardian god, *kuixinggong* or *kway-sin-gong* (H) (魁星公); to the right there is an altar for the earth god (*tudigong*, 土地公). Both the shrine hall and the adjoining courtyard are sufficiently spacious to allow for large congregations of lineage members at religious events.

This *zuzhai* is regarded as the residence of the ancestors and the location of their original home, and is therefore considered the physical source of the lineage. A *zuzhai* would not be created by a lineage branch, unless it wished to establish itself as a separate lineage and sever ties with the existing one. The *zuzhai* can be conceptualized as both a physical and a socio-religious space.[3] It is the place where the values of the first ancestors were laid down for descendants. The Ke lineage *zuzhai* has become an extremely significant marker for the two groups of Ke lineage members since it was rebuilt in the 1980s, and the intensity of social interaction between the Singapore and Anxi Ke has markedly increased, as evidenced by the numerous communal celebrations held in the *zuzhai*. The *zuzhai* has also allowed both the Singapore and village women to become primary reproducers of religious rituals within what had been a male-dominated village social structure, as women have been both active proponents of, and participants in, the elaborate religious rituals held there.

The *zuzhai* is a nexus of power. Emanating outward from this centre of power flows the traditional values of wisdom, compassion and morality. The Singapore and village elders are expected to perform the ancestral duties befitting their senior status. The values then ripple through the various layers of social relationship, moving from the centre to the outermost periphery, so that all kin may benefit from their association with the *zuzhai*. In this moral framework, wealth and social prestige of individuals are only recognized when they are converted into virtuous deeds that benefit the community as a whole: philanthropy and charitable works are thus essential to ensure that social status is recognized within the lineage, especially after death. To the Singapore Chinese, in this context, wealth alone has little value. Only when it is converted into social deeds do those in possession of it gain an everlasting 'fragrant' name.

Since the 1978 reform, in addition to the lineage ancestral house, the Kuitou zucuo (Kway-tau zhor-chu [H], 魁头祖厝), the three different branches, or *fang* (房), decided to establish their own branch ancestral hall but named it as memorial hall, *zongci*. It began with the third branch, *sanfang* (三房), building their own. The construction of Meiting zongci (美厅宗祠) began in the seventh lunar month and completed with the *zhuding* (祝丁) religious ceremony, a rite of gratification of the flow of descendants on the 27th day of the eleventh lunar month of 2002. This was followed by the second fang, *erfang* (二房), which built their memorial hall in the ninth lunar month of 2000 and completed in the twelfth lunar month of 2001. Finally the first branch, *zhangfang* (长房), also built theirs in 2004 and completed in 2006. The financing of these branch ancestral halls came from the overseas kin. Here, the creation of the ancestral hall is a reflection of the desire to consolidate the strength and status of their own branch on the one hand and competition and rivalry among these three branches on the other. When the third branch decided to build their own branch ancestral hall, the other two branches felt compelled to do so in order to keep up with the third branch and also not to lose face. In a sense, the establishment and the glorification of the branch ancestors in the branch ancestral hall also justified the continued creation of wealth in an overseas environment and the wealth disparity between the overseas kin and the villagers. Today, these three branch ancestral halls together with the main lineage ancestral house cluster together forming an ancestral house complex in Penglai.

In recent decades, many Singapore Ke lineage members have planned their visits to Anxi to coincide with communal ancestor worship. Although, in traditional China, communal ancestor worship was the responsibility of male elders, this is not so today, and women have become important participants.

It is the case that Singapore lineage members are given priority treatment when it comes to ancestor worship. One local lineage member said, 'we are host and they [Singapore kin] are guests, so they should be invited to worship the ancestors communally.' Another commented that their Singapore kin have priority because 'we must know our behaviour, they have come all the way from Singapore, so it is only right that they are given priority to worship our ancestors as they only come, at most, once or twice a year. We can always worship them on other occasions. There is no need to fight with them over this.' A third villager suggested that 'the Singapore Chinese are very enthusiastic about cultural and religious activities. They are firm believers and participants. That is why they are prepared to travel all the way back to Anxi for such activities. And they are willing to contribute substantially to these kinds of religious activities. If they pay so much for the celebration, then, it would not be right for us to stop them from communally worshipping our ancestors.'

Women, including married and unmarried daughters, and younger members, are now seen as an integral part of the lineage. One reason given for the incorporation of women from Singapore in communal ancestor worship is that Singapore women seem to be more interested in religious activities than their men. They not only prepare food, but also give offerings and give instructions for preparing religious occasions and ritual performances. The breakdown of traditional social structure under Communist rule and the changing social environment in Singapore have made it easier for women to be incorporated in communal ancestor worship. They sometimes represent their husbands, if and when the latter do not return for the occasion.

Young Singaporean men and women are especially invited to communal worship—by incorporating them, it is hoped that they will feel as part of the lineage and become interested in Anxi.

Such religious rites and communal celebrations have become significant events in the lives of Anxi villagers too. The daily monotony of working, tending the house and going to school is now broken by these periodic communal activities. One villager said, 'it is good to have these activities. They light up the atmosphere.' Another said, 'our children have more exposure to Chinese cultural activities.' Some said that, compared to the previous decades, 'with the increased number of Singapore kin visiting our village and their concern about religious activities, our village has become less dull'. Another affirmed, 'we will support these activities. We will buy some joss incense and papers and go and pray to our ancestors or the village gods.' A teacher said, 'it is also good for our village economy. These religious functions will need manpower to help with the various activities. Indirectly, they create some kinds of part-time jobs for some of us here.' And a trader said, 'they are good for our "incense and oil" business (*xiangyou ye,* 香油业) and for our village economy. That is why even though some of us might not believe in these religious practices, we will continue to support them.'[4]

The Rite of Gratification for the Flow of Descendants (*Xiezu juanding yishi,* 谢祖涓丁仪式)

The term *xiezu* (谢祖) means 'thanking the ancestors', while *juan* (涓) means 'continuous flow' and *ding* (丁) means 'descendants'. Thus *xiezu juanding* is the expression of gratification to ancestors for the continuity of the lineage. In the ritual of consecration of the Ke lineage *zuzhai*, over 20 Singapore lineage members participated. The ceremony was important to open the door of the ancestral house and to install the ancestors in their rightful positions. This ceremony was held in 1988, after the completion of the *zuzhai*. Since then, the doors of the *zuzhai* have been opened for communal worship and celebratory events several times a year, including the Spring Festival (Chinese Lunar New Year, 春节) and the Grave-Sweeping Festival (Qingming Jie, 清明节). On these occasions, members are expected to participate in both communal and individual worship of their ancestors. Individual households prepare several dishes, bring them to the *zuzhai* and offer them to the ancestors. These activities bring the women out from their private domestic spheres into the public sphere and establish them as *bona fide* members of the lineage.

Within the Ke lineage, there are 12 founding ancestors. These founding members were honoured during the *xiezu juanding* ceremony, and ancestral tablets (one foot high and four inches wide), each with intricately carved gold-inlaid edges and each inscribed in the middle with the name of an ancestor in painted gold characters, were prepared and installed in their rightful positions.

On the day before or on the morning of the celebration, individual households, and particularly the women, busied themselves preparing traditional rice cakes, slaughtering poultry and cooking. About mid-morning, women and men took tables and the prepared food to the *zuzhai*. They arranged the tables in neat rows in front of the *zuzhai* and placed the food on the tables as offerings to the ancestors. Because of their number, the households were divided into two groups, one of which made offerings in the morning and the other in the late afternoon. A variety of Chinese cakes, poultry, meat and fruits were offered to the ancestors; incense was also offered to the ancestors, but on an individual basis. At a stipulated time, priests or monks performed the liturgy and rituals. The sessions lasted about an hour each. After the religious performances, each household burned paper money for the ancestors. Afterwards, the lineage members collected the food they had brought, placed it in a basket, picked up their tables and returned home. The food was later eaten.

On the day of the celebration the appointed tablet-carriers, all elderly men, arrived dressed in a variety of styles—some in traditional high-collared gowns, or *qipao* (旗袍), others in Western-style suits. The rest of the participants dressed casually. The ancestral house was packed with lineage members, but other villagers were also present. The master of ceremonies, a local village cadre known for his speaking ability, read aloud the *zhangcheng* (章程). This informs the community of the history of the Ke lineage, of the achievements of its descendants, of the glorious past, of the achievements of the founding ancestors and of the desire to 'fragrance' the lineage through the restoration of the ancestral house. After the introduction, the tablet carriers stepped forward and honoured their ancestors. As the master of ceremonies read out the name of each founding ancestor the man with that ancestor's tablet carried it with both hands to the altar, while the master of ceremonies introduced the ancestor and read out his achievements. The tablet-carrier, with another lineage-member on hand to assist him, then climbed onto a chair, knelt forward and placed the tablet in position behind the deified Anxi guardian ancestor, Qingshui zushigong. Tablet-carriers were instructed to place the tablets carefully in position because, once they were placed on the altar, no adjustments would be made. The ceremony took about two hours to complete. Afterwards, fire-crackers were lit to mark the joyous occasion, and incense papers were burned for the ancestors and gods. After this formal ceremony, too, individual men, women and children strolled into the ancestral house and offered individual prayers to the ancestors. The ceremony had attracted many villagers, who displayed a great curiosity; some of them went in to investigate while others watched from outside. Such visitors were invited to a bowl of noodles while the lineage members were invited to a luncheon feast, which concluded the consecration ceremony. However, the ancestral house remained open for the whole day, allowing members and non-members alike to visit and witness the restored ancestral house. It was a proud day for the lineage members.

In recent years, many Singapore Ke lineage members have planned their visits to Anxi to coincide with communal ancestor worship. Such occasions provide them with a legitimate excuse to visit the ancestral village. On such occasions, younger members accompanied their elderly parents for a visit. In traditional China communal ancestor worship was the responsibility of male elders, but this is not so today, and women have become important participants—in fact, female members of the Ke lineage are often the main participants in communal ancestor worship.

Opening the Doors of Ancestral House (*Kai zuzhaimen,* 开祖宅门)

Individual members can also 'open the doors of the ancestral house' (*kai zuzhaimen*) if they want to honour and give thanks to their ancestors for their achievements and success. Several Singapore Ke members have done this, one example being a man who honoured the ancestors after his son earned his PhD. This was an honour that would 'give fragrance to the name of the ancestor and his family'. Such 'opening of the doors of the *zuzhai*' is considered an important means to share the achievement and joy with the lineage. Among the Ke, this privilege was extended to female members after much negotiation between the Singapore and the Anxi elders, and women who attain great achievement can now open the doors of the ancestral house.

Before one is allowed to 'open the doors of the *zuzhai*', however, both Singapore and village elders must agree on the appropriateness of the occasion. In the above-mentioned instance, having decided that the occasion warranted the opening of the doors of the *zuzhai*, the family and the son or daughter were invited to return for the ceremony. With the date set, the family made arrangements for opening the *zuzhaimen*. Prior to their return, village kin had made preparations, bought the necessary religious paraphernalia, had a plaque with the name of the son/daughter and his/her academic achievement prepared and had arranged for a feast. Invitations to all lineage members were issued.

By staging various religious functions, the lineage thus expresses its presence and social dominance vis-à-vis other lineages in Anxi. Through them the sense of lineage identity, which was hidden prior to the reform years, is strengthened and articulated openly. One lineage member said, 'it is good that the Singapore Chinese and we, the Anxi people, are able to identify with our ancestors again. It makes us feel like one people.' When wealth and success have become part of the social fabric of emigrants, other criteria are needed to measure social status and to differentiate lineages and villages from one another. Thus the old fashion criterion of knowledge, like the Confucian production of scholar-literati, has become important. Similarly, becoming an official has acquired more appeal than before.[5] Such types of recognition can only elevate the status of one's lineage vis-à-vis those of others. In the words of one, 'not every emigrant village could produce a doctor [*boshi*, 博士]'.

Meritorious Deeds (*gongde*) for Ancestors: The Rite of Inclusion

Among Chinese, disposing of the dead in a ritually correct manner is imperative for the dead to become transformed into ancestors. The passage from death to ancestor status involves various stages: cleansing the body of the dead, mourning, funeral, performing meritorious deeds (*gongde*), and burial and ancestor worship. The performance of these rituals allows the dead to transform from being a dead person, to become a spirit and finally an ancestor.

The transitions from one stage to another upon death can be regarded as rites of passage, which Van Gennep defines as 'rites which accompany every change of place, state, social position and age' (Van Gennep cited in Turner, 1969: 94). They are 'marked by three phases: separation, margin and aggregation' (ibid., 94; Van Gennep, 1960).

In Anxi, the dead person is separated from the living. Its soul is split into two parts, *hun* (魂) and *po* (魄). The *hun* part which is imbued with *yangqi* (阳气), or active, *yang* energies, moves into the heavenly realm, while the *po*, which is imbued with *yinqi* (阴气), or passive, *yin* energies, moves downwards to the netherworld (*yinjian*), where it undergoes various stages of punishment according to its karma and gradually moves through the ten gates of the netherworld. This is the stage of separation, when the soul is in a liminal stage, 'between and betwixt' (Turner, 1969: 95)—as a wandering spirit which has yet to find a permanent home either in the netherworld or in the heavenly world. Only after passing through the ten gates does the soul finally come to rest. This is the phase of aggregation, when the spirit is reintegrated within the cosmological world, re-emerging as an ancestor to the living and as a spirit with a permanent abode in the other realm. It is no longer a wandering ghost nor is it in a state of transience. Its permanent ancestral status is recognized through the acts of ancestor worship, conducted by its descendants.

In Anxi, the Communist policy of simple burial rites led to burial without the death rituals that Chinese have traditionally seen as essential for the dead to be transformed into ancestors. Death rituals were secularized and simplified, and cremation became common, as ground burials were considered to take up valuable space and resources (Whyte, 1988: 289–316). After the 1978 reform and the liberalization of religious practices, visiting *qiaoqing* and village kin reinstated several after-burial rituals to provide for the material and spiritual needs of their ancestors. The *qiaoqing* consciously reinstated the rites of *gongde* and selected a geomantically aligned burial ground (*fengshuidi*, 风水地). Performing rituals for the dead then again became important in village life, as many of the dead had not been given proper burial during the previous period, or had had their graves exhumed. Since the 1980s, *gongde* and *xiezu* have become the main religious preoccupations of many Singapore Chinese and their village kin, and a booming cottage industry has grown to specialize in catering for the material needs of the dead.

In the 1990s, I found that a majority of the households, and particularly those with Singapore connections, had conducted *gongde* for their dead ancestors during the 1980s and 1990s. In 1994 and 1995 there was a rush to perform *gongde* among members of the Ke lineage, who all wanted their ancestors to be included in the lineage genealogy. In 1995, the lineage started to 'mend the genealogy' (*xiupu*, 修谱). It was anticipated that the new entry of names into the lineage genealogy would be completed by mid-1996, and thus the *xiezu juanding* ceremony was scheduled for the tenth lunar month of 1996. I was told that only those ancestors that had been given *gongde* could be included as *bona fide* ancestors in the genealogy. Hence, members whose ancestors had not been given *gongde* felt obligated to perform the rite or be shut out of the lineage forever. Exclusion from the genealogy would leave a gap in the individual family tree, thereby sabotaging their descendants' attempts to ground their social identity in traditional terms.

What is *gongde*? Literally, the phrase means 'public virtues and morality', or 'meritorious deeds'. Its origins can perhaps be traced to a combination of Buddhist and folk religious beliefs. There are various interpretations of its origins and its ritual contents. However, among the Singapore Chinese, the Buddhist interpretation of karma and merit-making has influenced the understanding of this ritual,[6] although both the villagers and their Singapore *qiaoqing* found it hard to provide me with a satisfactory explanation. Orthopraxy here seems to be more important than the ideological intrigue of orthodoxy.[7] At any rate, for villagers and *qiaoqing* alike, *gongde* is essential for their ancestors for various reasons. First, it is the ritual which provides merit to the dead. This is the Buddhist notion that the transfer of merit to the dead can make up for the deceased's bad karma and provide the dead with the energy to move up from the underworld to higher planes of existence.[8] Some Singapore Ke explained this to me. However, unlike the Buddhist transfer of merit, *gongde* is also performed to inform the relevant gods of the virtues of the dead. By telling the gods of their achievements the dead can be elevated to various statuses within the religious hierarchy, at the apex of which the dead, because of their virtues, become deified as godly beings. At the base of the hierarchy, the evil of the dead is rightly punished. *Gongde* is thus also a rite of redemption whereby the wrongdoing of the dead can be redeemed through the efforts of the living, so that the dead eventually become ancestors.

Secondly, my informants told me that the dead, like the living, have wants and needs in the netherworld, including material goods such as a spirit/soul house (*lingwu*, or *ling-chu* [H], 灵屋), which are necessary to keep the ancestors from becoming 'hungry ghosts' and to help them live through the required period in the netherworld. Further rites are then required to install them permanently as ancestors. *Gongde* is the last major rite that needs to be performed for the dead, without which the cycle of death and rebirth would be incomplete.

Third, *gongde* is a rite of inclusion whereby the dead ancestors are incorporated into the wider lineage community, allowing the dead and the living to co-exist. In this especially important rite the dead are formally invited to become part of the lineage and are honoured in a communal manner with a position in the ancestral house and, individually, on the family's domestic altar.

The rite of *gongde* is thus an essential rite of passage, which serves to bring ancestors into the lineage structure, and failure to perform it will exclude them from the lineage. It allows the dead, as 'wandering spirits', to be transformed into ancestors and recorded in the genealogy.

In Anxi villages, *gongde* is performed by both the Singapore Chinese and their village kin for their closest relatives, such as grandparents, parents, siblings and, at times, parents' siblings. It might be performed for those who died in Singapore but who in life continued to regard themselves as part of the home village. Many of the *gongde* performed in recent years have been for those who had died over the forty years when such rights were not permitted, for political reasons.

Gongde Ritual Process

The rite consists of a series of rituals performed over a period of three to five days, depending on the family. The first ritual is usually the *yinhun* ceremony, and the last is the situating and positioning of the ancestors (*anwei*, 安位), through which they are given a permanent home. In most households, the ancestral tablet and ancestral altar are prepared beforehand within the household; at the end of the *gongde* rite the soul of the ancestor, captured within the ancestral tablet, is placed on the ancestral altar, his or her final and permanent resting-place. Each day while the rite continues, two to seven services are performed for the ancestors, those on the first and last days involving the participation of all kin, while those in between are performed only by Buddhist monks or Daoist priests (the Singaporeans prefer Buddhists) and the immediate family members for the dead. During the rites, mourners are required to perform as directed by the monks or priests. This involves directing the soul back to the village and to the home where it will reside as an ancestor. The rite of passage over the bridge of no return and through the ten hell gates rescues the 'soul' of the dead from the netherworld by directing it to the ancestral spirit world, the *yinhun* (引魂). During this rite, the monks or priests direct the eldest male descendent, who carries the incense urn (*xianglu*, 香炉), to also carry the *yinhun* streamer. The *yinhun* streamer consists of two bamboo sticks with the leaves attached on them; there are also yellow paper streamers hung at the end of the bamboo sticks. This is used to direct the soul of the ancestor to the ancestral house. The eldest male is followed by the rest of the family.

For this ceremony, a family usually employs three, five or seven Buddhist monks, usually from the Qingshui Temple or from other regions; the number depends on the amount that the family is willing to spend. The charge for Buddhist monks is higher than for Daoist priests, but the Singaporeans say they prefer Buddhist monks because they are better-trained; being full-time religious personnel with some knowledge of Buddhist liturgy, they are able to recite a variety of sutras required on the occasion. Daoist priests, on the other hand, are often part-time in their profession; they are perceived to have a different type of religious training and are thought to be more suitable for religious functions other than the care of the dead ancestors.

The *lingwu* prepared for the deceased in this ceremony is a two- or three-storey paper house, which is beautifully decorated with the intricate details that replicates the style of a living person's house. Although this *lingwu* is shaped in the traditional style, it is accompanied by numerous modern items, such as a motor car, a television, and a videocassette recorder, as well as maids, paper money, chests of gold and silver ingots, incense sticks and other religious paraphernalia. All these items are made of paper.

Mourners were traditionally required to dress in proper mourning attire, which includes mourning clothing made of coarse hemp material and a head-dress made of similar material. Presently, however, both Singaporeans and villagers simplify the attire. Mourners now wear their own clothing, with a thin hemp overdress over it. Grandchildren are required to dress in blue: they now dress in blue T-shirts and navy blue pants that replace the small square piece of blue cloth, called the *xiao* (孝) on the sleeve.

During the ceremonial period, an opera or puppet troupe may be invited to perform for the dead and the living. At the end of the *gongde* a feast is given for all lineage members; by attending the feast, the members accept the dead as part of the lineage structure, completing the process of inclusion and allowing for emotional closure to take place.

The cost of a *gongde* ranges from several thousand to over RMB 20,000. The cost includes all the religious paraphernalia, the spirit/soul house (*lingwu*, also known as the grand house or *dawu*, 大屋), the services of the monks or priests, service money for participating kin, food, drinks and all meals for the monks or priests and for the Singaporeans and their local kin. If the *gongde* is an elaborate one, with five to seven services a day, the cost for the monks goes up considerably, often by several thousand RMB. Higher-quality *lingwu* and religious paraphernalia may also add to the cost, and an opera or puppet performance, if held, will add another several thousand RMB. The final feast is a must and costs several thousand RMB. A budget of RMB 10,000 to 15,000 is thus a moderate one for a *gongde* ceremony. Most Singapore Chinese would spend at least RMB 10,000 to 20,000 for a sufficiently grand *gongde*, to impress their village kin.

A Case Example of a *Gongde* Performance

In 1995, the Chiu family, of the Ke lineage in Singapore, decided to hold a *gongde* ritual for Mr Chiu's father, mother, grandfather and grandmother. Discussions were held between Singaporeans and the Penglai villagers in the Xitou vicinity, and the tenth lunar month of that year was set aside for the ritual. Several family members, including Mr Chiu's wife, second son, eldest daughter and eldest daughter-in-law, were to be the representatives from the Singapore side of the family. From the village, the next of kin included Mr Chiu's eldest sister and her family, the family of his deceased sister, and an assortment of distant relatives. Chiu himself was in ill health and did not attend the ritual.

There were two main stages of this ritual performance, namely the preparatory and religious stages.

Preparation

After deciding on the date, the Singaporeans and their village kin discussed the scale and elaborateness of the occasion. They decided to have a three-day service and requested Buddhist monks (the Singapore Chiu were Buddhist) to perform seven ritual sessions each day. They wanted the *gongde* performance to be sufficiently grand to impress the villagers with their proper treatment of their ancestors.

Having decided on this, the villagers prepared all the necessary items for the occasion; the Singapore Chinese would send the money. The initial amount sent was RMB 20,000.

The usual site for *gongde* is the family residence (ideally the *laojia*, if there is one), but for the Chiu family it was a modern three-storey building sited next to the creek that flows by. They erected a covered canopy for the spirit/soul house on a vacant piece of land adjoining their building, which provided shelter for the mourners during the ritual and was subsequently purchased by Chiu.

A village kinsman arranged for the purchase of the required religious items, and placed orders for a three-storey *lingwu* of traditional Chinese architecture and quantities of incense, joss-papers, candles and other items. The *lingwu* came with a number of houseboys and maids, and modern items such as a television, a car, a videocassette recorder, and a bicycle, all made of colourful foil and paper. The *lingwu* cost RMB 3,000. Two big treasure chests, large candles, large quantities of a variety of joss-papers (for the dead, the gods and the spirits) and incense sticks were also ordered, to be brought to the site a day or two in advance. This religious paraphernalia had to be ordered well in advance because of the large quantity of items required. Four ancestral tablets inscribed with the names of the ancestors were also prepared.

Five monks were arranged through the chief monk at Qingshuiyan Temple. The cost for the monks for three days (seven sessions per day) was RMB 2,800. This was considered a bargain by the Singaporeans because the same service would cost a minimum of RMB 40,000 in Singapore. Monks need to be booked in advance, as the revival of religious activities in village China has brought about an increase in the demand for religious personnel, and there is now a general shortage of monks for various religious functions.

A restaurant was asked to cater lunch and dinner for the three days of the ritual. About seven tables were set for the participants at RMB 250 each, with another, vegetarian one for the monks at RMB 270. On the final day, more elaborate food was provided, and each table cost RMB 300. The food was cooked in the restaurant and brought to the ceremonial site. The restaurant also provided tables and chairs.

All villagers and those living in towns related to the family (including distant ones) were informed of the event and were invited to participate. Every member of the mourning team was given a sum of money. This is the so-called affinity money (*jieyuanqian,* 结缘钱), which establishes a relationship with the dead; it also ensures a good turn-out of mourners, thereby adding prestige to the occasion, as a big group of mourners performing ritual weeping is a testimony to the wealth and status of the family, reflecting on the social status of the Singapore Chinese. Not only the Chiu family relatives but also other villagers participated as mourners.

The canvas canopy was erected several days before the actual ceremony. Two days before the performance, the *lingwu* arrived and was placed in position, with a large table set up in front. The four ancestral tablets made for the occasion were placed on the table, and in front of the tablets were placed a set of each of the following daily items: wash basin, facial towel, tooth-brush and mug, and clothing. Fruits, rice cakes, a pig's head, poultry and dried food were also placed on the table as offerings. An incense urn holding lit incense sticks and two large lit candles were placed for the ancestors. In the family's house, there was also an altar where the Buddhist deities and the ancestral tablets were placed. Fruits and dried vegetarian food were also offered to the deities and ancestors.

The Singaporeans only arrived in the village two days before the ceremony, and were shown the preparations and informed of the itinerary. Singapore women then supervised the preparation of the ritual food for the ancestors.

The rites

On the first day of the *gongde*, at about four o'clock in the morning, the household woke up and prepared for the occasion. After a quick breakfast, family members dressed in the appropriately coloured attire. Village kin arrived at the house and also readied themselves. Close kin dressed in the hemp overdress; the distant kin and friends dressed in their daily attire, with a piece of coloured cloth (the size of a two-inch square) pinned to the sleeve signifying their social distance from the dead according to the 'five-grain' (*wugu*, 五谷) categorization. The monks arrived at the appointed time and were offered a simple vegetarian meal.

All participating members assembled in the shrine hall inside the house at around 8 a.m. The beating of a gong by a monk signalled the start of the *gongde*. The monks then began to recite a Buddhist sutra. The principal mourners from Singapore were instructed to recite Buddhist prayers, after which the chief principal mourner recited a *couwen or chobun* [H] (湊文), or petition seeking permission from the Buddhist deities to conduct the rite of *gongde*.

After preliminary prayers, an entourage made its way to the head of the Xi Creek, about half an hour's walk away, and began the rite of directing the ancestral souls or *yinhun* to the *lingwu* site, which would be their temporary home for three days. The monks led the way, followed by the chief male mourner carrying the *yinhun* streamer, followed by other kin.

By the riverside, the monks recited prayers inviting the souls of the dead ancestors to rise and follow them home to their rightful place. After the third invitation by prayer, a close kinsperson threw a pair of wooden cups, *mubei* (木杯, used in divination) to see if the ancestors agreed to be led home by the mourners. Before the start of this journey home, however, the ancestral spirits had to be ritually cleansed and to present themselves in a purified form because, as wandering souls, they were polluting and dangerous. They were thus told to 'take a bath' and a straw mat rolled into a cylinder was placed upright on the ground to serve as a temporary bathroom for the purpose. The monks then recited prayers that purified and cleansed the ancestral spirits. After this spiritual cleansing, the ancestral spirits and the entourage journeyed to the *lingwu*.

On arrival at the *lingwu*, a charm (*fu*, 符) was burned on the instrument *gong* to signal the start of the rite of ushering the ancestral spirits and transforming them into ancestors. The monks then recited several prayers, after which the tablets of the ancestors were dotted with red ink, symbolizing the taking of position by the ancestral spirits in the tablets. This dotting was witnessed by all thirteen local deities, whose temples were scattered throughout the district and who had been specifically invited by the monks as witnesses and guardians by writing their names on paper tablets placed at the site of the *lingwu* during the preparatory stage. These deities were given offerings and invoked at each session by the monks.

During each of the seven daily ritual sessions, a different Buddhist text was recited. The seven were the Diamond Sutra (*Jingangjing*, 金刚经), the Ksitigarbha Bodhisattva Sutra (*Dizangwang pusa benyuanjing*, 地藏王菩萨本愿经), the Amitabha Sutra (*Omitojing*, 阿弥陀经), the Heart Sutra (*Xinjing*, 心经), the Lotus Sutra (*Miaofa Lianhuajing*, 妙法莲华经), Medical Buddha Sutra (*Yaoshi Liulijing*, 药师琉璃经), and the Great Compassion Sutra (*Dabeizhou*, 大悲咒). During each ritual session, the monks led the mourners from the Buddhist shrine hall in the house to the *lingwu*, the principal male mourner carrying incense and four bamboo sticks bundled together to represent the four ancestral souls. This symbolized the carrying of the Buddhist light to the dead, where the burning incense was used to light up the *lingwu*. The Buddhist deities were also called upon to witness this ritual. Through recitation of the Buddhist sutras, the living imparted good merits to the dead to reduce their store of bad karma and increase their good karma. A 'motive text' (*biaowen*, 表文) was read, making the objectives of the *gongde* known to the Buddhist deities and local gods. This text was then carried by a second mourner from the Buddhist shrine to the *lingwu* and was placed on the table in the shrine, to be burned at the end of the ceremony.

During the first session of the first day the mourners were told to offer personal effects to the dead. Watches and jewellery worn by their Singapore descendants were placed on a tray as offerings; these were returned to the mourners at the end of the session.

During each daily ritual session, the monks led the mourners from the shrine hall to the *lingwu*, and continued the sutra recitation throughout the journey. When they reached the *lingwu* they assembled in front of it, with the principal mourners and other kin behind them. The rite of *zhoujin*, aimed at increasing good merits for the ancestral spirits, then began. Another Buddhist sutra was recited, during which the monks led the mourners around the *lingwu* in a circle. A second ritual act chanting (*nianshou*, 念寿) followed, during which the names of the four ancestors were recited and they were informed of the merits imparted to them. At the end of the ceremony for each day, the list of merits would be read out aloud and would be burned to inform all deities of the dead's achievements. During this recitation, mourners were required to kneel and pay obeisance to the ancestors. Towards the end of the ritual, wine was offered to the ancestors by each kin member. This wine was poured into a basin in which a young pine sapling had been planted, signifying the rebirth of the ancestral spirits as ancestors. This was the rite of *dianxie* (点谢). After the libations, the mourners were instructed to kneel three times, after which the monks led them back to the shrine hall, concluding the ritual session.

The ritual was repeated seven times daily, with an hour of rest in between, so that a total of 21 ritual sessions were conducted over the three-day period. Often the last session ended at around 10 or 11 p.m. each night. On the final session of the third day the principal male mourner presented a pair of lanterns to the attending married daughters and married granddaughters of the deceased, who then offered their merits to the ancestors. These were 'longevity lanterns' (*changshoudeng*, 长寿灯), the recipients of which were blessed with long life and prosperity. The final act was to seek permission, through the *mubei*, from the Buddhist deities to offer all material goods and treasures to the ancestors.

The final session began after dinner and ended at about 10 p.m. Afterwards, the *lingwu*, chests of gold and silver ingots, large quantities of paper money, all the ritual paraphernalia made of paper, the bamboo sticks, streamers, and clothing that were for the ancestors, were all burned in a bonfire. The ancestral tablets were taken and placed on the ancestral altar in the shrine hall, the permanent resting-place for the ancestors.

From now on, the ancestral spirits would be proper family ancestors, to be worshipped as such. Before the *gongde* they had been wandering spirits, dissatisfied and full of anger, polluted and unclean, and had been barred from entering the household by the guardian gods because of their status. Now their task was to protect and bless the family with good fortune and wealth.

The *gongde* was not considered a 'red' occasion, as death is a polluting event, so those who participated were given good luck charms—usually, of red thread—and money. Those who had accompanied the principal mourners to and from the river during the *yinhun* rite were given RMB 20, while those who had participated in the various sessions and offered incense to the ancestors were given RMB 30. Closer village kin were given RMB 60 per day, at the end of the final session each night. Persons of other surname groups usually stood as bystanders and watched the ritual performances.

For three days, the mourners, village members of the Ke lineage and some close friends participating in the *gongde* had been provided with lunch and dinner.

Throughout the day, during and in between the ritual sessions, visitors came and paid their respect to the ancestors, engaged in conversation with the mourners and showed their support. They also received cakes, biscuits, fruits, nuts and candy. Men (but not women) were served beer and offered cigarettes, the total cost of which amounted to over RMB 5,000. The total cost for the three-day *gongde* ritual came to RMB 50,000.

Resiting Burial Grounds

Other concerns of the Singapore Chinese have been to search for their ancestral graves and to rebuild the burial sites of their ancestors. The locals call this 'making *fengshui*' (做风水). As the Cultural Revolution had destroyed many graves and had converted burial sites into agricultural lands, the few sites remaining were those on the hillsides. For most Chinese, maintaining ancestral graves, commonly termed *fengshuidi* by the locals, was important traditionally, and for the Anxi Chinese it would have been an extreme act of unfilialness not to reconstruct an ancestral grave. It was also important to the Singapore Chinese to have an ancestral grave sited in a good *fengshui* location to bring good fortune to all descendants.[9]

Since reform, for 30 years, Singapore Chinese have returned to Anxi to restore their ancestral graves. Those that had been left in ruins for the previous 40 years have been repaired and restored, and regular maintenance has made them clean and tidy. They can be spotted dotting the terraced paddy fields on hillsides from a distance, as there is no need now to hide them in tall grass. Many villagers are now proud to display their ancestral graves publicly.

What about ancestral graves that were destroyed when the land was given to different families for cultivation? This is a situation that has created much dissatisfaction among Chinese overseas. While some families have been able to buy back original gravesites and to restore ancestral graves, others have not been so fortunate. These latter, however, may apply for new burial sites from the county government, and some Singapore Chinese have done so successfully and have been able to build new burial sites.

Competition for fengshuidi

Competition for good *fengshui* burial sites has been keen. Most Singaporean and their village kin were willing to search for a good *fengshui* site and pay a relatively high price for it. Usually this involved buying certain hilly sites from their owners, whether they were villagers or the *zhen* government. In most cases this had been a relatively straightforward transaction.

Although members of the same lineage had been known to fight for the same *fengshui* site, this was seen as unacceptable and was discouraged. It was very rare for a member of a lineage to buy another member's *fengshui* site, especially when an ancestral grave was already in place. There was such a case in Penglai, however, which created much rivalry, tension and ill feeling between the two families involved. The case involved two Singaporean families with village kin. The son of Family A had purchased the ancestral burial site of a member of Family B without his knowledge, the transaction having taken place between himself and the married daughter of Family B, who had agreed to the sale. Having purchased the land, the son of Family A built their ancestral grave there, and only later did the son of Family B learn of it. Within the traditional Chinese lineage, all land had been inherited by sons, and married daughters had no rights to land inheritance, nor did they have any say in the disposal of any land, especially ritual and burial sites. Even today, married daughters are considered to belong to their husbands' families and therefore do not have rights to make decisions regarding the land disposal of their natal families. Thus, in this case, the married daughter was seen as having overstepped her authority in selling the ancestral burial site without informing the living brother in Singapore, while the son of Family A was regarded by fellow lineage members as having behaved in an ungentlemanly fashion, since he failed to observe lineage rules and obtained the burial site by devious methods.

There is thus a conflict between the social expectations of kin relations on the one hand and the modern rule of competition on the other. *Fengshui* land is a scarce commodity and, according to the modern individualistic ethic, those with the means might compete in purchasing it, for personal gain. However, among local lineage members in Penglai, such modern rules of competition continue to be inapplicable to the acquisition of ancestral burial sites. The above case thus aroused much ill feeling and discontentment among lineage members, who viewed it with grave concern and it was seen as unethical and devoid of social gallantry for lineage members to commit such acts. The operation of lineage rules can only be effective if all members subscribe to them; otherwise, they fall apart.

Besides the violation of traditional practices, the case above involved 'face'. By taking away the ancestral site, Family A was not giving face to Family B— behaviour detrimental to lineage solidarity. However, the village elders did not dare to intervene, as the case involved a Singaporean who was aggressive and wealthy, and although the Singapore lineage elders had a word with him, they could do nothing about it. The honourable thing would have been for Family A to return the land to Family B, but this was not done. There thus continued to be a latent tension between the two families, although they continued to be polite to each other.

It has become a duty for Anxi Singaporeans to repair and restore their ancestral *fengshui* gravesites to its former glory. Like the ancestral house, where the ancestors' *yang* spirit resides, the ancestral grave is where the *yin* spirit of the ancestors rest, and is a visible reminder of them and of the benefits derived from them. For the villagers and the Singapore kin, restoration and taking care of the gravesite is also testimony of their filial piety, whom they feel to have prospered as a result of the good *fengshui* of the ancestors. In this connection the phrase *fugui buli zu* (富贵不离祖), 'wealth is not divorced from ancestors', was quoted to me—an argument indicating that the Chinese overseas should not neglect their home villages and their lineage members within them.

Ancestor Worship by Singapore Chinese

Within most Singaporean Chinese households there is an altar for the ancestral tablets of the immediate ancestors, and the offerings of incense to the ancestors are a daily routine. On festival and religious occasions as well as on the death anniversaries of immediate ancestors, offerings of food, incense and paper money are made. Since the 1980s, some family members have placed ancestral tablets in temples, and have gone there to make their offerings. Today, ancestors and ancestor worship continue to occupy a prominent central position in the Chinese community in Singapore.

Our survey showed that the Singapore Chinese concerned for their ancestors and their practice of ancestor worship stretched back to their ancestral villages, and that the majority of the Singapore Chinese were aware of the existence of ancestral houses and the practice of communal ancestor worship in their home villages in Anxi. The ancestral house in Anxi is a reminder of their origins and allows their ancestors to be remembered and worshipped in a collective manner. The house is also a place where their future descendants can go in search of their roots. One Singapore-born second-generation Chinese said:

> It is important to have an ancestral home so that we are reminded of our ancestors, of the sacrifice they have made in order that we have our present position. Without them taking the risks, developing the place, the lineage, and eventually allowing some to emigrate overseas, we might still be stuck in Anxi and not in Singapore. It is this unyielding ancestral spirit that we should not forget.

Three categories of Anxi Singapore Chinese can be delineated: those who emigrated as adults to Singapore, those who emigrated as children, and the Singapore-born. The responses of these three groups concerning their ancestors and ancestor worship allow us to understand their sentiments, as well as the tensions that arise as a result of intergeneration attitudinal differences. For the first and second groups, worship of the immediate ancestors is the most important duty, and they do this conscientiously, at altars within their domestic households. Daily offerings of incense are carried out at these altars by the women. On festive occasions and the death anniversaries of immediate ancestors, offerings of incense, joss-paper and food are made. Then on the Qingming and Chongyang Festivals, the sweeping of ancestral graves and the offering of food and religious items are standard practice. Most of these two groups do not fail to visit gravesites, where offerings are usually given, as well as within the household.

However, religious practices in Singapore have taken new forms and the new trend since the late 1970s has been to place ancestral tablets in temples, where ritual offerings continue to be offered on festive and death-anniversary occasions, often by entrusted monks and nuns.

The first-generation migrants fully supported the construction or reconstruction of *zuzhai* in Anxi, and either they or their spouses contributed to it. Such constructions were carried out and completed in the late 1980s and early 1990s, and were considered the most important activity which they had done for their ancestral village. One informant commented: 'How can we let the *zuzhai* become broken down and not care about it? Even if we have to save on our eating, we should contribute to help with the reconstruction. It is the house of our ancestors. So, it is our ancestral home.' In addition, several wealthy Singapore Chinese had converted their *laojia* into family ancestral houses. As the *qiaoxiang* became wealthier and as the villagers moved to live in new modern buildings, the *laojia* became vacant, and many were decaying. Some of the wealthier Singaporeans decided to turn them into sacred spaces solely for the use of their immediate families, symbolizing the relatively-high status of these families. This was not criticized by the official cadres, partly because they did not want to offend the Singapore Chinese and partly because the status of the *laojia* as surplus housing made such use more justifiable. By turning them into family ancestral houses, the buildings would be maintained in good condition. Few of the younger villagers wanted to live in them, as they were considered old style, even though some had been renovated and equipped with modern amenities. For this reason, some of these *laojia* were rented out to poorer villagers and to outsiders who lived in Penglai and many were left vacant.

One such case is that of a *laojia* that, with all its various extensions, amounted to a 13-room building that was only inhabited by several elderly people, whose children had all moved out either to cities and towns, or to live in modern three-storey buildings locally.

To worship their ancestors in Anxi has become an important rite of passage for first-generation migrants, and, by the late 1990s, a majority of first-generation migrant Singaporeans from Xitou had made visits to their ancestral villages to perform communal ancestor worship in their lineage ancestral houses. It is these activities that encourage them to return for visits, without which many would feel less inclined to visit. Some have stated that they would be very bored if there were nothing to do while they were in the village. The communal religious activities allow them to be meaningfully occupied. Perhaps for this reason, the Singapore Chinese, together with the village elders, decide on the scope of ceremonies and pay most of the costs, although, at present, some other wealthy village kin also contribute financially. Because of this, the villagers regard the practitioners as 'primarily interested in religious activities', and some label them—especially Singapore women—as 'being overly superstitious', *tai mixinde* (太迷信的). This label is especially given to the Singapore women who occupy their time in the village with all sorts of religious activities.

Among the third group, the second and third-generation Singapore Chinese, a fairly large number feel the need to know something of their ancestors—at least of their great-grandparents and grandparents, as well as of their parents. Some seek to fill in their family genealogies. For some of them, it is to answer childhood questions that they begin to search for knowledge of the ancestral home and their grandparents. Some are interested in reconstructing the social history of their immediate families—migration experiences, early life in Singapore, difficulties and sufferings, and success. Others are less ambitious. Yet many have visited their ancestral villages, and some have gone back several times. Many in this group in the late 1990s were aware that their parents had contributed money for the reconstruction of the lineage ancestral house, and they had supported this. Although they had not contributed themselves, they expressed their willingness to do so if asked. For this group, too, the ancestral house served as a visible reminder of the past of their lineage. For some, it is also a reminder of their good fortune. Here are some statements they made:

> Anxi people used to be very poor and because of this, we had very low status in comparison with other lineages in Singapore. Some members used to hide their origin. But today, thanks to our ancestors, the Singapore Anxi people have become rather prosperous and the lineage has elevated its status to become one of the top eight lineages in Singapore. Not only do we no longer hide our origin, we are now proud of it. In fact, some non-Anxi people try to become one of us by claiming that their ancestors were from Anxi too.
>
> Even though we are Singapore-born and consider ourselves Singaporean ... especially now that we are relatively well-off, we

should not completely ignore our ancestral root. The Chinese saying 'wealth should not be divorced from ancestors' (*fugui bulizu*) is very true. Without our ancestors, there will be no us and thus, no wealth. Thus, wealth comes from the blessings of our ancestors. If this is so, we should not forget our ancestors, for by forgetting them we would undermine future wealth.

However, a small group of this third category were indifferent to the construction of the ancestral house, and expressed no sentiments for it or for the ancestral village, which they had never visited. For them, Singapore was their home and the ancestral village and ancestral house held no meaning. Neither did they wish to participate in communal ancestor worship, nor did they see the need to return for visits. However, they did not prevent their parents or siblings from visiting and participating in village activities, as they recognized that their parents and others continued to harbour sentiments towards their ancestral home.

Ancestor Worship by Village Kin

Ancestor worship was banned in China until the early 1980s. During the early days of communism, some families continued to perform ancestor worship secretly behind closed doors, while others merely exhibited a ritual-less reverence, as recommended by the Communist regime. When the *qiaoxiang* began to stage communal ancestor worship and individual families began to worship their immediate ancestors, the local villagers overwhelmingly supported the reconstruction of the ancestral houses and were very pleased that the Singapore Chinese had been able to afford to do so. As we have seen, the villagers were primarily responsible for the actual work.

Support for the reconstruction of the ancestral home is evident in the following statements:

> There is a need to reconstruct *zuzhai* because it is important for us to remember our ancestors and having a lineage ancestral house will help us to remember them. It is a place for us to memorialize (*jinian*, *ki-liem* [H], 记念) our ancestors. It is important to understand our history and what our ancestors have done for us. Ancestor worship is important because it helps us to understand our ancestors. So, it is a good idea to reconstruct our ancestral house. Our Singapore relatives, whose roots are also from here, would be able to come here in search of their origin and history.

> The continuity of a group of people is dependent on the continuity of this house. Praying to ancestors will help the younger generation to remember their ancestors. It is especially important for the *huaqiao* because this is their root and without it, it will be hard for them or their future descendants to search for their own roots and identity. Ancestor worship is important because it is a tradition and a cultural practice of our people. The ancestral house is also a symbol of our respect for our ancestors. They [the *huaqiao*] should come back and pray to them especially now that they are well-off, because wealth should not be divorced from our ancestors. The ancestral house would also allow us and the *huaqiao* to recognize the significance of our common ancestors and their duty to help us.
>
> It has now become an important focal point where Anxi people from overseas come back and pray to our ancestors. This is very important for the unity of the lineage and allows for interaction and the rekindling of kinship and social ties between them and us. Ancestor worship is an important ritual and by participating in it, they would have stronger feelings for their home.

Why should the Singapore Chinese pay for the reconstruction? What part do the ancestors play in bringing the two groups of Chinese together? The following are the attitudes of some villagers towards these two questions.

> This reconstruction has been good for the local economy. It provided jobs for some of us. Also, the ritual activities and their need for religious items have also helped some of us to get extra income when we supply them with the religious items. These are important [activities] to pull back some overseas money. For the sake of this money, we will participate in these activities.
>
> The reconstruction of the ancestral houses is important to attract more overseas Chinese to visit our village, and this will prevent a break in kinship ties. It has encouraged more Chinese from Nanyang to come back. It is especially important to attract the younger Chinese back to our village. Otherwise, they would forget us completely.
>
> It is also very good for the dead. Now, our dead ancestors can enjoy a little and have a nice house to live. This is to compensate for the lost years after the Cultural Revolution.

They did it because they want face. Even if we want to pay, they would not have let us. They would feel insulted if we offered. They have such big egos.

Others feel that by contributing to the ancestral house and performing ancestor worship, the Chinese overseas

> ... must have thought of the home village and our ancestors. The *zuzhai* is a way of bringing together and galvanizing different sections of the lineage together. It is because of our ancestors that our people are spread to different parts of the world. Having an ancestral home will allow us to preserve our historical memory of our ancestors and to remember the different branches of our descendants overseas.

> It is important for the promotion of our lineage [vis-à-vis other lineages] and helps to unify future generations through 'blood relationship'. It is also good for the future of lineage and for a smooth life for all of us.

Attitudes of Official Cadres towards Ancestor Worship

In Penglai, the construction of lineage ancestral houses and the performance of communal ancestor worship ceremonies were made possible because of cooperation and support from the official district and county cadres. Since the reform years, the Singapore Chinese and the official cadres had maintained a close relationship which had facilitated the implementation of the many projects already mentioned, without much obstruction. Most cadres saw ancestral activities as significant cultural practices, and some local cadres participated in them. Naturally, they were concerned to encourage the flow of Chinese overseas capital into the *qiaoxiang* and other parts of Fujian, and encouraging and supporting the cultural activities that the Singaporeans desired was seen as important for strengthening the relationship between the Chinese overseas and the region.

Prior to reform, ancestor worship practices were considered superstitious; they were prohibited, and those who took part in them were persecuted. Today, they are construed as cultural traditions. To understand this transformation of attitude, we need to understand the roles of village cadres within the village politics.

Our survey showed village cadres to be very much part of the Singapore-*qiaoxiang* connection. Through the years, village cadres have maintained strong ties with their Singapore kin, and since the reforms they have played an important role in encouraging the Singapore kin to contribute and help with village reconstruction. For the most part, they have encouraged and supported religious fairs and ancestor worship in these *qiaoxiang*. By supporting the Singapore Chinese, they hope to revive the traditional cultural practices and at the same time, create a network of *guanxi* and reciprocity. Because of the goodwill that support for ancestor worship and religious functions creates, the flow of Chinese overseas capital into these villages has helped transform the economic status of the region. Some local cadres benefited personally from this and became important figures at both district and county levels, as their connections and ability to encourage their Singapore kin made them important in the eyes of the county government, who increasingly tapped into these *qiaoxiang* connections to help with county-level development. Although town, county and provincial cadres were openly more restrained than village officials in their support for ancestor worship and religious fairs, most would attend them when invited by Singapore Chinese hosts, thereby giving them official support. One cadre said:

> It depends on how you look at this. If it is purely religious practice, then it is superstition and we would not support it. But this is the ancestral house and they are engaged in ancestor worship. This is our ancestral place and it is very important for the future generations. It is a place to remind us of our ancestors and to remember them. Through it, we will be able to foster closer relationships among our blood relatives, within the villages and with Chinese overseas. This will also allow them to develop stronger bonds with their home village. The ancestral house is a place where we, the Chinese, search for our ancestors and roots. It is also beneficial to the lineage and provides an opportunity for Chinese overseas to express their love for their motherland and home village. Because this is a cultural practice and not a superstition, we would support it.

Table 4: Attitudes of cadres towards ancestral house and ancestor worship

Cadres	Agree	Disagree	Don't know	Total = N
Village/Cun	29 (97%)	0	1 (3%)	30
Town/Zhen	17 (94%)	1 (6%)	0	18
County/Xian	41 (82%)	5 (10%)	4 (8%)	50
TOTAL	87 (89%)	6 (6%)	5 (5%)	98

Table 5: Reasons for supporting ancestor worship by cadres at different levels

Cadres	Sentimental	Moral	Instrumental	Total =N
Village	45%	20%	35%	100% = 30
Town	42%	5%	53%	100% = 18
County	15%	0%	85%	100% = 50

Responses of the cadres at county, town and village levels can be divided into three types:

1. *Sentimental,* with emphasis on the ancestral house as a help for the Chinese overseas in searching for their cultural roots and ancestors. Such cadre responses categorize the early emigrants as a group of kinsmen who were forced to emigrate because of poverty in the villages, who should not be discriminated against when they search for their roots. Such responses imply the hope that such acts would strengthen their sentiments towards the home village.
2. *Moral,* with emphasis on ancestor worship activities as a concession to remind the successful and wealthy Chinese overseas not to forget their ancestral homes. These respondents considered Chinese overseas as *qiaobao*.
3. *Instrumental,* with emphasis that a concession concerning ancestral houses, worship celebrations, etc., is needed to establish further contacts and *guanxi*. With such responses, cadres hope the Chinese overseas will contribute money to schools and hospitals and help with infrastructure development in the county as a whole.

There is a small group of town and county cadres who felt that the Singapore Chinese had their priorities wrong. These did not agree to the reconstruction of ancestral houses and ancestor worship, but wanted the money to be used for educational needs so that future generations of Anxi villagers would be literate. They saw ancestor worship and its related activities as a waste of money, resources and labour.

Support and Rivalry

Local supporters and opponents of Singapore Chinese involvement with their local ancestral villages can be differentiated by generation and educational background. Generally, the younger and the better educated were less supportive, arguing that the Chinese overseas misused their resources, which should be used for village infrastructure development and to revitalize the village economy. These opponents were in their twenties and thirties. A few school teachers in their fifties who had Singapore kin also did not approve of such practices but did not oppose them, feeling that the revival of ancestor worship had indirectly contributed to the social life and economy of the village and stressing the need to adopt a flexible attitude towards their Singapore kin, as such involvement made them aware of the needs of the villages, and as many had contributed to village economic development. For such persons, it is a matter of trading one thing for another.

The staging of communal ancestor worship ceremonies and related activities resulted in competition and rivalry for leadership roles. Those with good relations with their Singapore kin and with the appropriate skills—usually village elders, but also some younger villagers—became leaders. The *guanxi* network among lineage members was important for selecting village kin who had character and were reliable, trustworthy and able to organize the activities, as they were entrusted with money and responsibility for preparation for the communal activities and religious fairs.

In Anxi, elderly men and women with intimate knowledge of the rituals of ancestor worship had been the main players in them, as the local authority structure was one based on seniority and knowledge. Several of the village elders became core members in planning and organizing communal ancestor worship. Assisted by a group of younger villagers, they worked closely together with their Singapore kin. Most were in their sixties and seventies.

Understanding ancestral rites was often an important criterion to becoming an active lineage member. Those with the knowledge and skills were the ones approached by the Singaporeans to assist in such activities, and so there was competition and rivalry among the villagers to portray themselves as skilful in matters relating to ancestral rituals. By becoming actively involved in ancestral rites, villagers could gain much social prestige and recognition, and also material and financial benefits provided by the Singapore relatives. In an environment where the elderly were increasingly considered a burden to society, the roles played by these village elders helped restore their self-esteem and reincorporate them as productive members of the lineage.

The relationship between Singapore and their village kin was not tension-free. When it came to worshipping the ancestors on a communal basis, all the Singapore kin attending in Anxi were given priority to participate in ancestral worship. All participated, irrespective of age, sex and seniority—in the front rows, carrying incense sticks and participating in the ritual acts—whereas, among the villagers, only the elders were invited. This created dissatisfaction among some villagers, who accused the Singapore Chinese of buying their way to a central position. One commented: 'Because they have contributed to this function, they are given such prominent placing in the worship. We should also be entitled to it. After all, we also have a share in the ancestor. Why should they be the prominent ones?'

Ancestor Worship as a Ritual Form and a Life Philosophy

Ancestor worship is regarded as a significant religious force as 'it allows us to express our sentiments to our parents and ancestors in a ritually correct manner'. The restoration of the ancestral house has allowed lineage members to perform the ritual acts of *xiezu* (thanking the ancestors) and *baizu* (worshipping the ancestors), two important forms of ancestor worship which are done communally.

We have seen how the revival of ancestor worship in the village transformed the *qiaoxiang* by enriching the calendrical cycle of activities with ritual performances and social activities. Here, the feasts became a symbol of the relative abundance of food and the higher standard of living in *qiaoxiang* villages than in non-emigrant villages. We have also seen that the important functions of ancestor worship include the socio-moral one of integrating the members of the family and the lineage, in a manner which dictates the roles and reinstates the positions of members within the community and which helps to bind two groups (Singaporeans and villagers) of the lineage together, re-establishes social and structural continuity among them, and provides a historical past within which the present generation of lineage members can find ancestral and cultural roots. By engaging in correct ritual forms (*li*), each member becomes a moral person, an honourable person, who fulfils his or her responsibilities to family and lineage and in so doing re-establishes a niche for him/herself in a social order that is fast losing its traditional moral values. Participants in ancestor worship rituals thus become champions of traditional moral and cultural values amidst the influence of modern education, modern mass media and technology. It is also through this bond of ancestor that enabled the Penglai villagers to increasingly use it as a form of cultural capital to extract emotional and material concession from the Singapore Chinese (Kuah-Pearce, 2006g).

Are we witnessing a renaissance of traditional culture among the Chinese in this part of the world? Can we see ancestor worship as a part of a wider social process at play in East Asian societies—one in which Confucianism, in its various forms, is emerging as an important ideological and social force driving all aspects of society, from economics to politics and down to individuals and families? Ancestor worship, as a transcendental ritual form of Confucianism, might thus be seen as an important socio-religious force galvanizing members of a lineage together and resulting in an interlocking social network where moral and social capitals have to be created periodically to establish one's honour and morality. Such a conception would indicate the re-emergence of a traditional moral economy and would explain the philanthropic activities of the Singapore Chinese in their ancestral villages.

In witnessing the emergence of a kind of cultural renaissance locally, one central issue of concern is that of cultural authenticity. To what extent have the rituals been subjected to varying forces that influence and change their contents and meanings? The ancestral rituals practised today in the village are an interactive product of villagers and Singaporeans, with the level of authenticity therefore subject to mutual negotiation. Old rituals are reproduced, simplified or elaborated and new ones invented to suit the occasions and the needs of those concerned. It is appropriate to say that ancestor worship is an evolving ritual form aimed at satisfying the cultural needs of the two groups.

In conclusion, ancestor worship remains a potent force among the Chinese, both within village China and in the overseas environment, as is shown among the Singapore Chinese. It recounts the story of family and lineage, draws on the moral economy of its members and forbids them to forget their ancestors, lineage, home village and village kinship structure. It is these things that are encapsulated in various formulae, such as 'not forgetting the source' and 'wealth not being divorced from its ancestors', that constantly prick the individual's moral conscience, and are instrumental in re-establishing continuity between the Singapore Anxi Chinese and their relatives in Penglai, Anxi County, Fujian Province, China.

Photo 10   The Buddhist monks perform 'the rite of ancestor spirit recalling' (photo by author)

Photo 11   The sedan chairs carrying the ancestors' spirits are placed in front of the lineage ancestral house (photo by author)

Photo 12   Monk giving a ritual bath to the ancestral spirits (photo by author)

Photo 13   A group of monks chanting sutras and informing the ancestors' spirits of the celebration while the elders pay their obeisance (photo by author)

Photo 14 Communal ancestor worship (photo by author)

Photo 15 Villagers offering food to the ancestors (photo by author)

Photo 16 Offerings of soul house to the ancestors by individual families (photo by author)

Photo 17 Preparing big-bowl noodles for the guests (author in the middle) (photographed by a villager on behalf of the author)

Photo 18   The black-faced Qingshui zushigong (in central position in the Lineage Ancestral House) (photo by author)

Photo 19   Qingshuiyan Temple (photo by author)

7
Religious Revivalism

Chinese religious orthodoxy is an important part of Singapore-Chinese socio-religious life. One of the earliest social institutions established by the Chinese in Singapore was the temple. Since then Singapore Chinese have continued to hold Chinese religious practices, both individually and communally. Today, Chinese ritual ceremonies and religious fairs continue to be part of the religious landscape among the Chinese in Singapore, enabling participation in communal expression that fosters a sense of group identity and solidarity.

Among the Singapore Anxi Chinese, the orthodox practices of Chinese religion continue to be important. In the 1960s, they built a temple in Singapore, Penglai Si (蓬莱寺), named after the home of the majority of them. Within this temple, their guardian god (Qingshui zushigong, 清水祖师公) is housed. Since the 1980s, the old temple was demolished for redevelopment purposes and Qingshui zushigong was relocated in the new site. On various occasions, communal fairs are organized for lineage members in Singapore.

The 1978 reform in China brought a revival of religious activities in Penglai, and visiting Singapore Chinese were instrumental in reinventing ritual practices in the villages of Penglai. The small-scale, individualized religious practices during the early years of reform gradually gave way and large annual religious fairs became common. Ninety per cent of village households belonging to the relevant lineage participated in them. In the 1990s, an increased number of Singapore Chinese visited their home villages to take part in them. This chapter examines religious reproduction in the *qiaoxiang*, focusing on the centrality of Qingshui zushigong; the revival of religious fairs and the implications for the lineage identity of Singapore and village Chinese.

Chinese Religious Orthodoxy: Its Contemporary Roles

Chinese religious orthodoxy can be seen as consisting of two structures, the ritual and the ideological. Each can exist independently of the other. Both remain important in Chinese culture. In one study, Watson sees the standardization of ritual as having been central to the creation and maintenance of a unified Chinese culture (Watson, 1988: 3). To Watson, it is the ritual performance rather than the meanings behind it that is crucial. He argues that 'what is clear and explicit about ritual is how to do it—rather than its meaning' (Watson, 1988: 5). On the other hand, Rawski has explored the meanings behind these ritual practices and argues that, although the practitioners themselves might not be aware of it, a complex structure of meanings does exist for all ritual practices and it is important to acknowledge its existence (Rawski, 1988: 22). I argue that the surface, manifest structure of Chinese religious practice is grounded in rituals and actions, but I also recognize a deep latent structure which provides the Chinese with an identifiable, common cosmological world-view. Taken together, these two structures allow Chinese communities throughout the world to practise an identifiable form of Chinese religious orthodoxy and orthopraxy; the latent structure often changes less than the surface while the manifest structure is subjected to addition, subtraction and modification due to changing socio-cultural, economic and political environments.

Chinese religious orthodoxy is an eclectic mix of three main ideologies—Daoism, Buddhism and Confucianism—interwoven with folk beliefs and animism. This syncretic mix did, and still does, determine the practice of the Chinese. Historically, ideologically 'pure' religious practices were confined to small elite minorities—in former times, these included state officials and the literati, who favoured institutional forms of religion—either Confucianism, Buddhism or both, at different periods; as well as many religious professionals. A more diffused form of religious practice was that of the masses (Yang, 1961)—formerly this meant, for the most part, the peasantry (Granet, 1975).

As a system of rituals, Chinese religious orthodoxy can be seen as a system of social action, the performance of which requires the co-operation of individuals who follow the direction of leaders (La Fontaine, 1985: 11). There are ritual rules and prescribed sets of actions that govern each action and each participant (La Fontaine, 1985: 11). Other rules concern those persons to be excluded.

In contemporary Chinese society, it is the better-educated and professional classes that favour scriptural purity. Among Singapore Chinese, only in recent decades has there been a rise in scriptural Buddhism and an emerging trend towards Reformist Buddhism, while Chinese religious orthodoxy has continued to be represented by communal religion; yet there is a new division between individual spiritualism and communal religiosity. The latter is now interpreted as part of Chinese cultural tradition by the Singapore state and thus is supported by various Chinese groups—and, by the 1990s, by the Singapore state (Kuah, 1998a). Many groups of Chinese—lineage groups, surname associations, temples and occupational groupings—participate in various communal religious celebrations in Singapore.

The reproduction of Chinese religious orthodoxy among the Singapore Chinese has not been a systematic process. The early migrants first engaged in religious reproduction, and ritual elements changed according to the perceptions and understanding of practices by the migrants through the years. What they remembered as traditions, they reproduced and practised— in many cases, with very little idea of the traditional meanings behind them. However, the process was important, as it provided the early migrants with cultural familiarity and continuity in a foreign environment. However, today these rituals constitute an important part of Chinese culture, and provide the Singapore Chinese with a distinct cultural identity in the face of new challenges. The challenge facing Chinese religious orthodoxy generally today is that of how to restructure it into a rationalized modern religion that fulfils the spiritual and social needs of individuals and the collective whole.

At any rate, for the Singapore Anxi Chinese, supposedly orthodox religious practices fulfil the function of providing a bond between them and their village counterparts in Penglai. Through it they are able to express their sentiments towards their ancestral villages and their village kin. By staging religious fairs and participating in ritual practices, these two groups of Chinese are brought together. Such practices serve as cushions against the initial shock of reuniting with village kin, and as an important dialogue platform for the two groups, who have been separated for several decades, providing a ready topic for conversation and thus reducing embarrassment due to lack of conversation topics. This is particularly important for the men, as many of them find it difficult to make small talk, so that involvement in some sort of work becomes a desirable aim when they visit the villages. The staging of communal religious fairs becomes a way out, as conversations are directed towards preparation and the actual ceremony. It also provides an important cultural bond for the women, as most Singapore and village women become involved in the preparation of food and religious paraphernalia for the ancestor worship ceremonies and are very active in individual and communal ancestor worship. Through cooperation in these chores, the women are brought closer together. Chinese religious practices thus provide the *qiaoxiang* with communal fairs that enable all villagers to participate and rediscover a religious culture that had been suppressed from the 1950s until the 1980s and to express overtly individual religiosity and spirituality that had been suppressed under secularism.

Centrality of Qingshuiyan (清水岩) and Qingshui zushigong

When the Singapore Chinese visit Anxi, one of their primary aims is to visit Qingshuiyan and make offerings to their ancestor, Qingshui zushigong. Something like 90 per cent of them do this. This deity provides the two groups with a shared religious connection and allows them to engage in communal religious activities as members of the same lineage.

The temple complex, Qingshuiyan, is located in the southeastern outskirts of Penglai District. It is 760 metres above sea level and nestled in a hilly area with beautiful greenery. From Penglai Zhen it takes about twenty to thirty minutes by car to reach the foot of the temple, and then another fifteen to twenty minutes to climb the steps on foot to reach the temple itself. It is an imposing temple complex built in traditional Chinese architectural style, with arched roofs. The main building is made of red bricks and granite slabs, giving it distinction in the rustic rural landscape. Its position at the top of a peak commands a panoramic view of the villages below it. To the villagers and Chinese overseas, the position of the temple—located in the hills with a river flowing by and overlooking the villages (*beishan wangshui*, 背山望水)—is believed to have exceptionally good geomancy (*hao fengshui*, 好风水).

The temple is dedicated to a Buddhist monk who is popularly known as Qingshui zushigong (literally, 'Clear-Water Deified Ancestor'), the name given to a historical figure who lived during the Song Dynasty and who was renowned for mystical powers that saved the lives of many villagers. There are several versions of both his origin and his mystical power. One version has it that his original name was Chen Pu (陈普) and that he was born into a family whose poverty forced them to send him to a monastery at a very young age. Because of the harsh conditions, however, he left the monastery, travelled, and eventually reached Anxi. He liked the place, settled there, and lived the life of a recluse, practising Chan meditation. He was rumoured to have attained a high level of spiritual power. He was seen as a compassionate monk, who often gave rice to poor villagers. After his death, the villagers built a temple in his honour.

Another version has it that he was a monk from nearby Yongchun County and was known as Chen Ying (陈应), who had become a monk at a very young age. His knowledge of dharma, and his possession of mystical powers and his compassion, were widely known to the villagers in the region. During the sixth year of Northern Song rule, Qingxi (present-day Anxi) suffered from a bad drought. The local inhabitants begged Chen Ying to perform the rite for rain. After the drought, he remained behind and lived in the temple. In addition to being a monk, he was a practising physician, who treated the villagers' diseases with herbal medicine, about which he was very knowledgeable. He also helped build bridges and roads. In his spare time, over a period of 18 years he rebuilt the temple he was living in, afterwards renaming it Qingshuiyan. His efforts, diligence and compassion won the hearts of the villagers. He reportedly arrived at Qingshui Temple (Qingshui Si, 清水寺) in 1101 and died at the age of 55 (*Anxi Xianzhi,* 1994, vol. 2: 1127–1128).

Qingshui zushigong is commonly known as Wumian zushigong (乌面祖师公) because of his black face. One version has it that during his nineteen years as a recluse practising meditation in the cave he was constantly disturbed by the spirits who, on one occasion, attempted to kill him by blowing on the lamp for seven days and seven nights. He survived the ordeal, but his face was badly burned and turned black.

He is also known as the 'dropping nose ancestor' (Luobi zushigong, 落鼻祖师公) among the Taiwanese today. One story has it that the nose of the statue of Zushigong was torn off when part of the roof of the cave collapsed. It was later fixed back in position, but since then, whenever he sensed natural calamities, his nose dropped off, to be found in front of his chest or buried in his sleeve—a sign for the villagers to prepare for the coming disaster. Another story claims that he disapproved of unclean worshippers making offerings to him, and that his nose dropped off whenever this occurred (Lou, 1977; *Zhenxiang zazhi bianjibu,* 1987).

After the monk's death, and in commemoration of his contribution to the place, the villagers continued to build various pagodas and to expand Qingshuiyan into an impressive temple. Gradually, the monk assumed a transcendental status and became deified, and was worshipped as a deified ancestor by the villagers. From 1164 to 1210, Qingshui zushigong was posthumously honoured by the Southern Song imperial palace four times, each time with two characters having the following respective meanings: 'ever-ready', 'great wisdom', 'ultimate compassion' and 'extremely charitable'. He was much loved and worshipped by the general population of Anxi County. Today, even though Qingshuiyan is known as a Buddhist temple, the main shrine houses this Wumian zushigong.

Qingshuiyan has undergone two main phases of development, the first during the Northern Song and Southern Song eras, after which it was honoured as a Buddhist temple by imperial decree during the Southern Song. During various dynastic epochs, additional honours led to new additions to the main temple, expanding it and transforming it into a renowned sacred place.

The second phase of development has been the modern period, starting at the end of the nineteenth century. In 1899, the main shrine of the temple complex underwent an extensive renovation, and two new buildings were added to it. In 1933, the complex was destroyed by a heavy rainstorm, which caused the walls of the main shrine, and those of other buildings, to collapse. It was then left in a state of ruin until 1953, when Chinese overseas started to rebuild it. From 1953 to 1976, a group of Chinese overseas collectively renovated and extended the temple complex. It now stands as a complex of three buildings. The main shrine is called the Zushi dian (祖师殿) and is devoted to Qingshui zushigong. In 1978, a temple management committee was formed to manage the complex, and the following year the complex was modernized with a telephone, street lamps and a sealed-surface road winding up the slopes to the temple.

Qingshui zushigong has, through the centuries, been the guardian deity of the people of Anxi County, and the villagers of Penglai have regarded him as their ancestral deity. His black face is now considered a symbol of virtue and righteousness. He is widely known for his deeds in helping those in need of assistance, and is a protector of the villagers from natural and human calamities. Because he was supposedly a historical figure rather than a mythological one, he is called a 'deified ancestor' (Zushigong, 祖师公).

An Emigrant's Deity

In rural China there was formerly very little flow of information, including that concerning the existence of other gods and deities than those already known. Villagers thus clung to their known gods and deities for all socio-psychological needs. On the eve of emigration, many of those who were to travel would pray to Qingshui zushigong for guidance and for a safe journey. Other deities, such as the Goddess of the Sea, Mazu (妈祖) (also known as Heavenly Empress or Tianhou (天后), only became popular with the emigrants after they came into contact with her in the coastal ports of Fujian.

To the Anxi Chinese emigrants of the nineteenth and twentieth century, Qingshui zushigong was a source of encouragement and moral support, a protector against banditry and the uncertainties of the journey, and the only deity known to many of them prior to emigration. He was also a source of compassion, and the villagers relied on him for blessings and to solve their communal and personal problems, big and small. He was known to answer most requests because of his mystical powers and was thus spiritually powerful (*ling*, 灵) for these Chinese.

The emigrants from Anxi made their way through the hills to the coastal cities and to Singapore. In the foreign environment, Chinese social institutions existed to help these newly arrived migrants with their social and economic needs, providing temporary shelter and employment; but their fears and innermost needs were assuaged by their faith in Qingshui zushigong, to whom they turned for support and comfort. The belief that Qingshui zushigong was their ancestral deity made their sense of security greater, as he was there exclusively for them. During the nineteenth and the first half of the twentieth century, there were religious fairs held in temples that provided a reprieve from the mundane routine of coolie life, and these served as a base for socialization and social networking; but Qingshui zushigong remained a figure to whom the Anxi migrants could turn to for both spiritual needs and social consultation.

Today, Qingshui zushigong reflects the proud achievement of the first-generation Anxi Chinese in Singapore and continues to be a constant source of support for them. He is also a visible reminder of who they are and where they come from—a testimony of their origin and cultural roots as they built their social base and sank their roots into Singapore society. Qingshui zushigong is there to prick their conscience, to remind them not to forget their ancestral home.

Qingshui zushigong was a historical person, and is now a deified hero and has become known as a Buddha given that he was a monk; but he also represented a socio-religious system that the Anxi Chinese came to embrace in their changed social environment, giving them a cosmological world-view and allowing them to reproduce aspects of their religion that fulfilled their needs in Singapore.

Temples devoted to Qingshui zushigong can be found in various Chinese overseas communities in Singapore, Taiwan, and Malaysia, where he is also known popularly as the 'dropping nose *zushi*'.

Situating Qingshui zushigong in Singapore

By the early 1950s, the number of recent migrants from Anxi to Singapore had grown substantially. There were about 60,000 people from Anxi in Singapore at that time, some from Penglai. Two social institutions emerged to cater to this increasing number of Anxi people in Singapore. The first was Anxi Association (Anxi Huiguan, Ann Kway Hui Guan [H], 安溪会馆), formed in 1921 to provide a social roof for the migrants. The organization recruited members from Anxi County and has organized several communal religious and cultural fairs on an annual basis, and today continues to provide a space for social interaction on a daily and weekly basis. It has its own premises and is open to all members.

The second institution established in Singapore was the Penglai Temple, built in 1951 to provide for the religious needs of the Anxi people and to house Qingshui zushigong. The original temple—small in size, with one main shrine and a small area for the temple caretaker—was built from contributions given by 12 persons. In 1985, it was subjected to urban renewal and urban redevelopment, and the land was returned to the Urban Renewal Authority (URA) for compensation. A choice of several locations for rebuilding was given, and these were to be leased to the temple authority at a rate several times below the market rate. The committee for Penglai Temple bid successfully for a site that has an area of about 20,000 square feet and a leasehold period of 35 years. The site was leased at a cost of S$270,000.

In the 1980s, many other small temples were also subjected to urban renewal and were given summons by the Urban Renewal Authority to relocate. At the same time, the URA earmarked several sizeable plots of land for religious purposes, for which the affected temples could bid for the rebuilding of their temples. In 1985, several more temples were served with relocation notices. The committee of two temples, Zhongting Miao and Mingshan Gong, first approached Penglai Temple with the intention of joining it, as members of these two temples were also from Anxi and also worshipped Qingshui zushigong. Given the fact that there were not so many parcels of land to be distributed to all temples affected by urban renewal, the government had encouraged temple premise sharing among temples. Since each temple had its own deities but worshipped a common Qingshui zushigong, members saw the feasibility of sharing temple premises. By combining resources, they were more likely to succeed in bidding for the government-designated religious plot of land. By claiming that several temples shared a plot of land, they were also in a stronger position to compete in the bidding with other Chinese, as well as with Christian, organizations. Furthermore, by pooling resources, they could also build a bigger temple. The parties all agreed to the use of the name Penglai Temple, or Penglai Si.

During this period of planning and construction, four other temples heard of the combined efforts and decided to join in the project, and so met with the organizing committee of Penglai Temple to discuss the possibilities of joining the temple as co-partners. These four were Che Chi Tang, Pu An Tang, Shui Kou Tang and Xiang Fu Ting. The committee members of these four temple organizations were also from Anxi County and also recognized Qingshui zushigong as their guardian deity. The groups were accepted into the Penglai Temple project. Thus, Penglai Temple became a combined project of seven temple organizations and was jointly owned by them.

In 1986, the Penglai Temple Fundraising Committee was established, with members from the seven temples representing the nine surname groups found in Anxi. These are Lin (林), Ke (柯), Li (李), Zhang (张), Liao (廖), Liu (刘), Wen (温), Xie (谢) and Chen (陈). With renewed effort and an increase in funds, construction work began on Penglai Temple in 1989 and was completed in 1991. The total cost of construction amounted to S$1.7 million.[1] The temple was constructed in traditional Chinese architectural style, with elaborate carved tiled roofs with dragons and phoenixes on top of it. It has one main shrine hall, with a high ceiling. At both sides are offices, on the first and second floors. At the front podium the building is supported by four cylindrical pillars, with carvings of dragons and phoenixes, transported from Suzhou. In front of the building is an open space where religious fairs are held.

The new Penglai Temple is co-owned and shared by the seven temple groups, and each has a management team to look after its own religious functions, while the overall Penglai Temple management team looks after the maintenance of the temple. Within the temple, Qingshui zushigong is the main deity and is shared by all. He is positioned in the centre of the main shrine. Behind him are seven pavilions, each housing a group of guardian deities from one of the seven previous temples, with the name of the original temples written above each group of deities. The Penglai Temple is opened to all, but especially those who claim ancestry from Anxi.

The temple holds several communal religious functions a year, both for Zushigong and for the guardian gods. To begin with, there is the annual celebration of the birthday of Zushigong on the sixth day of the first lunar month. This is the most important inter-lineage communal religious function, commonly referred to as Zushigong Dan (祖师公诞). Other communal religious celebrations include Spring, Qingming and Zhongyuan festivals, occasions on which members of all the surname groups go and make their offerings to Zushigong. Communal celebrations of this nature, shared by all surname groups, are organized by a joint multi-surname committee.

A committee composed of members of different surname groups is selected on an annual basis according to the 'will of Zushigong'. The selection process is conducted at the end of each Zushigong Dan. Members from all surname groups—representing individual households, family business groups or individuals—assemble in front of Zushigong. As each name is put forward, the person kneels and offers *mubei* to Zushigong. The person with the highest number of positive replies from Zushigong becomes the stove-master, followed by the deputy stove-master, secretary, financier and others. These persons then manage the organization of Zushigong Dan and other communal functions for a year. Both the names of individuals and of corporations are submitted for the selection process.

There are also birthday celebrations for each group of guardian deities from the seven temples, participated by members of the particular temple group. These are organized by their respective management committees, chosen in the same way as the Penglai Temple management, but with only the group concerned participating in the selection process. Penglai Temple serves members at two levels.

In terms of religious status, the deities of the seven satellite temples are equal with one another, but lower than Qingshui zushigong of Penglai Temple. They are of a parochial nature, represent districts within Anxi County, and serve their own members. Each temple group makes offerings to its own guardian deities. Each temple has one day per month when rituals (*fashi*, 法事) are performed for its members. On that day, only members of the relevant group come and make offerings.

For those who pray there, the temple visually represents a communal, collective consciousness involving themselves and their ancestral home villages. It presents to them their own deities, and those who recognize them are insiders—members of the same village, district or county. But it is also a social space, where interaction among members of different groups occurs—a place where friends are made outside immediate kinship circles. Such intra- and inter-lineage interactions are most common at communal functions. Penglai Temple, based on the *tongxiang* county (Anxi County), district and village affiliations of its members, is unlike other temples in Singapore, where individuals go and seek assistance of specific gods and goddesses, in that its members constitute one big socio-religious community, comprised of seven smaller socio-religious communities.

Celebration of Zushigong's birthday coincides with the Lunar New Year. On this occasion, the organizing committee arranges food, flowers, and incense and joss-papers, which are placed on the table and offered to Zushigong. A Chinese opera troupe is invited to perform for both gods and temple members, and Daoist priests are invited to perform religious rites. Besides the offerings made to the deified ancestor, offerings are also made to Heaven.

On this day, members, especially women, turn up in great number, arriving in the late morning with joss-sticks, incense papers, fruits and sometimes food to present as individual offerings to Zushigong. As on most religious occasions, worship is conducted on two levels: there is also a communal offering to Zushigong. For both, the form of worship is a simple act involving the lighting of incense sticks, the placing of flowers in vases provided by the temple, the offering of fruits and food on plates to Zushigong, and prayer. Incense papers are burned as an offering after these women finish their ritual, which takes ten to fifteen minutes.

Although most members arrive in the morning, others may arrive at any time of the day. By mid-morning, however, the crowd gathered in the temple has grown to a hundred or more people. During the morning, women visit and make their offerings. Many are elderly, and they generally spend several hours in the temple before returning home. Most stay for a luncheon prepared by the temple organizers. A small number of women in their thirties and forties often accompany their mothers or mothers-in-law to the temple. Some of these stay behind and join in the conversation while others, after offering incense to the gods, leave the elderly to socialize among themselves and go out.

On this occasion, the social and kinship networks of the members are clearly displayed to everyone. The majority are related to each other, either sharing surnames or coming from the same ancestral village. Each member is thus known to others, and there is a high level of sociability. At the lineage level, women are related to each other through their husbands, and many of the elderly have known each other for three to four decades—many, in fact, knew each other in their ancestral villages prior to emigration. Their relationships have been strengthened through their years of association in Singapore, where they have provided moral and other support in times of hardship, especially during the early years of migration; and where, at present, the younger ones provide mutual support for the elderly and for those who are suffering from illness. These cross-lineage ties of support and friendship have developed into important networks within which the women can draw strength in times of hardship and happiness.

Celebrating the birthday of Zushigong is a joyous occasion for all members. After their obligatory worship the women greet one another, settle down in small groups and talk among themselves, catching up with one another on marriages of children and grandchildren, health, recreation, food, fashion and other mundane issues, mostly centring on their families. It is a time to exchange news and to renew kinship and friendship ties with those whom they meet less regularly. After lunch, many make their way home, leaving a handful behind to continue their conversations.

Other religious functions, such as those for the guardian gods of the seven temples, are celebrated in much the same way, but within the smaller component groups.

On these communal occasions, individual religiosity is consigned to a secondary position, to the individual acts of worship and offering. Men usually gather in groups during the night, after making offerings of joss incense to the various gods, to engage in conversation on topics ranging from business to politics to events in their home villages in China. Although it is mostly elderly men at the temples, younger men in their thirties and forties are also present, as well as a handful in their twenties. These younger men have either accompanied their parents to the temple or come as representatives of their parents to worship and to pay dues to the temple.

Membership in Penglai Temple is exclusive, the criterion being based on ancestral territorial affiliation. All members are of Anxi origin, although outsiders do visit the temple. Membership is based on the household rather than on individuals. In fact, participation and belief are two separate issues: those who participate in communal worship need not be believers. In most cases, it is the ritual participation—that is, orthopraxy—that is significant.

Anthropologically, these religious activities fulfil several functions. First, they provide opportunities for the elderly to meet and rekindle their relationships. Second, they provide opportunities for younger members to get acquainted with one another. They also allow economic networking among the younger members: among the younger men who visit the temple, many have now taken over family businesses—thus, going to Penglai Temple allows them to develop *guanxi* and form business partnerships. The activities at the temple also enable younger women to be inducted into the wider patrilineal kinship network and become recognized as daughters-in-law. By encouraging the participation of younger members, identity with the lineage and ancestral county and district can be ensured.

Reviving Religious Orthodoxy in Anxi

A common remark made by Anxi villagers is that when Chinese overseas return to their ancestral villages, they are predominantly preoccupied with religious activities and are willing to spend large sums of money on them. Why are the Singapore Chinese preoccupied with conducting large communal religious fairs in their ancestral villages? What are these communal religious fairs? What is the impact of these affairs on their social and kinship life?

Before 1978, the conduct of religious activities in Anxi was extremely low key. Individual worship took place, but was conducted quietly, with hardly any burning of incense or offering to the gods. The small number of Chinese from overseas who visited Qingshuiyan gave incense, paper money and food offerings, but the majority of villagers continued to conduct their worship discreetly with incense and a little joss paper. Even at the beginning of the reform years, discretion continued to be the rule regarding religious activities. By the mid-1980s, however, closer relationships between official cadres and Singapore Chinese brought about a greater degree of freedom for religious activities. Communal religious fairs, since then, have become public events that many local people participate in.

When the idea of reform was gaining popularity in the mid-1970s, village and county cadres were looking for means to boost the economy. The cadres in the *qiaoxiang* negotiated religion in exchange for capital investment and infrastructure support at the village level. They first agreed to the renovation of Qingshuiyan by the Chinese overseas, agreeing that it was an important historical temple worthy of preservation. The temple had long been an attraction to the Chinese overseas and they made pilgrimages to it. By renovating it and according it the status of a tourist place, it was hoped that it would become a major tourist attraction in interior Fujian and encourage more Chinese overseas to visit the area. Such rationalization was in congruence with the new national ideology of heritage preservation—in contrast to the ideology of the Cultural Revolution years—and was also in line with the national push to encourage Chinese overseas to visit China and ultimately to invest in China—hence the temple reconstruction of 1976 described above. Afterwards, however, there was little religious activity by the villagers beyond the discreet domestic worship of deceased grandparents and local gods carried out mostly by elderly women, with only occasional visits to the temple to make offerings and ask for the blessings of Qingshui zushigong.

Beginning in the 1980s, however, religious fairs became common in the *qiaoxiang* villages. Among these were the welcoming procession of Qingshui zushigong (*ying Qingshui zushigong*, 迎清水祖师公), the worship of Heaven (*bai tiangong*, 拜天公), the 'welcoming of god and lighting the fire' (*yingshen yinghuo,* 迎神迎火), and the birthdays of various buddhas (*fodan,* 佛诞). Groups of Singapore Chinese returned to participate in these celebrations. Usually a local household would be selected as the main organizer and sponsor of each event, the chosen person being known as the 'buddha head' (*fotou*, or *puo-tau* [H], 佛头).

Most households in our survey participated in communal religious functions. Only three families who were Christian did not participate in any village religious events, although they continued to perform ancestor worship, including communal ancestor worship. Generally, the villagers practised orthodox religious traditions and were interested in rituals, as were their Singapore counterparts, but most did not concern themselves with religious ideology—whatever concerns they had in this regard were expressed in ritual form rather than as doctrine. The revived ritual practices were significant to them because they were considered part of the wider Chinese tradition. They answered this-worldly needs—local deities, gods and Buddhas were consulted about health and illness, material concerns, marital problems and social relationships.

As in Singapore, the elderly were the most religious and participated wholeheartedly, while younger persons were less enthusiastic, although they, too, continued to support religious activities. Elderly villagers saw religious practices as important in satisfying both this-worldly and otherworldly needs, whereas younger villagers felt ritual practices, and religion in general, as less relevant to their lives. Some viewed religion as superstition, not to be encouraged. However, given the highly emotional attachment of their elders to these rituals, many felt it best to go along with elderly parents, grandparents and Singaporean kin. Many of the young said that they did not believe in religion at all, and attributed their attitude to their secular education; yet a large majority continued to assist and participated in the ritual celebrations.

A middle-aged Jin commented this religious revivalism as follows:

> Before they came, the village was very quiet. Now that our relatives come regularly, the place is full of life. They usually come in a group and organize religious fairs. We have ceremonies like welcoming the deified ancestors (*ying zushi*), the rite for the flow of descendants (*juanding yishi*) and, most recently, the rite for thanking the genealogy (*xie puyishi*). I think it is very good to have these religious celebrations to enliven our life here. It is also good to see so many of them returning and visiting their ancestral village. Before this, there were very few outsiders to our village. Now, it is different. We feel that the village has come alive.

Another villager Chen in his thirties stated that:

> I personally do not really believe much in these rituals and their efficacy, but the old ones do. But, I think these ritual activities are not just religious in orientation. They are more important for creating a communal spirit among the villagers, but also between the villagers and their Singapore relatives. It is also important for us to show interest in these activities so that the Singapore Chinese will return more frequently. If there is nothing for them to do when they visit the village, then they may not be inclined to return as often as they do now. These ritual activities occupy their time and minds and so when they return, they are always busy and doing something. In this sense, it is good that we have these religious celebrations. Furthermore, they create some kind of festive mood and villagers tend to be more gregarious. The general atmosphere tends to be one of happiness and excitement. This is good for the social and spiritual life of the villagers and the district.

The communal religious fairs attract much attention because of their grandeur, and the atmosphere of excitement has encouraged individuals and households to participate in them. Like the ancestor-worship celebrations, the several yearly religious functions add life to an otherwise mundane social environment. As in Singapore, they can be divided into two types: that of individual or household worship, carried out on festive occasions or when the need arises; and that of communal participation in religious fairs.

Today, there are three types of communal religious fairs. The first is the district-level fairs which involve all the lineages of the district, of which the most important is the annual welcoming of gods and fire (*yingshen yinghuo*) celebration. The second is the annual lineage-level fairs, which, for the Ke lineage and for others, is the welcoming procession of Qingshui zushigong on the sixth day of the first lunar month. The last are the small-scale fairs organized by individuals or groups of visiting Singapore Chinese.

It is possible to argue that the this-worldly needs of the villagers are similar, in general, to those of the Singapore Chinese, and that it is this shared religious practice with its focus on ritual practices, which both groups embrace and understand, that allows the two groups to come together to recreate those aspects of religious practice which are relevant to their needs. This shared ritual practice provides a common platform to discuss other concerns, which may be irrelevant, or only obliquely relevant, to the ritual system.

Fotou and Religious Fairs

The district-wide religious fair (*yingshen yinghuo*) was revived only in the late 1980s. The important selection of the *fotou,* or chief organizer, of the fair was traditionally based on an annual rotation cycle among the nine surname groups in the district, and this procedure was re-established when the fair was revived. Thus, each lineage gets to have a member appointed *fotou* once every nine years, and when this occurs it becomes imperative that both the lineage's Anxi and Singapore members become involved in the fair, both as helpers and as participants. By involving themselves, the lineage gains much 'face' and creates a good name for itself and its members, which is important for maintaining its overall social standing vis-à-vis other lineages.

Although the position of the *fotou* is rotated, the year that a lineage is asked to serve is done through a selection process rather than according to an annual rotation scheme. When the Penglai district revived its first religious fair, all surname groups were required to submit their names for selection. In the second year, the surname group that was the *fotou* for the previous year was required to refrain from submitting its name. This left only eight surname groups bidding for the position of *fotou*. This process continues until every surname group has been selected to provide the *fotou* once, when a new cycle begins. For this selection, the members of all the relevant surname groups rely on the following method. In simplified religious rites, a representative from each qualified surname group is required to throw *mubei* in front of Qingshui zushigong, who stands as witness to the selection process. The surname group with the most number of positive throws chooses the *fotou* from among its members for the coming year. Usually a lineage learns that it will choose the *fotou* one year in advance as, at the end of each celebration, those lineages that have not had a *fotou* are required to compete for the position. After the selection, the lineage concerned is required to select a team to head the preparation for the following year's celebration.

Having a member who is elected as a *fotou* is prestigious for the lineage concerned, but it also involves a huge burden of responsibility—for the expenses, preparation, staging and scale of the fair. When a lineage is selected to name a *fotou*, an ad hoc committee of members from among both Singaporeans and Anxi residents is formed, the majority of whom are lineage elders. The actual preparatory work—booking the monks and/or Daoist priests and the opera troupe, arranging the feast and the religious paraphernalia, etc.—is carried out largely by the locals, the Chinese from overseas arriving in the district only shortly before the fair.

Within the lineage, members vie for the position of *fotou*. The selection procedure is similar to the one held at the inter-lineage level. Interested individuals or households are invited to participate in the selection process, which is again witnessed by Qingshui zushigong. This too involves the throwing of *mubei* in front of the deity, the person with the highest number of positive throws becoming *fotou*. Because he is expected to arrange for labour and to provide financial contributions for the fair, it has become a norm that the position of *fotou* would fall on the shoulders of a lineage member who is relatively wealthy—generally a wealthy local or overseas member. In the late 1990s some village households, who had the support of their overseas kin, successfully vied for the position. When the *fotou* is living overseas, his related village kin are required to carry out the preparatory work.

For the Ke lineage, the main lineage religious fair at the lineage level is the welcoming procession for Qingshui zushigong. The committee members had one year to prepare for the celebration. Giving oneself sufficient time to prepare for the celebration is important, as this is the first time that most *fotou* are organizing a large-scale communal religious fair and it allows them to seek help and advice from others, perhaps of other lineages, who have been *fotou* and who have the experience of organizing the event.

Within any lineage, there is usually a core group comprised of both Singapore and Anxi members who are most active and interested in its affairs. These are mostly men, ranging in age from their fifties to their eighties. In most cases, it is the local members who decide the details, and who recruit manpower for the jobs that need to be done prior to the actual days of celebration. Usually, younger men are recruited for a variety of tasks, including cleaning and decorating the shrine, erecting the opera stage and purchasing the religious items. These young men are normally available on short notice and are counted on to do odd jobs and run errands for the celebration. The Singapore elders, having agreed to the general outline of the celebration, do not concern themselves with these details. Although they remain intensely interested in the preparation, about which they are kept informed by their Anxi counterparts, they are more involved with funding, and they easily attract contributions from Singapore lineage members. They also encourage and co-ordinate the attendance of the Singapore lineage members. A third concern is the invitation of village and county cadres to attend the function and the feast.

During the preparatory period, the two groups of kinsmen remain in close telephone contact with one another, and the Singaporeans might make several trips to the village, although most of the actual work is left to the Anxi locals. The cost of the celebration is calculated, and the funds collected from lineage members in Singapore are handed to the core members of the Anxi group to be spent on the necessary items for the celebration. All expenses are carefully recorded by the treasurer of the lineage committee for the fair, and the names of contributors are posted outside the ancestral house during the celebration. The total cost of a large-scale communal religious fair, such as the welcoming procession of Qingshui zushigong, may range from RMB 40,000–50,000 to over RMB 100,000 or more.

Anxi members attest to the need to develop trust between the parties when it comes to large-scale joint celebrations where one party contributes capital and the other has labour power. I was told that during the early 1980s there was much corruption, with individuals pocketing expenses. Now, strict accounting is carried out.

Sometimes individuals or groups of Singapore Chinese decide to stage a religious fair in appreciation of the assistance given by the local deity or by Qingshui zushigong. They and their village kin then arrange and prepare for a much smaller celebration. For these small-scale religious fairs, the cost includes the following:

1. An opera troupe for about RMB 5,000, or a puppet show for about RMB 3,000, for several nights of performance. Often both are staged. The performers must also be provided with accommodation and food. This entertainment and the feast are the two most important and costly items in the celebration.
2. The hiring of Daoist priests or Buddhist monks to lead the religious procession and to perform religious rites. This could amount to another RMB 4,000 to 5,000, depending on the number of monks or priests and the duration and intensity of the performance.

3. Religious paraphernalia, often costing as much as RMB 3,000–4,000.
4. A feast, for at least RMB 10,000.

Thus the total costs are from RMB 20,000 to 30,000, at the minimum. Lineage-level religious fairs often cost RMB 100,000–200,000; district-level fairs sometimes cost double. In Penglai, district-wide fairs have amounted to RMB 400,000.

For both district and lineage-level celebrations, the grandeur of the celebrations is ensured through co-operation with various authorities. In most cases, the occasion is declared a public holiday, with schools closed. The primary and secondary school principals respond to requests by getting pupils and students to perform dances and musicals. On such occasions, each student participant was provided with dress, drinks and RMB 20 in the late 1980s and early 1990s. However, the sums vary with the lineage. Many students look forward to these occasions, when they can enjoy themselves and have new clothes and money, and when they do not need to attend classes.

Trust and Rivalry

To organize a big communal religious fair requires trust and co-operation among the organizers, a fact attested to by both Singapore and Anxi Chinese. The Singaporeans often worry about the failure of the villagers to make the preparations successfully, while the villagers worry about too much interference from the Singapore Chinese who do not know much of the cultural traditions. Since the reform years the two groups have developed mutual understanding of their respective needs and have worked amicably to stage religious fairs. However, the Anxi members continue to feel that they have to be vigilant in their efforts. In the words of one village member,

> When they entrust us to do something, we should be reliable and do it well, otherwise they would lose trust in us. We cannot blame them for being cautious, as there have been cases in the village where some [Anxi] people had been entrusted with a large sum of money for some projects. Instead of working on the projects and spending the money on them, they spent it on themselves. The result was that things were done halfway and incompletely. The Singapore people had to put in more money and get other people to do the job. When these kinds of incidents happened, the Singapore members were very unhappy and lost trust in us. We were also very upset by these incidents as it reflected very badly on us. Not all of us are like that. We like to see ourselves as reliable and trustworthy

and able to be counted on to do the job well. Thus, we will do our best to ensure that there are not even little incidents that would disrupt this religious celebration.

Sometimes, when members of different parties fail to trust each other, mutual co-operation does not occur, and tension arises between the two groups. In one incident, a village lineage member was entrusted with the full amount of expenditure for a large religious celebration. He took the money but the celebration was not organized on a grand scale, the quality of the religious items was considered to be inferior, and the feast was not considered up to standard. There was dissatisfaction among both Singapore and Anxi lineage members. At the last minute, some members provided additional funding to rectify the situation. They ordered better-grade religious items and asked local restaurant owners to improve the menu for the feast and thus saved face for the lineage. However, in some cases there was close co-operation among the Singaporeans and the locals. When they realized that the entrusted member was not carrying out his duty, others were assigned to take over.

However, such dissatisfaction was never allowed to surface and become outward, public antagonism. Sometimes the guilty party would be pulled aside by the lineage elders and given a warning. In most cases, the party would be blackballed and no future work would be entrusted to him. The Singaporeans would exercise restraint in their comments about such persons when they were in the village. However, upon returning to Singapore, they would not hesitate to speak their minds to other lineage members.

Usually, however, those who are known to be honest and capable are selected, and there is a high level of trust.

Participating in the Religious Fairs

As mentioned, when a lineage is selected to choose a *fotou* for a communal, rather than for a lineage, religious fair, the participation of his lineage members, especially the overseas ones, becomes extremely important, and becomes a visual display of the social solidarity and strength among both local and overseas members. Although whenever there is a religious fair, most village households participate in it, persuading the Singapore members to visit Anxi and participate is not easy. This is especially true for the younger Singaporeans, who have very little understanding of Chinese religious tradition. In the 1980s and 1990s, however, largely due to efforts by the older Singaporeans to persuade their children and grandchildren, many younger Singaporeans came. Group travel arrangements had become the norm, and such communal religious events regularly drew a group of 30 or more Singaporeans. The *xiepu yishi* celebration at the end of 1996 drew over 70 Singapore Chinese.

At such events, those without relatives, or with relatives without a house to put them up in, usually booked into the Overseas Chinese Guest House (Qiaoliansuo, 侨联所).

By the late 1990s, some Singaporeans had begun to visit their ancestral villages on a regular basis, some as annual pilgrims, and were no longer considered 'newcomers' or 'uncivilized guests'. The constant flow of Singapore Chinese into Anxi by then had become a routine part of the social landscape, and their arrival no longer raised eyebrows or caused the excitement, enthusiasm and expectation that it had in earlier years. Upon arrival, they would be briefed on preparations for the particular event for which they had come. The men would gather and discuss final preparations, while the women were busy with food preparation and purchase of incense, candles, joss-papers and fruits so that they could make individual offerings to the ancestors in the ancestral house. Over the next few days, the women visited the Qingshui Temple in Anxi and made offerings to Qingshui zushigong.

Although the *fotou* and other active members were the religious elders and led the Qingshui zushigong procession throughout the various ritual performances, in fact, on most occasions, younger members substituted for the elders after one or two rounds, to relieve them of the tediousness of the performance.

The village atmosphere transformed dramatically with the coming of the Singapore Chinese and the impending celebration. There was intense communication between households, and reciprocal visits between Singapore Chinese and their kin. At night, the men might gather at a particular household, sipping tea, drinking liquor and discussing the coming events. Likewise, women gathered together and talked. The social atmosphere was one of festivity and the mood increased as the celebration drew nearer. Children too were keenly aware of the upcoming celebration and became wildly excited about the event, as the schools announced the holiday. Village routine gave way to festivity and celebration, and most villagers became involved in the celebration one way or another.

Emergence of Household Temple and Wayside Shrine

Apart from Qingshui Temple in Anxi County, other local temples have been reconstructed (the most famous being the Zhouyue Miao). Such local temples often have a shrine hall where one can worship the deities. Smaller wayside shrines housing local deities are found in street alcoves, and they too have been rebuilt. Most of these are relatively simple in appearance but are distinguishable by their traditional arched roofs and the constant smoke streaming from the incense placed there by worshippers and passers-by. Such small shrines are maintained by nearby households which have three enclosed sides, with the front facing the street left open. Within, the local god rests on a concrete platform, together with a medium-sized incense urn, two candle stands and an oil burner with a wick that burns continuously. However, not all wayside shrines are in good condition, and some are left to await rehabilitation by the villagers or by the Singaporeans—although such temples and shrines do not, in fact, attract much attention from the Singaporeans. Some villagers and Singapore Chinese might give offerings of incense and candles if they are in the vicinity, but few would seek them out. They are mostly patronized by local villagers, especially by elderly women, although occasionally a younger woman might pass by and offer an incense stick. These village gods are nearby, and so it is easier to go to them than to Qingshui Temple.

Religiosity or Superstition?

In the village world, where religion and overt religious practices were suppressed for several decades, the sudden revival of communal religious fairs and large-scale worshipping brought about mixed feelings and confusion for some. Some Chinese overseas who visited their ancestral home village to participate in large-scale communal worship expected their village kin to have the same level of religiosity as themselves, but this was not generally the case. I have argued that ritual practices provided the two groups with a shared activity that allowed for social bonding to occur. Yet differences in religious experience, religiosity and interest led to a boundary between the two groups, between 'insiders' and 'outsiders' to Anxi. Local villagers had varying attitudes towards religious practices. Almost every villager felt that religious functions were very closely linked to the Chinese overseas and their needs, and that it was the Singaporeans who were responsible for the religious revivalism and for the expenditure on religious activities. These are some local responses to this situation:

> It all depends on what they want to do (the types of rituals) and we do not agree or object to these. We just do as what they suggest. Because they believe in these practices, we should try to accommodate and support their practices. By supporting them, we hope that they will visit us more often.
>
> It is now fashionable to stage religious activities and we have to participate in these activities. If we do not participate, we will not

> be giving them [the Singaporeans] face and this will not be good for our family and the lineage as a whole. Our village would also lose much face. On an individual basis, sometimes, I participated in them more actively than other times.
>
> We feel obliged to support these practices as they [the Singapore Chinese] want these rituals. These rituals are important to them and fulfil their needs. If we do not give them this support, they might not befriend us. Also, many Chinese overseas believe that their success is due to the blessings of Zushigong. So they return to give thanks to Zushigong and organize big religious fairs in his honour. We should be understanding regarding this.

Despite such comments, the majority of villagers were supportive and participated in the communal religious functions. They also visited Qingshui Temple occasionally and prayed to Zushigong—although mostly in company with their Singapore kin. In addition, some prayed to the local village gods. They felt that the large-scale religious events provided 'heat and noise' (*renao*, 热闹) to the village, in contrast to the years during and after the Cultural Revolution, when everything was quiet and socially lifeless.

The younger villagers generally found the religious practices to be wasteful, arguing that the large funds for ritual events could be put to better use, such as to help with village development. They felt that there should be a limit for such celebrations. Some, however, looked upon the religious revival as a way of exercising religious freedom, which had not been possible since the 1960s, so that being able to carry out these activities freely was refreshing. Yet they also expressed the fear that if the *qiaoxiang* did not exercise discretion over the conduct of religious celebrations, the government authorities might impose restrictions detrimental to such religious freedom. Many saw the religious behaviour as a leisure pursuit of rich Chinese overseas, which highlighted the differences in social status between themselves and the villagers, and others considered the Chinese overseas to be superstitious.

There were three Christian families in Penglai District. Among those Christians who did not participate in the rituals were a 21-year-old woman and a 51-year-old housewife and her household. Members of the other two families considered themselves as passive participants, and contributed some money when asked to do so, but did not actively participate.

To the villagers, religious revivalism and the staging of communal religious fairs were significant. First, these cultural traditions served as a bridge between Chinese and village kin, helping them to unite. Second, the activities encouraged the Chinese overseas to visit their ancestral home village on a regular basis, which was also instrumental in cementing social and kinship ties with the *qiaoxiang*. Third, these were important social functions, which brought the villagers themselves together and helped create social solidarity. Fourth, they, as significant social events, created variations in village life and enliven it. Fifth, the religious events and accompanying production of religious paraphernalia and services were important for the local economy, supporting the small cottage industry catering for the dead, the living, and the gods.

Official Patronage and Religious Legitimacy

Village, district and county cadres were subtle in their support of large-scale communal religious fairs and ritual activities. The village cadres were the most open in their support while the county-level cadres were the least open, the degree of openness being tied closely to their own needs to display political correctness in their treatment of social events and activities. At the village and town levels, the 1978 reform was seen as a watershed for both economic and socio-religious liberalization. The relaxation of policies pertaining to institutional religion by central government resulted in a more liberal interpretation and support of village religious practices, so that the cadres nowadays interpret ancestor worship and communal religious fairs as support for Confucianism, Buddhism and Daoism. Communal village fairs are therefore interpreted specifically as part of the Buddhist and Daoist systems of rituals and rites.

However, village and district cadres were more liberal in their interpretation of these communal rites than were county cadres, for two reasons. First, some were genuine believers. Secondly, they felt that, with tolerance and support for the ritual activities, they would be able to encourage regular visits by the Chinese overseas, and that these would eventually lead to contributions and investment into the region.

The cadres who supported the reconstruction of Qingshui Temple did so for three reasons. First, they saw the temple as having historical value and being worthy of preservation, as it is over 800 years old. Since the central government had officially named the *Qingshui* Temple as a national historical monument, so obviously the cadres found it necessary to preserve it. Secondly, support for the temple and its related functions was a crucial concession to Southeast Asian Chinese to encourage them to invest in the region. Thirdly, the temple was seen as a tourist site and hence significant for the development of the tourist trade in Anxi, and tourism by Chinese overseas brought substantial revenues to Penglai.

Despite their greater support, village and district cadres also expressed a need to maintain a balance in the celebrations, the scale of which had to be justified by substantial capital investment and aid to the region. The majority did not favour large-scale, ostentatious celebrations, citing waste of resources as the main reason. They did not attempt to interfere in the functions, and this can be seen as tacit support, although most did not participate. Those who felt the events were superstitious nevertheless felt that it would be unwise to stop or boycott them; others saw them as important cultural events that would alleviate the drudgery of village life. Irrespective of the reasons, the village and district cadres wanted to be seen openly in support of village cultural and religious activities, as they needed the support of the villagers to be successful cadres and they also needed the Singapore Chinese to help develop the *qiaoxiang*.

The county cadres were less supportive of religious activities; 85 per cent of those interviewed expressed disapproval. These felt such activities were not in line with the ideological orientation of central policies. Their official line of argument was that the functions were superstitious and thus should not be encouraged. They also felt that they were a waste of precious resources that could be put to better social and economic use. However, these cadres conceded that, given the socio-economic situation, they could not and would not eliminate the religious ceremonies, and some were even willing to attend the Qingshuiyan fair's associated feast, to give face to the Chinese overseas who together with the village elders issued the invitation. Thus, some were flexible. County cadres understood religious activity to be a part of village cultural tradition that continued to have profound impact on the life of its adherents. They saw that communal spirit had increased with the staging of these religious fairs and the coming of the Chinese overseas and that the villagers were generally happier and less dull—despite what they might think about superstitions and central government policy. To maintain a balance between pure social and religious functions and the economic interests of the region was a major consideration for the cadres. Overall, the communal religious fairs passed muster, and have become an entrenched part of the local social landscape.

Religion as Socio-economic Capital

When villagers support communal religious celebrations, it is often a means to an end. Irrespective of age group, religion is seen as socio-economic capital. For example, after the reconstruction of Qingshui Temple, the local economy benefited from an annual income of RMB 2–3 million from contributions for incense and oil by the Chinese overseas. Part of this income went to the Penglai district treasury and was used for social and economic projects.

The pragmatics of treating religion as socio-economic capital are expressed in the following comments from the villages:

> We used religion and religious celebrations as the starting point to tap into the sentiments of the Chinese overseas and their contributions. So, we will support and facilitate their religious needs.

> Since these overseas Chinese are so superstitious and have instructed us to perform these religious activities, we should obey their instructions and perform to their satisfaction. If it were not for the sake of their money, then we would not go all out for them. We would put in our minimum for such activities.

> We also hope these religious functions and Qingshui Temple will attract the younger Chinese overseas so that they would understand the history of the village, love the ancestral village and help us with our social and economic development.

At the same time, such religious activities also spurred the establishment of an 'Incense and Oil' cottage industry that produces religious paraphernalia such as candles, joss-incense sticks, and joss-paper to cater to the needs of their villagers. Village women have also become actively involved in the production and retailing of the products (see Kuah-Pearce, 2004b).

Conclusion

Religious revivalism brought about much change in the life of the villagers and the *qiaoxiang*. To a certain degree, the religious communal fairs revitalized the religiosity of the villagers, especially the older ones, whose formerly suppressed religiosity could come out in the open. Socially, the revivalism provided Singapore Chinese and villagers with a common ideology which allowed for a renewal of kinship ties and social networks. It also provided the villagers with a new set of activities to liven the village atmosphere. It also led to the emergence of a cottage industry geared to the production of religious paraphernalia and other related religious services.

8
Rewriting Genealogy and Reclaiming One's Cultural Roots

For many members of the Ke Lineage, inclusion in the lineage genealogy constitutes the ultimate goal in reclaiming one's cultural roots. The final task is thus the addition and rewriting of the genealogy (*xiupu*, 修谱, literally, mending the genealogy), as this establishes one's membership, position and social status, and expounds on one's achievements within the lineage.

Genealogy: Historical Significance

Chinese genealogies are commonly called *pu* (谱), of which there are several widely recognized types. Family registers are *jiapu* (家谱), lineage registers, *zupu* (族谱), clan registers, *zongpu* (宗谱), and sometimes information on various families are also included in the locality registers, *difangzhi* (地方志).

It is generally agreed that the composition of Chinese genealogies began in the early Zhou period (1111–256 BC). However, it was only during the Chunqiu period (770–477 BC) that the practice became fully developed (Lo, 1972b: 38). Though developed at such an early date, the fate of the genealogical records was highly dependent on the regime that succeeded in controlling China at different historical epochs. Throughout history, there have been several phases when large-scale destruction of records occurred. Records showed that the first phase of destruction occurred when Qinshi Huangdi came into power and ordered the wholesale burning of maps, census registers and other works, among which were genealogies of some important families.

There were also periods where preservation of genealogies was encouraged by the imperial order. From the Han Dynasty through the Sui Dynasty (206 BC to AD 220), most royal houses, aristocratic families and clans of good standing kept genealogical records, some establishing offices solely for the purpose of keeping records and framing new genealogies (Lo, 1972b: 38–39).

The significance of genealogy was elevated to a new height, as social background became an important factor in gaining entry into the imperial bureaucracy and thereby achieving upward mobility and social success. Thus, during the Ming and Qing epochs, the gentry class focused their attention upon framing, printing and preserving their genealogies. After the founding of the Republic of China in 1911, many big clans and families all over China had taken a keener interest in the making of a genealogy. Lesser clans and lineages did so as well.

When the Chinese Communist Party took power, it engaged in a massive effort to destroy all existing records that were considered bourgeois in origin. Many family, clan and lineage genealogies and locality registers were destroyed in this 'cleansing' campaign. Most were destroyed on a voluntary basis for fear of persecution, but others were destroyed forcibly by Communist cadres. The result was a massive loss of some of the most important records for shedding light on the social history of China during previous historical epochs (Lo, 1972b: 38–55).

Composition of a Genealogy

The existing genealogical records are usually composed of various sections that provide a wide range of information. There is usually a section on the descent pattern of the lineage and the branches of the family. The five-generation tabular form created by scholar-politician Ouyang Xiu (AD 1007–72) of the Song Dynasty, is most commonly used to record the lineage and branches of genealogical records (van der Sprenkel, 1973: 14).

The Ouyang style records the family tree, beginning with the primogenitor where he first settled in a place and raised his family there, and ending with the contemporary generation that records the genealogy. Those in between are elaborated upon. The primogenitor and his great-great grandsons constitute five generations and are tabulated in one line, with the offspring listed laterally. There are descriptions of each generation, often very short narration, which include names and aliases of each ancestor, dates of birth and death, academic degrees, official ranks, location of graves; names, dates of birth and death of wife (wives) and location of graves; and the names of sons and daughters. This style is used for both the main lineage and the branches (van der Sprenkel, 1973: 14).

Other important information included in the tabulation is the existence of ancestral halls and graveyards. Ancestral halls were not built until the Ming epoch, where Emperor Ming Shizong, during the period of 1552–56, decreed that the people of the nation made regular sacrificial offerings to their ancestors (van der Sprenkel, 1973: 14), after which families of some social standing built them for the purpose. Often, there was also detailed information regarding the *fengshui* and sites of ancestral tombs. At times, wealthy families assigned portions of farmland to ancestors' tombs as ritual land, so that sacrifices could be held regularly and in style (van der Sprenkel, 1973: 15).

The academic degrees and official ranks of individual members were recorded in genealogies in great detail. This was important during the later regimes, for it provided the social background of family members who sought entry into the Mandarin bureaucracy. Often a candidate taking the imperial examination was expected to be from a family of good standing. In practice, once a person had launched himself in the Mandarinate, there would be great attempts to record his position and that of other members of his lineage, thus adding prestige to the lineage. It was a common practice for lineages to record the positions of *xiucai* (秀才), *juren* (举人) *and jinshi* (进士) attained by their scholarly members. On rare occasions, scholars of the lineage had been promoted as an official of the Hanlin Academy (翰林院) and this achievement would be elaborated in the genealogy (van der Sprenkel, 1973: 16).

Records of educational activities conducted by the clans and lineages are also found in the genealogy. As education was the most prized commodity and attaining the literati status a dream desired by all, clans and lineages organized classes, established schools and provided scholarship for bright young boys to pursue literary skills. During the Republican era, many ancestral halls were converted to schools for this purpose. There were also records on the teaching of Confucian moral values to the members (van der Sprenkel, 1973: 16).

Included in the genealogy was also information regarding the contribution, wealth and occupation of the members. Members who engaged in philanthropic and charity works or provided great services to the lineage or clan were listed for their contributions. Likewise, morally upright clan elders and leaders were also given special mention in the genealogy.

Literary works of family or clan members, of both poetry and prose, were also documented in the genealogy. Many genealogies also included a 'miscellaneous' section where additional information was offered. Included here were the mythological origin of the lineage and new skills and inventions by members (van der Sprenkel, 1973: 17).

Genealogy as a Resource Base

The types of information found in a genealogy provide clues to the social history of a specific family or lineage. Here, the longer the historical depth of the genealogy, the greater the amount of information. Some genealogies have a depth of over 300 or 400 years of documentation. If sufficient genealogies could be assembled and studied in their entirety, the wealth of information would allow for a macro-societal analysis of the social morphology of Chinese society. At a more generalized level, specific functions of the genealogies can be listed as follows.

Family and kinship patterns

One important source of information in the genealogical registers is the detailed records of births and death of all male members and their wives. This kind of information provides clues to kinship and marriage patterns of the family, lineage and clan as well as the demography of the wider society. At the individual level, genealogies tell us about the marriage links between or among families. Through examining members with different surnames who married in and out of the families, it is possible for us to ascertain the extent to which marriage served as an alliance system, upon which families asserted their social influence, raised their social status and consolidated their power base. It also provides us with clues to the extent of reciprocity between the families. The details of births and deaths allow for deduction concerning birth rates and fertility patterns, as well as life expectancies.

However, some scholars have argued that the information given in the genealogies fails to provide an accurate picture of the actual demography of the family or lineage. This is especially so for the early genealogical registers with selective entries. To begin with, the practice of not including the daughters in the genealogy provides a biased picture. However, this was rectified in later genealogies where not only daughters, but (at times) sons-in-law, were also mentioned. There was also the problem of infant mortality rates. Only those children that survived were recorded, which means that we could build a picture of the living but not the actual birth rate. This is compounded by the fact that those children who did not survive more than a few years were not included either. Likewise, genealogies do not provide accurate pictures of the sex ratio of infants. Female infanticide was widely practised, but there was no way of finding this out from the genealogies. Eberhard argued that the gross imbalance in the sex ratio (in favour of the male members) could be regarded as testimony to the practice of female infanticide. While plausible, this remains at best speculative (Eberhard, 1972: 33). It was also a common practice in

Chinese families and lineages to exclude those members who had committed serious crimes or had behaved immorally, further distorting the picture found in the genealogies.

The entry of birth and death dates of sons in the genealogy makes it possible to study the life expectancy of the Chinese males who had survived childhood. It is also possible to deduce the length of fertility of couples by comparing the dates of birth of children with those of their parents. Eberhard found that there was a progressive drop, over time, in the age of the parents with a first-born. Around AD 1200, parents were over 25 years of age when they had their first-born; by AD 1800, the age had dropped to 22. At the same time, life expectancy had also dropped progressively through the years, until the mid-nineteenth century. From this information, he concluded that there must have been a lowering of the marriage age, pointing to difficult living conditions and poor economic conditions. We may also calculate age differences between husbands and wives from the birth dates and horoscopes that were recorded. Under normal circumstances, the age of a husband was usually a few years more than that of his wife. If a wife's age was much greater than her husband's, it meant that the family was poor and had taken a girl into the house as future wife for the son. Such a girl, *tongyangxi* (童养媳), would provide free labour when the boy was still young (Eberhard, 1972: 31).

The economic might of certain families was also reflected in the marriage pattern. Only wealthy families could afford to have secondary wives and concubines. In the genealogy, there were usually records of the status of women, either as principal wife or as concubines, and of their respective offspring. These reflect the extent to which polygamy was closely linked to the economic wealth of the family. As a general rule, the principal wife usually bore more children than the concubines, who usually came from a lower social class. Sometimes, these children might enjoy similar status as the offspring of the principal wife. However, it was usually the first-born son of the principal wife who would be the successor, and it was he who would perform the last rites to the father upon his death. These families at times devised methods to differentiate between the offspring of the principal and secondary wives. One method was for the principal and subsequent wives to use different naming systems. It was a common practice to differentiate a generation from the next by having one common Chinese character (usually the middle character) in the name of all male members of the lineage of the same generation. It was also a common practice for the lineage to use a classical poem or a verse derived from a Confucian classical text for this naming purpose. This system is called 'ordering the generations', *paibeifen* (排辈份). In cases where children were born to both the principal wife and concubines, this second character might differ between the children of the principal wife and those of the concubines.

Thus, by looking at the name, it was possible to establish the identity of the children (Eberhard, 1972: 31–32).

A second wife could also be taken into the family upon the death of the first or when the first was divorced. As divorce was very rare in China, it was more frequent that a second wife, *tianfang* (填房), was taken as a substitute, after the death of the principal wife, to mend the household and take care of the children left behind by her.

Genealogies also inform us of the extent of adoption within the lineage. It was a common practice for families to adopt a brother's sons, particularly when the adopting brother had no son. Such an adoption would enable the adopted son to carry out the last rites. At times, 'ritual adoption' was conducted where the adopted son continued to share two sets of parents and lived with his biological parents but performed the last rites for the adopted parents. In most cases, adoption outside the family was frowned upon, but there were cases of this being practised (Eberhard, 1972: 32). The diverse methods of adoption allow us to estimate the fertility and infertility of couples, as well as to investigate changes within the family structure over time. This is possible through comparisons among existing genealogies and biographies of well-known individuals (Eberhard, 1972: 33).

Genealogies also inform us of the practice of uxorilocal marriage and residence. Often, wealthy families with only daughters would invite the sons-in-law into the family, whereupon the first-born son of the couple would usually take on the surname of the wife's family. The second and other sons would then resume the husband's surname. This often took place when the man was from a poor family (Eberhard, 1972: 32).

Another sociological significance of the genealogy is that it allows us to calculate the rate of upward mobility through the centuries. The elaborate details on members who succeeded in imperial examinations and received appointments in the bureaucracy often signify elevations in a family's social status and the beginning of its upward mobility, or its ability to maintain and upgrade its status through the centuries. It is estimated that during the earlier centuries, many families tried to get their eldest sons into the examination and obtain civil appointment. However, in later centuries, families tried to get the most able son into it, reflecting the progressive difficulties in passing the examination (Eberhard, 1972: 35).

Migration and establishment

The genealogies also show great details on movements of families and lineages, often detailing the migration of the first member of a family to a different region, either voluntarily or by coercion. Throughout Chinese history, it was not uncommon for criminals and those who fell foul of the administration and their families to be exiled to different regions. There were also veterans who were relocated by the government to newly opened lands in South China. Though there is no mention of criminal records, the genealogies nevertheless provide information on the social movements and inter-marriages between these families. Other persons migrated in search of greener pastures. This form of migration followed well-established routes, following the rivers and the lines of communication (Eberhard, 1972: 36).

The genealogies also show the diffusion process of the family structure. Once settled and having acquired some wealth, families began to acquire new lands. The original family often continued to reside in the same location, while their sons were sent out to manage new fields at a distance. Through time, new branches were set up, creating a 'family colony' (Eberhard, 1972: 36). The branch families continued to pay allegiance to the main family, which continued to be an important ritual and economic centre for the extended family. Important ritual events were held within the main family household. It provided economic assistance to those branches that needed aid; likewise, the branches sent money to the main family if they were able to. It was this form of social obligation and reciprocity that bound the main family and its branches together; and this also explains why the overseas Chinese have continued to be bound to their main families for generations (Eberhard, 1972: 36).

It was also not uncommon for government officials, sent to administer distant places, to acquire lands of the region under their administrations. At a later stage, these officials retired into the regions and assumed high status in the district. Often these families would separate from their main families and establish themselves as main families (Eberhard, 1972: 36).

At times, deviant sons, who did not follow in the scholarly footsteps expected of them, would leave the family. Some ended up as merchants and amassed great wealth. While some contributed gifts and money to the main family, others acquired property in distant lands, establishing permanent settlements and finally acquiring independent identities (Eberhard, 1972: 36). This was especially true of those who emigrated and settled in Southeast Asia.

Rewriting Genealogy and Its Contemporary Relevance

After the Communist victory in 1949, any kind of major lineage activity, including the compiling of genealogies, came to a complete halt. Indeed, many of the genealogies were destroyed during the Cultural Revolution. However, among the lineages of Fujian, attempts to conceal them have been successful.

It is only in recent years members are made aware of the existence of the lineage genealogies.

There is a resurgence of interest in genealogy among Singapore Chinese. Those who have continued to maintain strong ties with lineage members in their *qiaoxiang* are now busily engaged in the process of recompiling their genealogies (*xiupu*), as many elderly members feel an urgent need to make new entries before their generation dies out. To them, it is important that a new genealogy be compiled so that their descendants living in the overseas environment can be included, as the incorporation of overseas members will allow for lineage continuity. Thus, in rewriting genealogies, Chinese overseas seek to incorporate not only the members of the lineage in China, but also themselves.

The writing of genealogies, which can document the existence of individuals and their success, wealth and contributions, is important, because successful and ambitious individuals can reassert their identities and assert their dominance within the lineage. For Singapore Chinese, this is an assertion of power and wealth made possible as a result of their emigration to the Nanyang region during earlier years. Genealogy thereby helps to establish or re-establish a hierarchy of dominance and power amidst complex social relationships. Such a hierarchy of power is now based not so much on seniority and wisdom, as it would be according to Confucian tradition, but on wealth and *guanxi* with wealthy and politically powerful elite.

In a sense, genealogy serves as a cultural idiom, reinforcing the traditional social divide between insiders and outsiders. Now, however, the divide is deeper and wider. Those who have the wealth to perform philanthropic and charity works, who are politically prominent, or who are scholarly-oriented, are given prominence in the genealogy. In this regard, the genealogy reflects the present-day reality of the inversion of the traditional class order, where businessmen and entrepreneurs are given disproportionate attention. It also reflects on the predominance of Chinese overseas entrepreneurs and businessmen and their contributions to home villages, to their countries of domicile and to their communities. While blood ties remain an important criterion for one's inclusion in a genealogy, the actual boundary of the lineage becomes slightly negotiable in favour of those with wealth and status, as every lineage wants a share of members with wealth, knowledge, status and power. Thus, Chinese without a lineage can buy their way by becoming an adopted son of a lineage member because adopted sons are counted as part of the lineage structure. Biological or blood ties thus continue to be only one criterion for admission. This flexibility of the lineage boundary allows the Chinese overseas to gain significant inroads into the inner circles of lineage committees. The situation is not unlike during the nineteenth century when the Qing government, with a bankrupt coffer, sold imperial titles to Chinese overseas.

Genealogy serves as a symbolic representation of kinship relations, cutting out those who are at the margins. The social deviants, non-conformists and political radicals can, theoretically, become excluded. However, included in the genealogy will be those sons that are not recognized officially by the Communist regime (those families who failed to adhere to the one-child policy and thus did not report the birth of subsequent children to the authority). As such, those children have no official status or identity, but they are recorded in the genealogy, thereby providing us with much information on the demography and the success or failure of the centrally administered family planning policies.

Recompiling the Chinese genealogy—which incorporates both the Mainland and Chinese overseas as part of a single lineage—is, to a certain extent, an attempt by the Chinese to rewrite their history and cultural identity in a rapidly changing environment. This is particularly so for Chinese overseas who have found that their cultural identity has been increasingly subjected to challenges by forces of ethnic pluralism, corporatism and homogenization, as well as by those of modernity and social liberalism. To them, the only way to arrest this is by looking back to their source of origin and understanding their position within the wider lineage structure. Exploring the genealogy is one main way of identifying oneself and giving oneself a cultural identity.

Ke Lineage Genealogy: As a Cultural Connector

In our survey of Penglai, 95 per cent of the villagers had been aware of the genealogy and had felt that it was important for a lineage to have a record of its members. As mentioned above, they were also aware that the Ke lineage was recompiling a new genealogy. They had a favourable impression of the project, and those who were of the Ke lineage felt that all members should be included in it. Many villagers said that after the PRC was founded, and especially after the Cultural Revolution, they had been very uncertain as to whether the other branches of their lineage—i.e., those in Singapore, Taiwan, Malaysia, etc.—would continue to recognize their Anxi ancestors. They had also been under the impression that the younger Chinese overseas and some of the older ones as well had some unfavourable opinions of the Anxi villagers. They thought that these overseas members would want to break with their ancestral home. They were very surprised that the elderly members started visiting the ancestral village, especially after the 1978 reform, and that they brought the younger members with them. Thus they felt that the Singapore Chinese and those living overseas should be included in the genealogy.

One male village elder explained the enthusiasm of the Singapore Ke lineage members and the need to support *xiupu* in this way:

> *Xiupu* is very important. They [Singapore Chinese] are very enthusiastic about *xiupu* because they recognize their ancestors. These activities are being promoted by the overseas Chinese. It is therefore very important for them to be incorporated into the genealogy so that their achievements can be recorded and their future generations will know of their ancestral origins and of their ancestors. Such initiatives on the part of the Singapore members have allowed for continuity of generations and of the different member groups coming together. We should also understand that. During the earlier years, they took initiatives and went out because of economic difficulties. Now that they are successful and have taken initiatives to recompile the genealogy, we should support such a move and include them wholeheartedly. What they want is also what we want—to ensure that our lineage relationship is not broken.

In addition, said a 69-year-old village male, 'genealogy is important because it is good for the home village and would strengthen our traditional ties as it is the members that make up the lineage collective', and so 'we should send people out to search for all members and ask them to provide information on themselves and their families so that we can record them. They are our people, our children and grandchildren. Such a move is important because recompilation is only done every few decades. By having all members together, we would know our strength and hopefully each member would play a role in strengthening the lineage ties.'

Likewise, the older Singapore Ke lineage members saw the genealogy as a reminder of one's cultural roots, and felt such a reminder was especially important for the younger generations, as they were concerned to prevent an eventual loss of cultural roots and self-identity among the Singapore-born.

Most local Ke lineage members felt that the Singaporean lineage members' project to add new names to the genealogy was a good idea, and that the Chinese overseas, as lineage members, should be included in the genealogy. They felt that this would help present and future generations retain their connection to their ancestral village, and that this was a good thing.

Eighty-five per cent of the villagers surveyed viewed the position of the Singapore Chinese in a positive light with one arguing that 'since they have recognized that our [i.e., all Ke lineage members'] ancestors were from here, they [the Singaporeans] should be included'. Villager Gan stated that 'my cousins are Singapore-born and they should be included in the genealogy. It is important that they know Anxi because this is their ancestral home. They bear the same surname. It is therefore important for Chinese overseas to understand us so that they will be interested in us.' Eighty-two per cent of the villagers were of this view, as one villager Hor said,

> this [inclusion in the genealogy] will ensure that the contacts and relationship will continue. Otherwise, it would be broken. As relatives, we would not know one another if there was no contact and no record of them.

Other comments include: 'we share the same ancestors', 'they are from Anxi', and 'it is natural that they be included'. Anxi is a source of origin in so far as the villagers are concerned. Thus, 'this is their ancestral land even though the younger ones rarely visit here' and 'this is their *jiazu* and it is important for the young ones to recognize their ancestral home'. They further stated that 'because the roots and the source are located here, this is why the overseas Chinese come back to search for their roots and inquire about their ancestors'. Some pointed out that the genealogical records would help them validate their ancestral origins. Another reason given for the inclusion of Singapore Chinese in the genealogy was: 'so that they know that they are Anxi people and to help them deepen their sentiments towards their home village. As Chinese people, they and we should like our home village.'

Eighty-seven per cent of the surveyed villagers echoed a variety of views supporting genealogy recompilation such as:

> so that the young ones would know of Anxi as their ancestral land;

> The younger generations would be able to understand that they are descendants of Anxi. This is their origin.

> They are part of the lineage and they should remember their ancestral home and that they do not oppose the ancestors.

> This was important for future generations as they [the overseas lineage members] are the children and grandchildren of this place. They only went overseas to seek a livelihood. They should return to their roots [*luoye guigen*]. They are the leaves and we are the roots. So, it is natural that they be included.

> This [genealogy] is important to them when they want to search their roots and their relatives in future as it provides a written record for future generations.

It is thus important that

> ... they are all included.

> To be included is important so that we know who they are and if the younger generation did not recognize our ancestry, then they would become *fan*.

> The Chinese overseas need to know their roots; that is why rewriting the genealogy is so important.

> If the lineage is broken, then it is impossible for them to locate their ancestors.

> They are an offshoot from here and it is especially important for the younger generations to come back and get to know the village members. Otherwise, they would not know us. They should come back and understand their village.

To be included in the genealogy and be seen as lineage members was an important asset for the villagers, as membership brings along a certain amount of social obligation on the part of the Singapore members. Sixty-four per cent of the villagers in the survey argued that as lineage members, the Singapore Chinese should feel obligated to make important contributions to village reconstruction, and that these should be acknowledged in their genealogy. Village elder Gan said,

> They [Singapore relatives] should be included in the genealogy. They have contributed much to schools, their ancestral house and other public infrastructures. We should record their achievement and contribution in the genealogy. He [a Singapore kinsman] has always thought of home and contributed to all public projects—ancestral home, hospital, etc. He was also very enthusiastic to become a *fotou* and contributed to this.

He further stated,

> they played a significant role in the recompilation of the genealogy. After all, the cost of rewriting the genealogy comes from them (about RMB 70,000).

Another elder said,

> they are members of this lineage and village and have contributed millions to village development. By incorporating them into the

genealogy, it is a way of letting them know that Anxi is their ancestral home. Hopefully, once included, they will be aroused to become more interested in village affairs and their relationship with the village would be further enhanced.

According to 52 per cent of the villagers, genealogy records the lineage history. The following views were recorded:

> this is a record of our history and is meant for our future descendants. It is very important that the future generations know and recognize Anxi so that we will know one another.

> [Since] it is a historical tradition, its records need to be preserved. If there is no record, then, there will be no way that they or we could trace our roots, especially when we are separated and have no contacts.

> [Thus] inclusion is important because it is our roots and a record of our historical ancestors and families. [Here], genealogy records our lineage history. The younger ones should know Anxi so that the ties will not be broken. If they know their ancestors are from here, they can then find their ancestors.

> Members residing overseas should be included so that we know who our descendants are and know of their success in other countries.

> [Also] it is important to know of their contributions to the home village and their adopted country.

> [Genealogy should be seen as] a record of our contributions and achievements in both to our home village and the adopted countries.

Sixty-nine per cent of those surveyed felt that (as one said), it was important that lineage 'members, both the Singapore and village members, understand the generational and genealogical order among us' so that they could accord them the necessary respect befitting their elderly status. However, the village lineage members were aware that some of the Singapore Chinese did not wish to be included in the genealogy, and 93 per cent felt that this was not right, since these Singapore members would be depriving the lineage of a complete record of their descendants. Despite their dissatisfaction, however, there was little they could do but to accept this. They saw such Singapore members as uncivilized and babaized. A 79-year-old village female elder said,

> Some of them, especially the English-educated, do not want to be included in the genealogy because they do not consider themselves as part of the Anxi community.

Despite this, she felt the reluctant members should be included

> so that the future generations have a record of their roots, their ancestors and their home village, as this is not for their personal interests but for the whole lineage. Those who are English-educated have become *fan* and do not understand the significance of the genealogy. But it does not mean that they should be deliberately excluded.

A 26-year-old male villager Keong said,

> My aunt told me that her children had expressed disinterest in the village and did not want to be included in the genealogy. We told them that if they did not want to recognize the ancestors, if the future generations could not find their roots, they should not blame us for the exclusion.

Thus, despite the fact that the villagers regarded these people as having turned *fan*, they were apprehensive at their being excluded. A 63-year-old village man Han said,

> Though some who have been there for 40 years or more have turned *fan*, their descendants might want to search for their roots in the future. A record in the genealogy is important, for it allows my nephews and grandnephews to come back and search for their relatives.

With the perceived pressure, even though some Singaporeans might not want to be included, they eventually rescinded on their decision. In our survey, there were two families who initially chose not to have their names entered into the genealogy. One said,

> I do not think that it is necessary or important for us to be included in the genealogy except for the sake of knowing our roots and where our ancestors were from.

In this case, he finally submitted his name and those of his family members as he did not want to be blamed for leaving a gap in the family tree. A second man said: 'Inclusion in the genealogy depends on individuals. Most of us are more Westernized and are less concerned about it.' Nevertheless, they also submitted their names so as not to be blamed for an incomplete genealogical register.

Recompiling the Ke Lineage Genealogy

It was the Singapore Ke lineage elders who first mooted the idea of compiling and updating the genealogy when they visited their Xitou (溪头) (also called Kuitou, 魁头) ancestral village in 1989. In 1990 several Singapore Chinese, after a subsequent meeting with elders in Singapore, returned to the village to gather support and prepared to launch this project. In 1994, at the first meeting of the World Anxi Association, held in Anxi, the decision to recompile the Ke Lineage Genealogy was finalized. Upon returning to Singapore, a group of Ke elders voted to support the project. During the spring of 1995, a Singapore elder returned to Penglai and invited every Ke household to a meeting to discuss recompilation of the genealogy. During the meeting, it was agreed that a recompilation was necessary and that there would be two committees for the project: an executive committee of 11 Singapore elders in Singapore, and a managing committee of 7 village elders in Anxi. The managing committee would be divided into editorial, compilation, treasury and management sections. On the auspicious date of the eighth day of the second lunar month, 1995, the 'opening of lineage genealogy' ceremony (*kaipu yishi,* 开谱仪式) was held to inform the ancestors of the start of the recompilation of the genealogy. A chief compiler was appointed to enter new names and amend any mistakes and omissions found in the earlier versions. The recompilation was to be completed, and the new genealogy made available to all lineage members, by the third day of the tenth lunar month of 1996, when the 'closing of lineage genealogy' (*xiepu yishi,* 谢谱仪式) ceremony was planned. This was to be followed by the 'celebration of descendants' (*juanding yishi,* 涓丁仪式) ritual five days later.

The reason for compiling and updating the genealogy was simply that it had been over half a century since the last entry and a whole new generation of Chinese had to be included. This need to recompile the genealogy was made more urgent by the fact that the younger Singapore Ke lineage members had less emotional attachment to, and hence less concern for, their ancestral home, their genealogical roots, or recompiling the genealogy. However, for elderly Ke members, to inscribe the present generation in a recompiled genealogy was a moral responsibility so as to prevent a permanent break in the genealogical record during their generation.

There had been two to three generations since the last compilation. By bringing together the names of all members, the recompilation would allow lineage members to know the expansion of their members, including those overseas. A search for lineage members globally was then conducted as, while the majority of Ke emigrants went to Singapore and Malaysia, others went to Indonesia, Burma, Thailand or the Philippines, as well as to Western countries such as Australia and America. However, the immediate concern of elderly Ke lineage members was to allow their own children, grandchildren and great-grandchildren to know their own origin and source, and to prevent a permanent break in the genealogical record. They argued that their basic responsibility was not to allow such a break during their own generation. If the younger members had no interest in maintaining lineage continuity, it would be the problem of the younger generation and they would have to face the consequence of answering for the break to their descendants. The conscience of the elderly Ke members thus required that they do their part to ensure the genealogical continuity of their lineage, and so perform their filial duty to their ancestors and carry out their moral responsibility to their descendants.

An added factor in this urgency was the relatively relaxed political climate in Communist China and the amicable attitude of the Communist cadres towards cultural events and items. In the emigrant villages, official cadres not only supported the process of recompilation, but some became involved in it. To them too, it was important for all members to 'recognize the ancestors', *renzu* (认祖), and particularly the babaized Singapore Chinese. They felt that by supporting the compilation of the genealogy, they were indirectly encouraging and fostering goodwill and winning the trust of the Chinese overseas, and hoped that this would encourage the Singapore Chinese to become culturally involved in village activities and contribute to village reconstruction and development. Many cadres too, therefore, had felt that the time had come to embark on recompiling the genealogy.

Who Should be Included?

The main consideration during the recompilation was who to include, as the inclusion and exclusion of members in a genealogy requires a difficult and delicate decision-making process. Ideally, all members should and would be incorporated. However, it turned out that not all members wanted to be included; and there were others who wanted to be included but were refused entry, as they were not considered part of the lineage. Discussion concerning the entry of new members was thus a lengthy process.

The target was inclusion of all living members of the Ke lineage of Anxi ancestry scattered throughout the world. About one-third of the members continued to live in Anxi, although a small number lived in other areas in China. Although some two-thirds lived abroad, with a majority of emigrants having gone to Singapore or Malaysia, others lived in Taiwan, Indonesia, Burma, Thailand, the Philippines, Australia and America. A search for lineage members globally was conducted. Many of those in the United States and Australia had gone there from Southeast Asia for their studies in the 1970s and then stayed on after their education. Who were these people and how could they be included in the genealogy? What was the possibility of total inclusion? Would the genealogical update be incomplete?

Inclusive strategy

In the emigrant villages, 95 per cent of lineage members were eager and excited over the recompilation of the genealogy and expected to be included. The territorial confines of the villages and the relatively low mobility of the members—especially important for locating sons who had not been recorded as part of the household system as a result of the one-child policy[1]—enabled a complete list of the members to be drawn up with relative ease. Such sons were important, as they would eventually assume the headship of households and continue their family lines. The genealogy thus would provide further generations of these families with a legitimate means of recording and proving their membership in the lineage.

However, including every member who had moved overseas proved to be a more difficult task than anticipated. There were three recognizable categories of overseas members. First, there were those who had, through the years, maintained some kind of contact with the home village or with other kin known to the lineage in their adopted countries. They were thus already part of the lineage network, and there was no difficulty in contacting them and including them and their families in the genealogy. Many of these were members of the Ke Surname Association in Singapore, Malaysia or other parts of Southeast Asia. Fortunately, this category formed the majority.

The second category were those who had not maintained any contact and were not known to other kin, either inside or outside the ancestral village. There was no way of contacting them, and so they could not be included in the genealogy.

A third category of lineage members consisted of those who were known to their kin inside and outside their ancestral village but had chosen not to acknowledge their status within the lineage and did not wish to be included in the genealogy. There were only a handful of them. Lineage elders told me that these persons had openly refused the invitation of the committee to be included in the genealogy, and no longer had any contact or desire for contact with their ancestral home villages as they no longer considered themselves as part of the Kuitou community and did not want to have their names and those of their children written into the genealogy. The committee members told me that if such persons insisted on having their names omitted, then they would be. However, the committee would explain to them that their family tree would thus stop with their immediate forebears and that once the compilation was completed, no addition could be made. This was to prevent any conflicts that might arise as a result of non-entry. In fact, often, after such explanation, such persons then agreed to be entered, even though they had only nominal interest in the lineage and its activities, because they desired not to break the family tree. Some Singapore Ke members told me that while they might not be very active or keen in lineage activities, they would certainly put the names of their ancestors and families in the genealogy, and that it was important for the younger generations to know their ancestral origins. By the time of genealogical compilation, there were only two families who had refused to have their names entered into the genealogy.

Existing Genealogies

The first genealogical compilation of *Kuitou Keshi zupu* (魁头柯氏族谱)—the Ke Lineage of Xitou (Kuitou)—was completed in the spring of 1541 (211 years after the first arrival of Wanshangong, 万山公). He was widely recognized as the first ancestor of the Ke lineage travelled from Quanzhou (泉州) and resided in the village of Kuitou in Penglai in 1330. Today, a tomb within the village is maintained in honour of him. The first genealogy detailed the arrival of Wanshangong and his descendants marking the start of the first generation of the Ke lineage; their permanent settlement in Kuitou; their pioneering efforts in opening up the land for agricultural and other purposes; and the expansion of the membership of the Ke lineage. The entry of the first genealogy was recorded by Muxuangong (木竿公) of the sixth generation. Update of names was made to this genealogy by Fengchungong (逢春公) of the eighth generation in 1541.

A second major genealogical recompilation was done by Guangshenggong (光胜公) of the twelfth generation in 1717 and this version has undergone seven times of updating names and for each entry, the genealogy elaborated on special events and achievements of its members. The third update was done in 1755 by Yuanliao (元僚) of the twelfth generation; the fourth update in 1835 by a team from the fifteenth generation led by Jiuzhong (鸠众); fifth update was done in 1877 while the sixth update was done in 1907 and the seventh was in 1948.

The third major genealogical recompilation which comprises of two volumes was done in 1995 and completed in 1996. During this compilation, women of significance and achievements were annotated in the leaves section (Volume 2) of the genealogy, signalling a departure from the earlier versions where only achievements of male descendants were annotated.

However, in 1995 the lineage had in its possession only three earlier compilations: the genealogies of 1835–77, 1877–1907 and 1907–48 (two earlier versions had been lost during the early part of the twentieth century and two had been destroyed during the Cultural Revolution). These three versions had been kept in the possession of the lineage elders in their ancestral house and were consulted when the 1995 recompilation of the genealogy was in process.

Procedures for Genealogical Recompilation

When the lineage decided to recompile its genealogy, they engaged one main *xiupu* master, a retired teacher with the requisite experience, and two lineage elders as assistants, to enter names and to look at inconsistent entries and omissions. The retired teacher was good in Chinese calligraphy—an important attribute, since he would be the person who actually wrote in the entries. The two lineage elders helped to verify and authenticate the existing names of lineage members and family branches, make decisions, and weed out inconsistencies found in the various versions. The three of them consulted the Liu lineage genealogy. The Liu of Anxi County had recently been recompiled. Lineage elders decided to use the existing formal name of Kuitou Keshi Genealogy for the new version.

Genealogical content

The new version of the genealogy consists of two volumes. The first contains the primary stems and branches (*zhi*, 枝). Kinship links are traced from original ancestors downwards, showing the progression from the first generation through the most recent (29th) generation. In the chronological progression of unilineal Chinese patrilineal family trees, the individual branches spread wider and wider, encompassing all male members. The Ouyang style is used in this genealogy, with those of the same generation linked by a black horizontal line and those of different generations linked with red lines. The genealogy shows only male descendants and their wives; daughters are not shown, unlike some other genealogical styles. When asked about this omission of daughters, the elders told me that this was a tradition. There had been no record of female members in previous versions of the genealogy, so they found it inappropriate to add the females in the first volume of this one, pointing out that daughters were recorded in the second volume. Through the stems and branches, all male members are able to trace their ancestral origins from their generation back to the first ancestor, Wanshangong.

Along with the stems and branches in Volume 1 are annotations indicating the birth order of sons, the dates of the deceased and those who were adopted. There are numerous cases of a son having been adopted by a newly married couple who subsequently had several biological sons. In such a case the adopted son, being the eldest, would assume the role of first-born and, upon the death of the father, would become the head of the household. Adopted sons, in Chinese society, are legitimate sons of the family with the rights and power of biological sons, and are also expected to perform duties upon the death of their foster parents.

Volume 2 consists of annotations and descriptions of each family and generation member (ye, 叶), including the females. This new type of entry was insisted upon by the Singapore Ke, who felt that daughters were an important part of the family.

A large part of Volume 2 is devoted to describing the achievements and contributions of lineage members. Those who had attained wealth or scholarly achievements, started successful businesses, or acquired technical skills, are described in this volume. Also included are members who held public office or contributed to home village development or development in their adopted countries. A substantial portion of these descriptions concern the contributions of overseas members, especially those from Singapore, both to their home village and to the countries in which they live. Details are given of Singapore members concerning when they left Penglai, their village backgrounds, their family members in Singapore, the types of occupations they engaged in, their business enterprises, and their contributions to village infrastructure and to the development of Singapore. Many had contributed to the building of village schools, bridges, roads, hospitals, ancestral houses, residential buildings, the power plants in Penglai, village cottage factories, tea-processing plants and other economic institutions.

In this second volume, the entries and achievements of daughters become significant. Daughters were traditionally not considered part of the lineage structure, but temporary members who, after marriage, belonged to their husbands' families. The change of surname, and sometimes given name, was thus more than symbolic—it ushered in a new phase in the life of women, as daughters-in-law, wives and mothers in their husbands' families. However, the status of daughters had changed considerably, especially for the Singapore members, who viewed women and daughters in quite a different light from that of their village counterparts. To start with, urbanization, education and the strict family planning policy of the Singapore government in the 1960s and 1970s led to many families with two or fewer children. Even after the policy of encouraging more children was been implemented in the 1990s, many women continued to choose to have two or fewer children. Correspondingly, there was a change in the attitude of the parents towards their children; both sons and daughters tend to have more or less equal treatment, especially in terms of education. Likewise, in China, the one-child policy has also led to a greater recognition of the role of daughters in the family and many now have opportunities to receive higher education and some are successful in the Mainland China. In the villages, there continues to be a desire to have at least one male heir although this attitude is also gradually changing.

A second factor is the fact that, as women in Singapore and elsewhere had become better educated and economically independent, with some having attained high positions, their voices could not be excluded. Their very success made them visible. They were thus not only daughters-in-law, wives and mothers in their husbands' families, but also daughters of their agnatic families, with independent status not linked to affinal identity. Such a change in attitude towards the female members of the family had implications for the treatment and attitudes towards women in general. Thus it was to the advantage of Ke lineage members in Singapore and Penglai to have daughters included in the genealogy, as many had attained high status and made achievements in society which added prestige to their immediate families and brought glory to the lineage. The genealogy shows a disproportionately large number of daughters of the Singapore lineage who had high levels of education, many with university degrees, in contrast to a modest number of sons with higher education, whereas the majority of daughters in the Anxi branch had received no more than ten years of education, with a large number having received only nominal education or none at all.

In Singapore, many first-generation migrant parents had chosen to introduce their sons into family businesses at a young age, reflecting traditional attitudes that sons were expected to help out and succeed their fathers. Daughters, on the other hand, were not burdened with such expectations, and so had the freedom to pursue education without being pressured to stop in order to help out with the family business. This was the attitude of Ke lineage members in the 40–50 age group. However, those in the 20–30 age group had a great desire for both sons and daughters to complete university education, which had become easy to access in Singapore. An increasing number of younger Singapore lineage members were receiving education in Western countries, and this ability to send children to Western universities reflected the growing wealth, affluence and importance placed on such education.

Incorporating daughters into the genealogy was a subject of negotiation between the Singapore and Anxi members. The Singapore members felt that, because daughters as well as sons were offspring, they should not be left out of the lineage system. Because of the power of the Chinese overseas and the wealth that they had contributed to the village economy, and because they were wholly funding the updating of the genealogy, they were able to get daughters added to the second volume. However, they would have upset the whole community if they had insisted on the incorporation of the daughters into Volume 1.

Costs

Compiling a genealogy is an expensive project. The cost of compiling the genealogy was estimated to amount to RMB 700,000. This included the cost of hiring the *xiupu* master and his two assistants for a year, printing costs, and the cost of the ritual ceremonies that marked the opening and completion of the genealogy. As mentioned, funding came primarily from the Singapore members. Four of the eleven initiators of the project contributed S$10,000 each, or a total of about RMB 200,000. The other seven contributed S$1,000–5,000 each. The Singapore committee in charge of the genealogy project agreed among themselves to charge each well-to-do Singapore member S$1,000 for entering all his family's names. They would then be given a set of the new edition of the genealogy when it was completed. Those who were not well-to-do could contribute whatever sum they could afford. The Anxi villagers would have their names included without paying. Those who wanted neither to contribute nor to have their names included had to make known their objections. According to one Singapore elder, 'there are very few who do not want to be included. Almost all want to have the names of their families recorded in the genealogy. When we tell them of this project and of the need to contribute, they sign a cheque and come forward with a list of names of their family members.'

A breakdown of the costs includes the following. The *xiupu* master was paid RMB 3,000 per month plus food and housing, as he was not a Ke lineage member and did not live in Penglai and his assistant was paid one-third of the *xiupu* master. The cost of production, including employing a company to input the two-volume genealogy into computer files, was RMB 150,000, and the printing of 200 sets cost RMB 100,000. The rest of the money collected was used for the 'closing of the genealogy' ceremony, which came up to over RMB 400,000, while the simple opening ceremony cost only a few thousand dollars.

The Compilation Work

The entire project took about three years. The conception of the project and the format of the genealogy have been discussed above.

Collection of the names of members in each household was done systematically by committee members. The Anxi elders were responsible for informing all households in Anxi of the project. Each household head was asked to submit a list of all living members of all generations, including married and unmarried daughters, as well as their achievements and contributions to their present homes and to the ancestral home. Some members who had significant achievements and/or who were successful were asked to provide additional information.

The elders of Xitou (Kuitou) precinct compiled the information for those who were illiterate by distilling data from their birth documents and oral information. In Singapore the same method was employed, except that local elders there also asked for contributions.

Filling gaps and adding names

To start with, there was a need to ensure that there was a continuity of the names belonging to the various stems and branches of earlier generations. This was done by comparing the three versions of the genealogy available. Missing names and gaps in the earlier generations were filled after consultations among the committee members to ensure accuracy. Amendments were made when names were added to earlier generations, and information on the status of sons (such as whether they were eldest, youngest, adopted, etc.) was added if it had been omitted in the earlier versions. Through cross-referencing, the compilers were able to fill some of the gaps in earlier generations.

Going through the various versions was a tedious exercise. The compilers read each version several times and made notes, comparing places where inconsistencies and gaps occurred, searching for reasons for omissions and establishing reasons for reincorporation. They had to interpret information provided in the genealogy, ascertain its accuracy, and then add, subtract or amend it. They made notes on the page wherever this was done.

In filling the gaps and amending the wrong entries, the three versions were cross-referenced and checked. The newest of the three versions was copied in its entirety, and any omission that could be remedied would be added on to this copy. The corrections and amendments were written in with a writing brush in the same calligraphic style but with annotation, so that future genealogists would know that amendments and additions had been made. After cross-checking the new data, it was entered formally with a Chinese brush. After this was completed, the new generations of names were then written in for a full entry of names in the new genealogy. Two copies of this genealogy would be handwritten, making a total of three handwritten genealogies. They were all bound in the traditional style. One copy was sent to the typesetting company to be printed in a modern form, while the other two were kept in the original form for future reference.

Entry of new names

When the names of all members of the households had been collected, the three-member team collated and assembled them according to the stems and branches to which each belonged. The next step would be to trace the immediate ancestor/line of descent for each household. Having traced the name of the ancestor, the names of the present members were then added to each household. The search for the right tree and branch was an enormous task. Once the right tree was found, the names of the recent descendants were added; the trees were then linked together by the branches. After all had been carefully laid out and checked for accuracy, the names were entered into the genealogical register.

Inclusion of daughters

Although the names of daughters were entered into the annotations volume—the so-called 'leaves' volume—they were left out of the tree-and-stem section. I was told that if they had been included in the latter section, the Chinese patrilineal structure would have been undermined. It was also felt that it would have created too great an inconsistency to begin the entry of daughters from the present generations onward, as traditionally this had not been done, and the compilers did not want to change the whole format of the genealogy.

Much negotiation and insistence on the part of the Singapore Chinese Ke lineage members was necessary before the Singapore elders were willing to depart from tradition and include the names of daughters. This insistence had to do with the fact that many of the Singapore Ke lineage women were highly educated, held high positions and contributed much to family prestige and status. It was also because urbanization and family planning policies in Singapore had resulted in smaller family sizes, some families did not have sons. While, among present-day Singapore Chinese, having a son to carry on the family name continues to be an important consideration, daughters are now seen as important members of the family as well, although they do not continue the family name. The filial-ness of daughters and their willingness to care for elderly parents are considered important qualities in contemporary Singapore society, and the shrinking family size has made both sons and daughters important. A village elder asked rhetorically, 'Who would not like to include a millionaire CEO daughter, a daughter who is a politician or one with a PhD in the genealogy? For they add much prestige, "face" and glory to the family and lineage.'

An elder in Anxi, who was also a cadre, told me that it was good to have daughters like myself to help change the way the villagers looked at their own daughters, and that it helped him to feel more comfortable, as he had only one daughter and no son and would not feel so guilty for not having a son to carry on the family name or to carry the incense stick upon his death.

Final product: The Kuitou Keshi Zupu

Having completed the entries, the committee decided that a total of 200 copies would be printed and distributed to all those who had contributed financially to the project. It was also decided that the genealogy would be typeset into a computer database for easy retrieval, amendment and future addition, although the committee would retain the handwritten copy as the original version of the genealogy.

Genealogy: Cosmic Rite of Renewal

The recompilation and updating of a genealogy is a dignified and solemn ritual process, as the genealogy is seen as a sacred book. Both before and after the compilation, elaborate rituals are conducted in order to call upon the local gods and deities to witness the recompilation and completion. At the start, there is the ritual pertaining to the opening of the genealogy (*kaipu yishi*). When the genealogy is completed, there is the thanking ritual (*xiepu yishi*) and the closing ritual (*guanpu yishi*).

Opening the genealogy (*kaipu yishi*)

The Singapore and local elders consulted the almanac and sought the advice of monks in selecting the most auspicious date for the 'opening of the genealogy'. A separate altar within the ancestral house was created for the King of the Netherworld, Dashiye (大士爷), who is the overseer of the founding ancestors' soul. In *kaipu yishi*, the monks performed a ritual ceremony to invite Dashiye and the ancestors as witnesses to the recompilation of the genealogy. Offerings of incense, paper money and food were made, the three existing compilations of the genealogy were brought forward, and the genealogy master was introduced to the ancestors. After the ritual, the genealogy master started the task of recompiling the genealogy.

This was a relatively simple ritual and involved few people. Its main function was to invite the ancestors, overseen by Dashiye, to witness that only members of the lineage were being entered into the genealogy.

Thanking ritual (xiepu yishi) and closing ritual (guanpu yishi)

After the new names and annotations had been entered, the *pu* was considered to have been completed. An auspicious date had been chosen one year ahead for the thanking and closing rituals, which were held together, and in conjunction with the 'rite of gratitude for the flow of descendants'. The two rituals took three of the total of five days for the combined events.

The combined thanking and closing ritual celebrations involved a procession in which the new genealogy was carried from Zhouyue Miao to the ancestral house, where the thirteen local gods and deities had been invited to witness the closing ritual ceremony. After various necessary ritual acts, the *pu* was placed in a box and padlocked, the monks then sealing the lock with a religious amulet. The wooden box is now kept in the ancestral house and is not to be opened until the next recompilation.

In this ritual, the thirteen gods and deities, all past ancestors and members of the lineage present were called upon to witness the completion of the new version of the genealogy. This was a time of cosmic renewal, when past ancestors and living lineage members were brought together to celebrate the birth and continuation of the lineage. The ancestors were not only present as witnesses to the growth and achievement of their lineage, their early sacrifices, achievements and contributions were also highlighted to firmly entrench their roles in everyone's mind. Members alluded, in Confucian ritual fashion, to the original source and birth of the lineage.

The celebration was a time for the renewal of kinship ties among members and a celebration of the coming together of the different branches of the Ke lineage. As mentioned earlier, in addition to Singapore Anxi Chinese, those from Malaysia, Indonesia, and the Philippines also attended this event. Over a hundred members from the overseas communities attended the celebration, about two-thirds of whom were elderly or middle-aged; young adults and children made up only one-third, but the celebration made a great impact on them because, apart from its grandeur, this was the first time many of them had come into contact with their ancestral village and village kin. These visitors were generally impressed with both the organization and the generally friendly atmosphere of the festival, and many said they were prepared to return for subsequent visits. The village elders provided the new visitors with some insights into village life and took the younger Singapore and Malaysian members around the village, explaining to them the religious rites, showing them the farms and explaining to them what farming life was all about. They thereby hoped to arouse the interest of the younger Ke in their ancestral village. The celebration kindled interests among the younger generations.

Conclusion

The genealogy serves to inform Singapore and Anxi lineage members of their common social history and to record the existence of the immediate family and its membership in the Singapore branch of a wider lineage structure. It is a record of their ancestral roots and allows them to search for their cultural and social history. It also allows the Singapore Chinese to come to grips with their emigration background, to resolve their tensions with their village kin, and to mark their ethnicity and their cultural identity within the wider Singapore polity. They thereby become part of the wider lineage structure, with continuity to village China, from which they derive aspects of their cultural understanding and practices. The Anxi village is seen as an ancestral home, to which they have kinship ties, although their orientation and national identity remain firmly with Singapore.

9
Chinese Lineage as a Cultural Network: A Model

When the Singapore members of the Ke lineage visit their ancestral home in search of ancestral and cultural 'roots', they inevitably feel a renewed sense of lineage identity. They are forced, whether they like it or not, to acknowledge the existence of the other branches of the lineage.

This is even the case for the generations of Singapore-born Ke lineage members as the various degrees of kinship relations unfold before their eyes. They are asked to acknowledge the extended kinship and lineage circle. Some of the youngest generation may be surprised by the details of their relationships, while others, perhaps older, may have understood more prior to their visit. However, coming to grips with their kinship and lineage structures are emotional affairs for many, and while some are delighted to do so, many resist.

At any rate, the Singapore lineage members inevitably establish a web of social relationships that links them into new, or revived, socio-cultural and socio-economic networks. These networks enable a moral economy to become operationalized, thereby enabling the Ke lineage members in their ancestral village to tap into moral and social capital according to new meanings given to the lineage structure. The operation of this moral economy can be understood as an attempt by the Singapore Chinese to recompense for their inattention to their ancestral homes and villages, and to allay their guilt over their failure to discharge social and economic duties to their immediate kin and to the lineage in general. On the other hand, the ability of the village kin to extract social capital out of their Singapore counterparts demonstrates the intricate nature of the production of social capital.

Why does the lineage structure continue to be of primary significance among the Ke lineage in Singapore? To what extent is this an aberration within the wider Chinese community? How does the lineage structure operate in contemporary Chinese societies? Has the way it operates changed according to contemporary situations? How do various groups of Chinese of the same ancestry, but separated by history and geography, perceive the lineage structure? How do they attempt to reintegrate themselves into a common ancestral lineage structure? How can we best conceptualize the modern lineage structure as a social institution or as a system of networks? What is its structure and membership composition, and what are the roles and linkages among its members?

This chapter argues that the contemporary operation of the Ke Lineage is not an aberration but is similar to that of other lineages in Singapore and Southeast Asia, where there continue to be strong ties with ancestral villages. However, this operation requires a reconceptualization of the Chinese lineage as a cultural network in contemporary society.

Lineage Formation

The term 'lineage' has been interpreted by various scholars in their attempts to understand wider kinship organization. The social anthropologists Evans-Pritchard and Fortes (1970) focused much of their scholarly work on understanding lineage as an important form of social organization, basing their understandings on studies of African tribal societies. Other studies followed. Maurice Freedman was the first anthropologist to focus on the study of Chinese lineage structure in two Southeastern Chinese provinces, Fujian and Guangdong. Freedman saw land as the most important element motivating the formation of single-lineage villages. 'The centrality of the ownership of land is so important that where there is enough land, a nucleus of agnates strive to build themselves up to form a large homogeneous settlement. If to begin with they must share a territory with members of one or more lineages, they will await their opportunity to dominate and eventually drive out their neighbours. Land, which constitutes the most important material focus of any agnatically constituted group, determines the status of a lineage within a village vis-à-vis lineages in other villages' (Freedman, 1966: 8). Thus the powerful and wealthy lineages were those that occupied the most fertile stretches of land (Freedman, 1966: 12). Freedman further argued that what constituted a lineage was the corporate group of agnates living in one settlement, or in a tight cluster of settlements. He termed this a 'localized lineage' (Freeman 1966: 20). The grouping of a localized lineage with other local lineages was often based on an agnatically defined common ancestor. The central focus of this whole unit was the ancestral hall or another piece of property (Freeman 1966: 21).

The connection between the status of individuals within a lineage and the enlargement of the lineage was also directly connected to the possession of landed property, particularly, of ritual land. Freedman pointed out the great desire among Chinese who accumulated substantial wealth to purchase ritual land and construct ancestral halls. Possession of such landed property was used to differentiate between groups within a lineage and created status and class differentiation, as well as corresponding differences in power distribution within and among the various groups. It was wealth in the form of land that allowed a segment or segments of a lineage to construct an ancestral hall, thereby establishing its identity separately from the rest, resulting eventually in the formation of sub-lineages, often of an asymmetrical kind.

J. L. Watson extended Freedman's definition of lineage to include other features. He wrote that a lineage was a corporation, in the sense that members derived benefits from jointly owned property and shared resources, and joined in corporate activities on a regular basis. They were highly conscious of themselves as a group in relation to others, whom they defined as outsiders. A lineage 'is not a loosely defined collection of individuals' (Watson, 1986: 5), but a corporate group that celebrates ritual unity and is based on demonstrated descent from a common ancestor (Watson, 1982: 594).

Watson saw lineage as comprising three main phenomena, namely: (1) descent through patrilines from a common ancestor; (2) ritual activities through which membership was collectively expressed; and (3) the incorporation of membership through the joint possession of property, usually land. Like Freedman, Watson saw the localized lineage as consisting of members living in a well-defined area—usually a village or a set of neighbouring communities—which had a high degree of interaction among local members (Watson, 1986: 5–6). Several patrilineally-related localized lineages might combine to form a higher-order lineage, which would usually be well endowed with resources, including ancestral halls and other properties located in the market town or county. Members of the higher-order lineage usually conducted regular ritual activities that served to bind them together in a closely knitted fashion (Watson, 1986: 6).

Faure, however, sees lineage as corresponding to the patrilineally-organized *zu* or *fang* (Faure, 1989: 5). The formation of a lineage is closely linked to access to resources by a group of people and their ability to produce a legitimate claim to such resources. 'The right to exploit natural resources within what villagers consider to be their communal territories is so consciously recognised that it may be said the possession of them has demarcated villagers from outsiders. These rights include the right to build houses in or near the village, to gather fuel on hillsides, and to open for cultivation land that had not been privately claimed' (Faure, 1989: 6). To

Faure, the formation and perpetuation of the lineage is a consequence of a broad agreement on ancestry and lineage history. The ability of members to articulate their genealogical links with their ancestors and with their fellow members is a basic criterion for acceptance as members in the village, in territorial alliances and in ancestor worship (Faure, 1989: 6). Cultural and religious activities (such as religious sacrifices), together with welfare facilities, are organized in the territorial boundary of the group and are meant for the benefits of its members only.

In recent years, social historians have joined in the study of Chinese lineage from the Song Dynasty onwards. Historically, they have argued, most kinship groups formed during the imperial eras did not conform to the definition postulated by Freedman (Ebrey and Watson, 1986). Rawski argues that while land played an important role in enhancing the prestige of individuals, estates did not play a determining role in promoting kinship solidarity or dependence.

At any rate, most studies agree that a lineage is formed when a group of people demonstrate to themselves and others that they are of the same descent line. Descent serves as the core of all descent groups. Although descent points to biological links, the primary concern here is demonstrated descent, a social construction (Watson, 1982: 594). In traditional Chinese society, the standard device for demonstrating descent was the written genealogy. However, among the peasantry, where illiteracy prevailed, it was the oral recollection of the genealogical links that proved to be the most important source of information for the group concerned. While the written genealogy at times was used to stimulate the *formation* of a lineage, at other times it signalled the *completion* of lineage formation.

Hymes sees the formation of a local lineage as a kind of localist strategy 'for the elite-gentry class where a member of the elite is seen carving out from the local population an agnatic pool of potential allies and clients' (Hymes, 1986: 122). Genealogy writing is thus 'a strategic act' by which members of the local elite seek to strengthen their position in local society. At times, it is an important method for positioning the local elite for their social interaction with the regional elite.

Hazelton (1986) points out that the existence of written genealogical records among the local elite is a step forward in further entrenching their power and creating a stable socio-political order at a localized level. The result is a kind of patron-client relationship between the elite-gentry and the rest of the lineage members. Despite this social differentiation, or perhaps because of it, Hazelton argues that, an environment conducive to social interaction is created among lineage members.

As the common descent groups develop and are stabilized by their genealogical records, it becomes possible for a dominant lineage to incorporate segments of lineages with the same surname into its fold, thereby extending its territorial claim. The terms 'higher-order lineage' and 'lower order lineage' can be used to distinguish those with power from subservient groups. Dominant lineages can thus project their elitist images and further consolidate their positions through a series of political alliances with members of the local elite. In so doing, they create a large network of kinship relations (Hazelton, 1986: 137–169).

An important aspect of the lineage is the role of ritual. In an article written by Ebrey about kinship life during the pre-Song and Song epochs, rituals, especially the worship of ancestors at graveside, constitute a key organizational element. Writing from a functionalist viewpoint, Ebrey sees the various ritual elements as important prerequisites for the establishment of various interaction patterns among groups of agnates. Such ritual elements reinforce and strengthen the kinship solidarity and group consciousness that will ultimately lead to the formation of a lineage (Ebrey and Watson, 1986: 16–61). Watson, on the other hand, argues that such a view neglects other aspects of social organization.

Brook argues that kinship and ritual systems have exercised considerable influence on the structures of many pre-capitalist societies (Brook, 1988: 75). Kinship has, under certain circumstances throughout history, assumed an important role in structuring relations of production and especially in fostering specific forms of domination. To ignore non-economic factors such as kinship organization and political overlordship is to ignore their profound influence on the structure of society (Brook, 1988: 75).

An important feature of lineage is the role of the elite-gentry class in shaping the communal social life of peasants. Fei Hsiao-tung, in his various works, has illustrated this point (Fei, 1939, 1953). Likewise, Hazelton treats the elite as engaging in a localist strategy that pursues a mission to translate 'transitory achievements of individual degree winners and office-holders into an enduring elevation of the status of their line and segment' (Hazelton, 1986: 149). What intensifies agnatic interaction from the level of casual groupings to that of organized lineages is the elite—even at its highest bureaucratic levels—in their promotion, celebration, and, in some sense, creation of such structures (Hazelton, 1986: 131). By the Qing era, the lineage and the panoply of rituals attached to it were seen as part and parcel of the gentry's strategy for success. Those with gentry as their leaders were able to compete better than those without.

In assessing Freedman's paradigm, Ebrey and Watson suggest that the word 'lineage' be avoided when dealing with agnatic groups that do not fulfil all elements of the definition, especially the joint ownership of property. Anything less than a full lineage is a 'descent group'—that is, a group (in contrast to a loose collection of agnates) whose members are aware of their kinship connections, but whose corporate behaviour may be limited to activities such as ancestral rites or the compilation of genealogies. A descent group becomes a lineage when 'it provides material benefits for members'. They argue that this distinction shapes the individuals' outlook on their membership within the lineage and influences how the social relationship within the lineage as well as the interaction of the lineage with others in the wider society (Ebrey and Watson, 1986: 5). Brook rejects both Freedman's and Watson's definitions. He argues that leading members of a lineage seek to build reliable networks of ties of dominance and dependence that place their own patrilines in advantageous positions. Corporate property is used to achieve such ends. The institutions do not create the lineages. Rather, they serve to formalize and extend kinship ties that create the lineages. It is for this reason that Brook argues that the concept of lineage may be better analyzed in terms of networks than institutions. He argues that lineages should be perceived as structured networks of agnatic kinship ties, and that institutional arrangements that mature out of what Hymes calls the 'lineage orientation' are in secondary position to, though powerfully supportive of, the primary function of the lineage, which is to tie individuals and families together systematically within the structure of local society. The lineage thus provides them with an organizational context within which to mobilize potential ties with lesser agnates in order to gain, consolidate and perpetuate the lineage's elite status and to maintain advantageous relationship vis-à-vis outsiders. In this way the lineage produces a ready-made set of accessible clients, identifying patrons and allies and placing them in a hierarchy of power. As to its possession of corporate property, this is highly dependent on the socio-economy of the wider region (Brook, 1988: 78). In Brook's view, a lineage can exist when a group of agnates—or, more particularly, certain families within a group of agnates—are conscious of their ties to each other and create institutional formats to reinforce the consciousness and maintain the visibility of those ties.

Chinese Lineage: A Cultural Network Model

The views offered above help us to understand the socio-economic base for the formation of lineage in early Chinese society. They identify various factors that are instrumental in the consolidation and expansion of a lineage structure, the inter-relationships among various lineages, and the interactions among their members. Lineage, for all these scholars, is an important social institution of traditional Chinese society.

However, how should Chinese lineage be viewed in contemporary situations? What is its present structure? What are its contemporary roles and functions? To what extent is Chinese lineage an integrative force in the perpetuation of Chinese culture? How can we reconceptualize the lineage in light of its changing environment and the players involved? We will explore the changing nature of Chinese lineages at two levels: first, Chinese lineage as a chain of cultural networks; second, at the macro-level, Chinese lineage as part of the global socio-economic *guanxi* networks in the restructuring of *qiaoxiang*.

Subcultures and Microcultures

Culture is subject to varying interpretations. In the *Mirror of Man*, Kluckhohn defines it as 'the total way of life of a people', 'the social legacy the individual acquires from his group', 'a way of thinking, feeling and believing', 'an abstraction from behaviour', 'storehouse of pooled learning', 'a set of standardised orientations to recurrent problems', 'learned behaviour', a 'mechanism for the normative regulation of behaviour', 'a set of techniques for adjusting both to the external environment and to other men' and a 'precipitate of history' (Kluckhohn, 1960; Geertz, 1973: 4–5). Geertz views it as 'the webs of significance he [man] himself has spun' where the search is not so much for meanings but rather interpretations of these actions (Geertz, 1973: 5).

Hannerz looks at culture as a social organization of meaning made up of a set of complex interlinkages (Hannerz, 1992: 68). At any one time, the individuals within the culture are subjected to a set of culturally shaped meanings which influence his or her ordering of experiences and intentions. At the same time, the individual is capable of interpreting culturally given phenomena, and this individual interpretation can differ from the culturally sanctioned one. These differing modes of interpretation result in a tension zone between culture and social structure (Hannerz, 1992: 65), and Hannerz considers the latter to embody a network of perspectives because of the variations and diversities found within it. Within the wider culture, there thus exist subcultures, microcultures and countercultures (Hannerz, 1992: 69–81), all of which are collective phenomena associated with particular sets of social relationships. Within these subcultures, microcultures and countercultures, there exist only those aspects of the total flow of meaning that are directly relevant to them. They are therefore distinctive in their own right and contrast with the meanings flowing in the wider culture.

The Chinese lineage structure is important for Chinese culture. As stated previously, it is widely conceptualized as a social institution within which the reproduction of Chinese culture takes place. Today, some Chinese lineages have branches scattered throughout China and the world, each branch having developed its own subcultures and microcultures. Within the broader lineage framework, there continue to be shared cultural elements and collective memories; but within the subcultures and microcultures, there are distinctive elements that belong uniquely to each. Thus we may expect the attitudes of the Singapore Ke to differ considerably from those of their village counterparts.

Within the wider lineage structure, the shared collective memories and attitudes serve as integrative forces which bring together the various branches, and the convergence of its members at the lineage ancestral house is a testimony to this. Religious and ritual reproductions serve to unify and allow for expression of this cultural identity (of being Anxi Chinese, which implies speaking the Fujianese dialect, etc., for example). This sense of cultural identity serves as a habitus that contains members and rejects outsiders.

However, subcultures and microcultures are also clearly displayed when various branches of a lineage gather together for communal ancestor worship or religious celebrations. In such a situation, Singaporean, Malaysian, Hong Kong and other Han-Chinese subcultures appear distinct in attitudes, dress, social habits and social etiquette. At such times there may exist a high level of tension among them, with individuals from different groups attempting to outdo each other in displays of wealth, power and social status, thereby challenging each other's level of social existence—although, in a broader perspective, they share common characteristics that identify them as members of a shared culture.

Nodal Links

Given the fact that subcultures and microcultures among the various lineage branches that may be separated geographically from one another, the Chinese lineage can no longer be seen as a locality-bound social institution. Emigration has led to the formation of separate Chinese overseas communities. The various branches of a lineage created by migrants residing permanently in adopted countries cater to their needs and those of their locally-born descendants. While these are distinctively Chinese, many of their activities have taken on a contemporary look to suit the needs of local members with local political allegiances. Overseas Chinese communities thus set up social institutions such as surname and territorial groupings (*zongqing,*宗亲; *tongxianghui,* 同乡会) to cater for their needs. Such groups have grown powerful and functioned independently in providing for much of the cultural activity of their members, and established informal social relationships with similar local institutions. The roles of these institutions within their communities are largely cultural and ritualistic in nature. They continue to play the role of cultural identity marker, although their significance has increasingly been reduced by professional groupings in recent years. However, they can still be found in many Chinese communities throughout the world.

There has been an awareness of recent migrations of the Chinese from Southeast Asia to the United States, Australia and other English-speaking and European countries. Along with the migration was the establishment of traditional social institutions in an attempt to maintain Chinese cultural identity.

All these migrations, accompanied by the setting up of lineage branches, mean that such Chinese lineages are no longer social institutions with distinctive geographic boundaries, as Freedman observed. However, although lineage members outside China have established political, economic and social allegiance to their countries of domicile, and although their descendants are born and raised in these countries, many of these Chinese overseas communities have begun a process of searching for their ancestral roots and cultural identity back in China—without denying their roots in their present countries.

Given this global spread, the lineage structure should now be seen as a cultural network, with links connecting *nodes*, including those representing Chinese communities scattered throughout the world, those located within the village polity, and those located within Mainland Chinese cities. Each node is an encapsulation of Chinese culture, but represents it as a different subculture or microculture. Each node is linked to others in a socially horizontal manner, as it is a branch of the main lineage structure and enjoys equal social status, irrespective of its other attributes. Nodal links can be strong or weak, and can expand or contract depending on the needs of the groups concerned. Local Chinese subcultures can function independently as well. Although, in fact, power, wealth and social status play an important role in determining the strength and dominance of each branch, they theoretically have very little impact on the social relationships among the nodes: the nodes are *theoretically* among social equals.

A Web of Lineage Culture

Within the lineage network described above, there are two kinds of link. The first link is between node and 'source' (the ancestral village) and the second is between one branch, or node, and another. Each branch, however, is a transmitter of Chinese culture, and constitutes a regional cultural centre.

The relationship between the source and the nodes is qualitatively different from the relationship among the various nodes, as it is based on a different set of dynamics, with the village representing the origin, or source, of the branches that are its offshoots. Theoretically, the primordial centre should have power and dominance because of its status as source. However, in the *qiaoxiang* relationship, the traditional social stratification system has been replaced by a contemporary utilitarian system within which wealth has become an important marker of social status. In this system, the nodes with wealthy members have become the dominant players in the transnational relationship between the source and the nodes.

Lineage members, both at the source and at the nodes, share a collective memory and a real and/or an imagined sense of history based on at least some common knowledge of the ancestral home and a common understanding of their cultural roots, although the nature of their relationships is subject to the effects of the variety of life experiences and socio-political changes that they have undergone. Those who left the source and migrated abroad early may have experienced great upheavals, but their livelihoods have now stabilized and the majority have been able to move up local and global economic and social ladders and have achieved relatively comfortable standards of living, while some have become wealthy. As for second and younger generations born overseas, their political and social experiences differ from those of their elders.

Lineage members at the source, and those at nodes within the village polity, have also experienced great political upheavals and uncertainty, and even with the doors open to reform in China, many continue to be apprehensive of political change. Only recently has life returned to greater stability, and only in the last three decades have there been renewed kinship ties between them and their overseas kin.

Members of the Chinese overseas communities have been able to carry out, reproduce and develop the socio-cultural and religious activities involving customs and rituals which they know without much hindrance. However, those who remained at the source were forced to curb their socio-cultural and religious activities as a result of political pressure. This has resulted in very uneven developments of Chinese culture between the source and the nodes, so that the 'residual Chinese communities' overseas (Freedman's term) have become, to a large extent, the guardians and proponents of 'traditional' Chinese culture. Many groups of Chinese overseas have been able to recreate aspects of Chinese culture in their communities, but with modifications and additions of new elements, thereby moving away from village culture in an urban, non-Chinese direction. With the interactions between source and the overseas communities in recent years, village and Chinese overseas cultural elements have begun to produce a wider synthetic Chinese culture. Yet certain core elements are retained, and therefore the additions and changes do not disqualify it as 'Chinese culture' in the eyes of its adherents, although they acknowledge its changing aspects.

The complexity of this web of source and nodes is determined by the relationships within it. The network embedded in the web operates as follows: first, there is the membership consideration within the lineage web. Lineage members can be divided into two main groups, those within China and those overseas. Within China there are: (a) the source; (b) nodes within the village polity; and (c) nodes in Chinese cities where lineage members have relocated. Those overseas are geographically scattered throughout the world. However, not every Chinese overseas community forms a node. The greatest concentration of nodes is found in Southeast Asia, where there is a large concentration of Chinese. Elsewhere, where there are only scattered individuals, there is no desire or incentive to form a node.

In the case of the Ke lineage, nodes have formed in Singapore, Malaysia, Indonesia, Thailand, the Philippines; there are several in Taiwan and a small one in Hong Kong. Members of these communities are permanent residents, function within their respective Chinese communities, and are citizens of their local nation-states.

For the Ke lineage, the relationship between the source and the nodes can be seen as follows.

The source

For Singapore Ke lineage members, the source has different components. At the broadest level, the source is the locality where they or their ancestors came from. It can be divided into outer and inner areas. The outer area is Anxi County, often regarded as the ancestral land. The inner area of this locality is Penglai's Xitou, which is regarded as the place of origin, the *qiyuandi* (起源地)— the place where the first ancestor in the region planted the lineage's roots. It is the place where the grave of the first ancestor, Wanshangong (万山公), and the ancestral house, the *zuzhai,* are situated. To travel to the inner source is to pay homage to the ancestors and reconnect oneself with one's ancestral roots.

Village members live within the Penglai and other districts in Anxi and so are in proximity to the source all the time. They thus are unlikely to experience a break in their relationship with their ancestors. Though they experienced political upheavals during the Cultural Revolution and were forced to refrain from acknowledging or worshipping their ancestors, they nevertheless continue to reside in the area, which serves as a powerful reminder of their origin, whether they consider it good to do so or not. Since the reform, they, together with their overseas kin, have reconstructed their links with their ancestors through individual and communal rituals.

In identifying with the source, the lineage member is confronted with the issue of allegiance. The relationship between the individual and the source is determined by the social distance between them. He or she is interconnected with it through the lineage web of agnatic and affinal kinship ties, and is able to recognize his or her immediate ancestors, to locate the ancestral house or *zuzhai*, and to trace the genealogical links with all other members within the lineage structure. It is these ties that are instrumental in establishing and operationalizing the moral economy. Embedded in the various ideological constructs, such as the moral reasoning of Confucianism and the Buddhist understanding of karma, the moral economy ensures that the players within it discharge their social and moral obligations to the source and to the members who live within the locality and those who have lived within it. Singapore members who visit the inner source area experience themselves as part of an extended kinship and lineage network based on a shared surname—in our case, the surname 'Ke'. Involuntarily, they have to acknowledge the existence of kin of all the different grades, both socially close and socially distant, and there is great social expectation that they acknowledge these kin and their common ancestors. To visit the ancestral village is thus not just to visit a physical place, but to enter into the social relations bounded within that space. It is this that some Singapore Chinese find it difficult to cope with.

In the ancestral village, many of the Singaporeans are introduced to agnatic and affinal kin that they have not previously met. They then assume the identities of brothers and sisters, uncles and aunts, nephews and nieces and cousins of village lineage members, as these identities are bestowed upon them by their village kin. Other possible individual identities remain unimportant—the reference point is always the family and the lineage. As members of a moral economy, they are culturally bound, by a sense of moral obligation and duty, to give assistance to their immediate family and lineage members within the ancestral village, as well as to others within the outer source area. Within the inner source, personalized gifts, in the form of money or material goods, are given to blood and affinal kin, the amount and type of which depends on them. A main characteristic of the moral economy is thus the variety and personalized nature of the gifts given, which tend to vary according to the needs of their village kin and the ability of the Singaporeans to provide for them.

There are also moral obligations to the ancestral village in Kuitou in Penglai itself. In addition to contributions to individual kin, members overseas are expected to contribute to the communal well-being of the village as a whole. Such assistance may take the form of village reconstruction, raising the material standard of the villagers, providing infrastructure for education or medical facilities, or for road transportation. This attempt to restructure the village life and economy has led to an identity for wealthy *qiaoxiang* emigrant villages distinct from that of surrounding villages.

In regard to Anxi, the moral economy operates in a less personalized fashion, focused not so much on primordial ties with individual lineage members as on affiliation with the region as a whole, with the ancestral village or ancestral home as the key reference point. Many Singapore Chinese recognize that Anxi is the county where their ancestors came from, but most refer more to the county than to the specific village of their ancestors, so that 'Anxi County' is a more familiar term than 'Penglai Zhen' and Penglai Zhen is better known than Kuitou precinct. A small group of Singapore Chinese said that, although they did not know the village of their ancestors, they felt that by knowing the county they at least had the opportunity to locate the inner source if they wished to, and so found their 'cultural roots'.

However, within the greater area of the county, social relationships are not closely bound to kinship ties that one is expected to acknowledge. As social relations here are not based on shared surnames, but only on territorial affiliation, ties are less intimate, social expectations less personalized and obligations fewer. Still, a moral economy operates to advance the general welfare of the county as well, and the Chinese overseas are asked to look at its overall development. According to governmental reports, Anxi is still one of the poorest regions in China, and Chinese overseas are encouraged to contribute and alleviate this poverty. Contributions here are not made to individuals but to the district and county governments. Investment in large infrastructure projects benefits both outer and inner source areas.

Some overseas lineage members find it more satisfying to interact with this entire outer source area than with the inner source, as they then experience less moral obligation to immediate village kin and remain less involved with village kin and lineage ties and remain better able to control the operation of the moral economy. These members feel that their contributions are put to better use, to benefit the whole region. However, when dealing with immediate village kin, many find that they are unable to keep out of the kin-based moral economy, within which they must share control with their local relatives; whereas, within the outer source area, they can more easily control their contribution agendas and choose those village, district or county projects to which they wish to contribute. As we have seen in Chapter 5, many Singapore Ke lineage members favour contributing to district-level education and county-level construction of the main arterial road. In making these contributions, they change the nature of the moral economy to focus on philanthropy and charity.

Within both inner and outer source areas, the dominance of a shared communal identity works to undermine individual identity. This shared communal identity involves both Singapore and village members in a broader Fujian Anxi Chinese identity, within which the Singapore Chinese are *Singapore Fujian* Anxi Chinese (*Xinjiapo Fujian Anxi Huaren*, 新加坡福建安溪华人).

Nodes: Overseas regional Chinese cultural centres

The nodes of the social network are made up of three overlapping components: the lineage and its members are sometimes represented by local lineage/surname associations, or *zongqinghui* (宗亲会); sometimes are constituted independently of such associations; and sometimes act within territorial associations, or *tongxianghui*. The three taken together represents the regional Chinese overseas cultural centres. Although the two types of social institutions mentioned have attracted varying degrees of support from their members since World War II, they have become less popular in recent years. However, they continue to be important conduits for the expression of Chinese culture in present-day Chinese communities throughout the world, especially in Southeast Asia. They can be found in Singapore, Malaysia, Indonesia, Thailand, the Philippines, Vietnam and elsewhere. During the nineteenth and the first half of the twentieth century, they performed important social and economic functions (Yen, 1986). During the early post-colonial days, in post-independence nation-states, their roles were greatly reduced because they were considered seats for Chinese nationalism and chauvinism, and today, in countries like Indonesia and Malaysia, they continue to be viewed with suspicion. In Indonesia they are permitted to function minimally; in Malaysia they may function only at a low level; in Singapore, earlier roles played by such institutions have been taken over by government-run institutions.

In recent years in Singapore, however, recognition of Chinese social institutions as seats of Chinese culture and tradition by the Singapore state has led to their revival. They now actively promote Chinese culture and cultural activities, carving for themselves a specific niche as custodial guardians and promoters. They promote the 'Speak Mandarin' campaign; Chinese cultural activities such as Chinese opera, folk dance and traditional Chinese music; education, allowing their premises to be used for after-class tuition for members' children; various Chinese religious activities; as well as 'modern' popular activities such as sports and karaoke-singing, to encourage the participation of younger members (Kuah-Pearce, 2006d).

Relations between nodes and sources have vacillated with the political atmosphere of the times. Practical links were very weak from the 1960s to the mid-1970s: formal institutional contacts were occasionally made, but most contacts were informal ones between individual members. Links have been strengthened since the late 1970s, with increased institutional exchanges and visits to Singapore by official cadres from Anxi County in recent years. One main reason for these visits has been to promote Anxi and the emigrant village phenomenon among the Singapore Chinese, and to encourage them to visit and contribute to the development of their ancestral villages, such as those in Anxi County. The Singapore Chinese began to visit their ancestral villages for sentimental reasons, and then established ties with cadres, which tended to lock them into *guanxi* networks. From the 1980s onwards, with the relaxation of the political atmosphere, interaction between the regional nodes and their sources intensified, with the key focus on cultural reproduction and economic revival.

Relations today are of two types. The first consists of relationships of individuals who visit and make contributions to their ancestral villages, engage in religious reproduction and assist in the setting-up of small retail businesses for the benefit of immediate village kin, as well as to infrastructure development of ancestral villages, the object being to raise the standard of living of village kin. This type of relationship is focused on the *qiaoxiang,* and the flow of financial and material benefits is unidirectionally towards Anxi. The second type consists of the relations of Chinese social institutions and corporate groups whose members claim ancestry from the district or the county generally. These involve contributions in the form of aid, or as joint business ventures, the primary aim being to help the district and/or county to develop economically and to obtain small investment returns. These overseas institutions and corporate groups thus combine sentiment with business interest in economic ventures with town and county governments. One example of this type of involvement is the development of power plants in the county.

Social relationships between the inner source and the nodes are now characterized by movement in both directions between the nodes and their *qiaoxiang,* and are more intense, while previously they were unidirectional, with the flow from the nodes to the inner source, or the ancestral village. Anxi villagers now make social visits to Singapore. The relaxation of policies from the 1990s pertaining to the employment of Mainland Chinese workers in Singapore has resulted in the recruitment of workers from both Penglai and Anxi generally, and there is now much pressure exerted on Singapore Chinese to help their village kin to find employment. This has raised the level of tension between the two groups and has resulted in much misunderstanding and dissatisfaction.

The greater flow of social and economic interaction between the source and the nodes has fostered greater emotional ties, but some of these have been negative ones, and feelings among Singapore Chinese are often mixed. The older generation want to establish closer links with village kin but are constantly frustrated by the villagers' lack of understanding of the Singapore situation, and the pressure and demands to arrange employment in Singapore for younger villagers. The younger Singaporeans, on the other hand, are emotionally less engaged and maintain a social distance from their village kin, thereby retaining a 'comfort zone' for themselves.

In Diagram 1, the inner source, represented by the ancestral village, is linked to the nodes and overseas regional cultural centres through the members and the associations (surname and territorial). Links may be strong or weak. In our case, the physical source of the Ke lineage is the Penglai, most strongly represented by the ancestral house, or *zuzhai*. The source is linked strongly with the Singapore Ke members and the Ke Association, as well as with the Anxi Association in Singapore. There are also strong links between

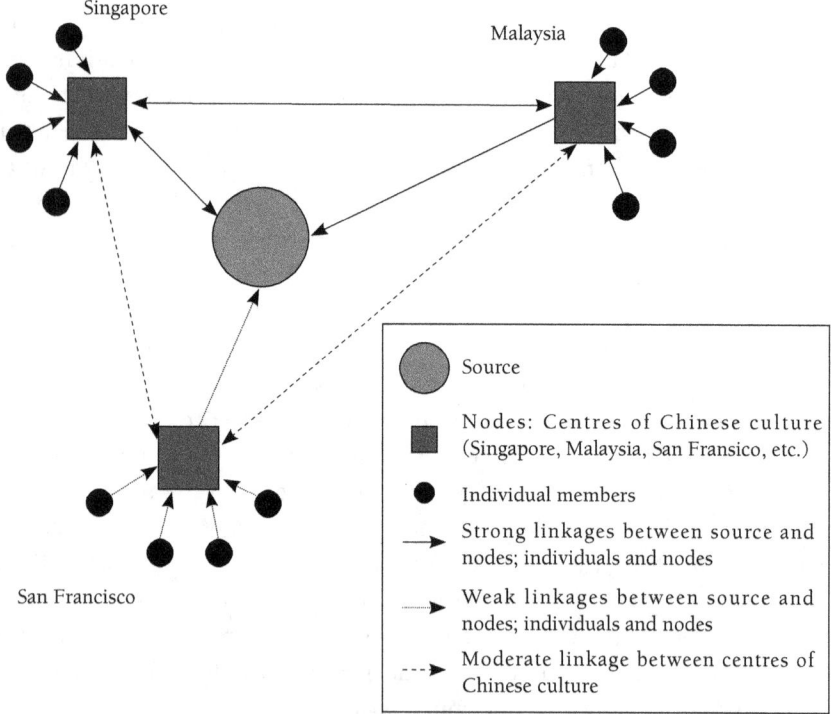

Diagram 1: Lineage network: Relationship between source and nodes
NB: Relationship between the source and nodes (centres of Chinese culture) is weak and unidirectional for some [San Franciso] but strong for others [Singapore and Malaysia]. The relationship between the centres of Chinese culture and the individual members is also strong for some but not others.

the source and the Malaysian and Indonesian nodes, and a weaker link with the United States.

At the institutional level, the links were weak and for many years, while there was some interaction among lineage members, there was very little institutional interaction between the source and the Anxi association. Only in the past 20 years or so have the links been revived and strengthened through various activities, one of the most important being the International Conference of World Anxi Associations in 1992, which was organized by the Singapore Anxi Association and held on its premises, with participation of members from around the world, including numerous members from Anxi County itself. In November 1997, the Anxi County government, in conjunction with the overseas Anxi Chinese, held another international conference in Fengcheng.

The Anxi Association is a mixed-surname association based on locality. In the 1980s, village, district and county construction and reconstruction—particularly the building of public infrastructure such as roads, bridges and hospitals—have become a major concern to the Anxi Chinese in Singapore and elsewhere in Southeast Asia, and they have contributed much to such projects. Members of various lineages, including the Ke lineage, have contributed substantially to these infrastructure projects, as territoriality has been an important marker of identity and Anxi County represents the common outer source. The Anxi Ke have also assisted projects related directly to their lineage, especially as individuals, through personal social networks. They have also made large contributions and funded many public work projects in the inner source, Penglai.

Guanxi networks

There are several types of intra-lineage social networks in operation. All are informal. First, there are the 'primordial' *guanxi* networks. There are two types of *qinqing guanxi wangluo* (亲情关系网络): the first is that among lineage members in the regional cultural centres, the second is that of relationships between the source and diaspora community, in our case between Singaporeans and Penglai villagers. For these two types of networks, membership is exclusive; the ties are established on the basis of shared common experiences, and on shared outlooks on, and attitudes towards, the outside world.

The Singapore regional *guanxi* network consciously attempts to exclude those that are not from Singapore, including Anxi villagers. The factors here include not only Singapore national identity but also social class, as the village kin of many Singapore Chinese possess low social status. For the source and diaspora community relationship, membership is inclusive and incorporates members that were originally from the source but now reside elsewhere and those presently live there. There is a sense of territoriality but it is also an acknowledgement of differences amidst similar cultural experiences.

A second type of network involves lineage members from both Singapore and the village lineage *guanxi* network, the *zongqin guanxi wangluo* (宗亲关系网络). This can be viewed as the moral economy network, or *daode jingji wangluo* (道德经济网络). Here, social expectations exist and interactions occur of varying degrees of intimacy, depending on the individual members involved, but attitudes and actions are governed by a set of moral values and a sense of duty and responsibility. Participation within this network is voluntary, but much persuasion is exerted to involve lineage members, and numerous members have been inducted into it in semi-coercive fashion. Some younger members may become involved because their parents are, and they often represent their parents. Once in the network, they are considered permanent members, unless they declare themselves otherwise. Many may choose to become inactive rather than to be seen as openly rejecting the network. Often, however, they are not left alone, but are pushed into activity through 'obligatory' ritual duties.

This Singapore-village *guanxiwang* involves the shared common ground of members, and is particularly used for ritual reproduction and village reconstruction. Members find this common ground as they engage in, for example, ancestor worship and communal religious functions, or the recompilation of the lineage genealogy. Throughout, it involves the desire to revive the lineage structure and to bring together the various branches of the lineage, and involves the objective of developing the emigrant ancestral village. The network provides a ready pool of people to help organize ritual activities, and to help with village reconstruction and economic development in the areas of education, village health care, the construction of roads and bridges, retail businesses and cottage industries. Within it, male members often involve themselves in the social and economic aspects of village life while women group themselves for socio-religious activities. The numbers of men and women involved are about equal. Most are village or Singapore elders with strong emotional ties to the village. They are the main proponents of communal activities. Members see themselves as being in the vanguard for the advancement of the economic interests of the villages.

Unlike the more formal institutions, these *guanxi* networks are not burdened by formal rules. Most activities are *ad hoc*, and participation is voluntary and elicited through informal recruitment. The extent of participation is dependent on personal interest and on the effectiveness of persuasion by kin. Because of this informality, movement in and out of the network is fluid, and involvement in any particular activity is dependent on time and interest. It is possible to distinguish several categories of participating members: there are the very active members who form the core of the *guanxiwang*, the passive ones who need persuasion, and the inactive ones whose participation is infrequent. However, most can be depended on to support major events in the ancestral village. This network is represented by Diagram 2.

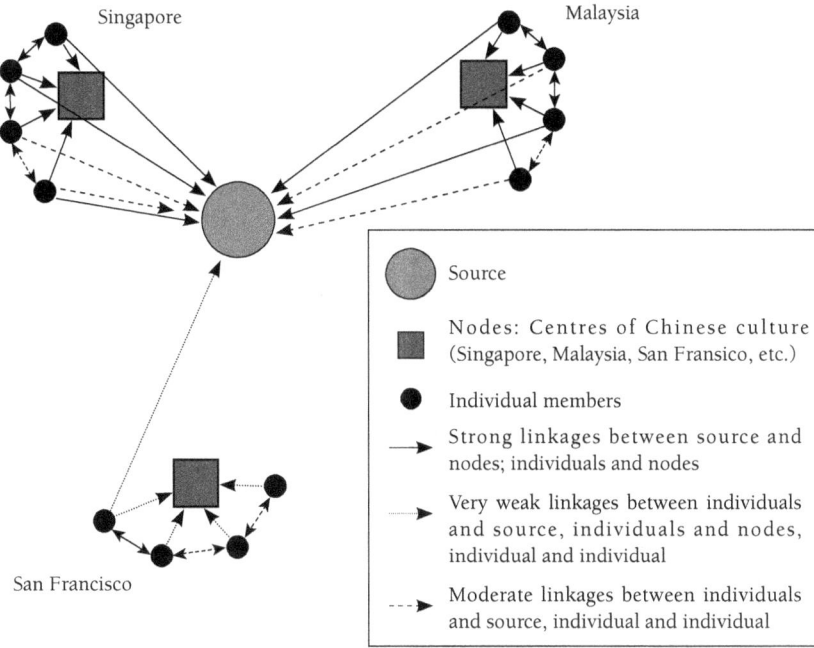

Diagram 2: Intra-lineage networking and relationship between individuals and source
NB: Strong interaction between individuals and the source and between individuals (Singapore and Malaysia). Very weak interaction between individuals and the source (San Francisco); interaction between individuals can be strong or weak depending on their personalized interaction.

Inter-lineage guanxiwang

Communication among branches or sub-lineages of the same lineage is a common occurrence. These intra-lineage *guanxi* networks are informal and fluid. However, members of various lineages routinely exchange news and provide information about activities and developments in their mutual *qiaoxiang*, and offer advice to those who need it.

In Anxi, there is much communication among members of the nine local lineages, and in Singapore such communication between members of different lineages and surname associations, both formal and informal, has increased since the 1980s. Formally, lineage and surname organizations have increasingly co-operated in social, cultural and educational activities. In Singapore, these inter-lineage *guanxi* networks are important in raising the profile of Chinese culture and Chinese activities. They are important for elevating the status not only of the lineages involved but also of the territorial associations, the *tongxianghui*, such as the Anxi Association, and help transform them into custodial institutions of Chinese culture and identity.

These *guanxi* networks have important socio-economic functions. Three distinct overlapping sets of players are involved: members of different emigrant villages; Singapore Chinese members with different surnames; and official village, town and county cadre members. Chinese overseas are consciously courted by village elders to help with cultural reproduction, village construction and reconstruction, and the rekindling of kinship sentiments. Official cadres network with Chinese overseas and village elders to encourage more overseas investments in the region. Like the villagers, the cadres transform ancestral and kinship affiliation into social capital to attract Chinese overseas into their networks, and the latter allow themselves to be inducted in the hope of establishing good *guanxi* for prospective economic investment in the region.

This three-way courtship permits certain observations. First, it enables large capital flow into the villages and, to a certain extent, into other parts of the county. Rapid development has thus been made possible, resulting in the social and economic betterment of the *qiaoxiang* villages. Secondly, by courting Chinese overseas, the latter are given social status and self-esteem by the three levels of cadres. They are treated as VIPs who have contributed philanthropically and charitably. While many of these people are successful in Singapore, they are not recognized for their contributions to the Singapore community as, in many cases, they do not have a sufficiently large pool of resources to make a mark in Singapore society. However, in the villages of Anxi, they are honoured for their contributions. They are thus 'somebody' in their home village, if not in Singapore.

Global Lineage Flows

In recent years the regional cultural centres have taken on extended roles and have globalized their outlook, using their institutional structures to provide bases for their members to form new networks and springboard into new areas of activity, while reaching out to lineage members and members of the same surname groups world-wide.

Chinese Lineage as a Cultural Network   237

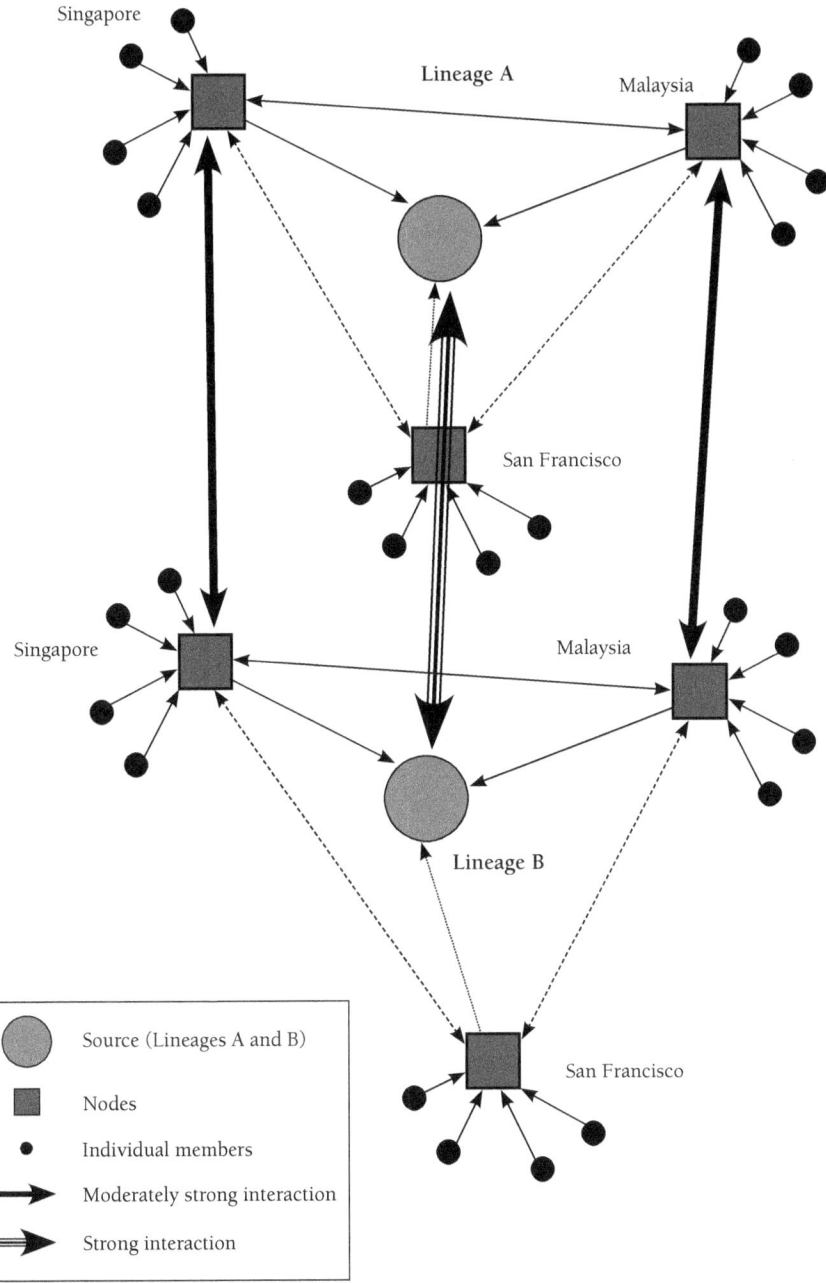

Diagram 3: Inter-lineage networking and relationship with the source
NB: Moderately strong interaction between the nodes and very strong interaction between the sources.

The Ke lineage in Singapore established linkages with their ancestral village and has now become active in village and county cultural and economic reconstruction. It next recompiled the genealogy, searching for members scattered throughout the world. Then the formal Ke institution in Singapore, the Ke Association, began to organize business tours for the Singapore members to visit China. Finally, this latter activity was expanded to encompass visits to other Southeast Asian countries.

Rewriting the genealogy involved reaching out to scattered members. A world-wide search for lineage members conducted through newspaper advertisements and word of mouth was launched. Most members residing in the West came from families in Southeast Asia (especially in Singapore and Malaysia), and continue to have strong ties with kin in Singapore. Through these ties they came into contact with relatives in Anxi, albeit obliquely, and thus came to know of the rewriting of the genealogy, and so had their names included in it.

The Ke Association serves as a natural setting for members to network among themselves and with their counterparts in other countries. It lends its name to help its members explore economic links and joint ventures with the governments and other economic corporations of Vietnam, Cambodia and Burma, and has proven to be important for establishing contacts with other foreign governments and non-government organizations, thereby establishing itself as an important socio-economic institution. Today, the Ke Association provides information and support for members to carry out economic ventures.

Relevance of Network Analysis

In this chapter, I have attempted a network analysis of the reformulation of the lineage structure. The Chinese lineage has undergone various phases of structural development. Unlike in the nineteenth and early twentieth centuries, it is no longer the same social organization that Freedman and other scholars have portrayed.

In the reconceptualization of the Chinese lineage structure, there are various considerations. First, there is a need to take into consideration its spread through geographical space. It is no longer confined to one geographical area but has developed various nodes and regional cultural centres that operate both formally and informally. Second, there is a need to take into consideration the power and influence of various sets of players within the lineage. Power is no longer derived from the Anxi source, nor is the source an influential player: in the contemporary context, the regional centres are just as, if not more, powerful. It is they that set the agenda with regard to the ancestral village. Third, the formal Chinese bureaucratic institutions of *huiguan* and *tongxianghui* have been set up to help implement socio-cultural activities, and these institutions have taken on important roles in recent years, networking among themselves in attempting to globalize and providing bases for members to network with each other. Increasingly, they are also used by their members to network with government bodies and other corporate groups for economic purposes. Fourth, *huiguan* and *tongxianghui* are also important social institutions within the countries with a Chinese diaspora community and play an important role in defining the Chinese community within the wider polity.

Analysing the Chinese lineage as a cultural network allows us to give due recognition to the continuity and diversity of the source and the regional centres. The source—primarily, the ancestral village—functions as the place to which lineage members can trace their ancestral lines—where they can participate in important Chinese cultural traditions on a large communal scale, and where they can gather from overseas to perform communal ancestor and religious worship and acknowledge their common origin. However, it is not necessarily a seat of power or influence.

Such analysis also provides an understanding of the diversities found among Chinese overseas communities. Each Chinese overseas community develops a distinct identity—the Singapore Chinese identity is different from those of Chinese communities in Malaysia, Indonesia, the Philippines, Australia or the United States. The varying social experiences in the adopted countries have led to changes and modifications in the original village culture that migrating ancestors brought with them. Today, processes of adaptation and localization to suit local needs are continuing in Chinese overseas communities. In this sense, they are independent communities with distinctive identities. What ties them together is the concept of 'being Chinese'—and this importantly includes Chinese lineage identity and activity.

Cultural continuity between the source and the regional centres is characterized by relationships that are neither dominant nor subservient, but that carry a sense of nostalgia and collective memory important for rekindling lost sentiments of lineage members in regional cultural centres and encourage them to look again at the source of their lineage. Sentimentality and nostalgia are instrumental in pushing them to visit their ancestral village and to participate in cultural reproduction and village reconstruction, all of which enables cultural networking to take place and finally leads to the creation of a lineage network incorporating the various branches.

Within the cultural network, some nodes and links are more active than others, and each can be studied on its own and compared with others.

Network links can be strong or weak, depending on the interests of their members. It is generally true that links between the source and the cultural centres in Southeast Asian countries are strong, with much flow along them; and among the cultural centres in Southeast Asia there are also strong links. However, nodal links between the source and the centres in North America, Europe and other parts of Asia are weaker. Several factors account for this, including political considerations and the attitudes in the regional centres themselves. Today, the political climate in Singapore has allowed for the establishment of strong relationships between the nodes and the source. Although there is desire by the Malaysian Chinese to do the same, the political climate in Malaysia continues to restrain them. For North America and Europe, the links are much weaker as a result of the lack of elders to motivate the younger generation to return to their home village. Other factors such as the eagerness to be integrated into the local society might also impact on this.

Conclusion

In late modernity, lineage structure continues to play an important role in Chinese overseas communities and in China itself. The usefulness of the lineage structure can be further enhanced through a reconceptualization of its structure. Contemporary Chinese lineages can be best understood if they are reconceptualized as cultural networks, in order to allow us to understand the dynamics of relationship between the various branches of a lineage and its source, as well as among the various branches themselves, taking into account global migration and the formation of permanent Chinese communities in various parts of the world.

10
Conclusion: From Lineage to Transnational Chinese Network

In this book, I have explored the relationship between the Singapore Chinese and their *qiaoxiang*. For the Singapore Chinese, visiting their *qiaoxiang* is a journey in search of ancestral and cultural roots. This search is facilitated by the fact that there continues to be a sizeable number of elderly first-generation Chinese migrants in Singapore, and they have played a large part in encouraging the younger Singapore-born Chinese to visit their *qiaoxiang*. It is this first-generation group of Singapore Chinese, who desire to maintain kinship and lineage continuity that set in motion the search for cultural and ancestral roots.

From Nostalgia to Cultural Reproduction

This search for cultural and ancestral roots has been very much accompanied by feelings of nostalgia and by collective memory. This older group recalled, with much emotion and sentiment, their childhood experiences in their villages, their migrant journeys to Singapore, and their village kin. Some of them had experienced life in the villages during the various phases of Communist rule. This generation were able to relate to their village kin and to empathize with them concerning their political plight and material poverty. However, they found themselves with mixed feelings concerning their own situations: on the one hand, they felt fortunate to have escaped the Communist regime; on the other, they felt guilty for leaving their kin behind or having been unable to rescue them. Sending remittances and money during the 1950s and 1960s was all they could do. However, as the political tension eased and reforms were introduced after 1978, the guilt feeling gradually gave way to a renewed sense of wanting to do something for their ancestral villages.

The period after 1978 witnessed an increasing number of Singapore-born Chinese making their way to their ancestral villages. They related to the *qiaoxiang* differently than did their parents or grandparents, as they had no social experiences pushing them to empathize with the then-recent plight of their village kin. For them, the *qiaoxiang* was an illusive or distant ancestral home. Many disliked or did not appreciate their village kin, and there was much tension between this group and their parents and grandparents because of different perceptions and expectations. There was also tension between the Singapore Chinese and their village kin, which was part of the moral economy that had been revived. Confucian morality, kinship obligations and parental demands dictate that the Singapore Chinese, being financially and materially better endowed, assist and provide for their poor village kin. Requests for material goods by those in the *qiaoxiang* in the late 1970s and early 1980s were perceived by some Singaporeans as insatiable demands, and some of the latter soon began to experience '*qiaoxiang* fatigue', and became wary of constant demands. They began to dislike receiving *tangshan* letters, and this feeling was reinforced, especially among the Singapore-born generations, by their lack of understanding of village economic conditions.

Despite these apprehensions, many Singapore Chinese participated in the moral economy. As the saying goes, 'blood is thicker than water'; the kinship ties and the call of duty from the ancestral home became socio-moral bonds which pushed many Singapore Chinese to contribute to village reconstruction and development and to provide material and financial assistance to members of their extended kinship groups. This continuation and revival of the traditional moral economy involved cultural and religious reproduction in the *qiaoxiang*. In attempting to widen the moral-economic networks involved, most village elders, cadres and villagers supported this reproduction, which was and remain as the main preoccupations of the Singapore Chinese when they visit their *qiaoxiang*. It has thus been an attitude of give-and-take that finally creates goodwill and reciprocity between the two groups.

From Lineage to Transnational Networks

The Chinese lineage has gone through various stages, transforming itself from a parochial social institution into a transnational network. From its ancestral source, the lineage has spread outwards and, at present, there are numerous branches throughout China and overseas, especially in Southeast Asian cities.

The source of the Singapore branch of the Anxi Ke lineage remains in Penglai in Anxi, where it is represented by the ancestral house, which has been reconstructed in recent years to cater for revived communal worship. It serves as a physical reminder and a testimony to the origin of the lineage and to the works of the ancestors. Its existence reminds lineage members to perform their duties to these ancestors. Lineage members, from within the village and overseas, have come together to acknowledge their ancestors and roots through communal ancestor worship and related rituals. It is in this context that lineage members acknowledge each other as such. The relationships between the source and the overseas branches of the lineage are governed by this ancestral bond of assumed blood ties. Despite this, kinship intimacy often remains confined within immediate or extended family structures.

As the Anxi Ke settled in their adopted countries overseas and established their own communities, some came to accept roles within them as elders and leaders of their lineage branches, which remained autonomous of the sources of their lineages. The socio-cultural activities and economic and welfare facilities they organized for their members became important organizations for the local transmission of Chinese culture and identity. Yet, ideologically, these branches remained satellites of the source, which was represented by the ancestral house. However, this centre-satellite relationship was not one of domination and subordination. Although, theoretically, the centre should dominate, the social status of the members of the branches in fact became much higher, due to their financial and material wealth. When broken contacts between the branches and the source were reconnected in the 1980s, tension arose from mutual demands and expectations. However, because of the common ancestral bond, the source and the branches influenced each other in the areas of cultural and religious reproduction. The resulting synthesis has created the Anxi Ke lineage religious culture that we witness today.

To understand the relationship between the source and the branches overseas, the lineage structure must be seen as a cultural network that allows for multidirectional integration among its members. With connectional flows among the branches scattered throughout the world, individual members have established mutual ties and created personalized interactive cultural flows among themselves. The branches, through their individual organized bases, now have strong renewed links with one another for co-operation in cultural, religious and other activities.

The various forms of social interaction between the various lineage members, either at individual or collective levels, are instrumental for our understanding of the Singapore Chinese and their *qiaoxiang* connections. Within this social network, relationships are characterized by informality and fluidity; members are free to communicate with each other individually or collectively. They are not bound together by strict rules or regulations.

The local cultural network can draw upon the support of other branches scattered throughout the world when the need arises. As the lineage sheds its parochial identity and embarks on the process of globalization, more of its members throughout the world are likely to form their own branches and join the network. As the lineage network adds its function of generalized communication medium for its branches and diversifies the roles it plays beyond those of a strictly social, welfare and/or economic nature, it becomes increasingly advantageous for the different branches to take part. The ability of the lineage structure to serve this modern need is imperative for its survival, and it is to this end that members of the Ke lineage are working to transform its image as part of this wider cultural network structure.

Re-inventing a Chinese Cultural Identity

The level of negotiation between the Singapore Chinese and the villagers on cultural issues shows the extent to which each group must compromise its understanding of what the culture should be. We thus see a *negotiated* Chinese culture being created—one that consists of the socio-cultural and religious elements of village China, those of early migrant society and those of the contemporary Singapore Chinese community. This combination constitutes Chinese culture for the Ke lineage. The Singaporeans' simultaneous acknowledgement of both their ancestral roots and their Singaporean identity allows them to formulate this particular Singaporean style of Chinese identity and yet maintain a sense of historical and cultural continuity with the past.

As for the identity of the Anxi villagers, it is now bound to that of their overseas kin. This relationship thrusts them into the global sphere. They are now able to move beyond their territorial identification with their village into a global space. They now have to reassess their cultural identity, as the Singapore Chinese have been influential in reproducing and modifying the types of cultural and religious practices that are conducted in the village environment, and this has impacted on how these village Chinese look at themselves and their cultural identity.

Village cultural and religious activities are now carried out at regular intervals (two to three times a year) and have become important aspects of village culture. This return to religiosity among the villagers has strongly influenced their cultural identity. The elaborate communal religious functions have partly resuscitated traditional understandings of their own culture. In these activities, the ancestors are once again given centre stage.

The Future: Chinese Overseas Communities and Their Identity

How can we conceptualize the Chinese overseas communities and their identity? This work has demonstrated how the Chinese overseas are constantly searching for their identity, especially so in new nation-states with multi-ethnic populations.

Singapore is one society within which Chinese are subjected to various types of identity. First, there is the Singapore national identity, which is tied to the status of the polity, where citizens are required to declare their allegiance to the nation-state. This imagined identity and imagined community is essential for the collective well-being of the state and its population. Second, there is the Singapore Chinese identity constructed through a negotiating process between the Singapore state and the Chinese community. This identity portrays the Singapore Chinese as a homogenized group to outsiders: a large segment of the Singapore Chinese population use Mandarin as the lingua franca, and they are economically successful, urbane, sophisticated, obedient and so forth. Culturally, this Singapore Chinese identity is largely represented by its food and religious practices. Other aspects of traditional Chinese culture (e.g., art, traditional music and dance, calligraphy, etc.) are less significant.

Third, there are the narrower regional and dialect-based identities that many Singapore Chinese continue to subscribe to. These are insiders' identities which differentiate the Chinese among themselves, and are relatively invisible to the outside. They are marked by dialects, slight variations in religious practice, mannerisms and food culture.

It is also possible to portray the Singapore Chinese identity as a matter of four concentric circles. Here, the centre is the primordial (lineage) cultural identity, followed by the dialect and territorial identity, then by the Singapore Chinese ethnic identity and at the outermost, the Singapore national identity. It is possible for us to see that the first three sets of identity often overlap with one another. When such overlaps occur, their common foundational bases also increase and this strengthens the social and cultural networks of the members within the system; where they do not, it is weaker. At the outermost layer, identity is shared with other ethnic groups. At this level, there are integrating factors that allow the citizens to proclaim themselves Singaporeans. The state attempts to shape this identity with a set of shared values.

At the second level, all Chinese in Singapore share their certain values associated with ethnicity and cultural practices. At the third level, the social base is narrower and differentiated, involving Chinese from different regions, who speak different dialects. Finally, each lineage is united, with a focus on its particular narrow social base, centred on its original ancestral source.

In their quest for cultural identity, the Singapore Chinese have looked to their ancestral roots for a sense of historical and cultural continuity. This has given them a renewed sense of 'Chineseness'. How they look at the issue of 'Chineseness' and 'Chinese cultural identity' is important for their identity as Singapore Chinese. Singapore Chinese use their four sets of identities in different social contexts to represent themselves to different groups of people, including those of other nationalities, ethnicities, dialect groups, and lineages. The four levels of identity form a total cultural baggage, which make them Singaporeans. Their different identities are only displayed in relation to whichever groups and people they are dealing with—that is, their identities are context- and situation-bound, and represent social distance between themselves and others.

Singapore, in the late 1990s, had moved away from earlier preoccupation with economic and political stability and was focusing on the cultural and social values of its citizenry. As we have moved into the twenty-first century, the urgency of the quest for a national identity is less pronounced, as new generations of Singaporeans have known no other home than a Singapore with policies of multi-ethnicity and multiculturalism fully entrenched. Given such a situation, individual ethnic and sub-ethnic groups will probably be given greater room for cultural expression. This greater cultural autonomy that is allowed by the state is likely to foster greater cultural dynamism among ethnic groups, enabling a flowering of cultural activity and cultural identity. Of course, such a movement might also promote ethnic rivalry.

The encouragement by the state and the active roles taken by the various Chinese social institutions—clan and lineage associations—have enabled the Singapore Chinese to undertake initiatives and embark on a cultural renaissance, in which a focus on art, literature, music, philosophy and aesthetics becomes possible.

New Social Dynamics of the Young Generations

With the gradual passing of the first generation, a new cycle has also begun. The first generation had previously worked hard to bring the younger generation to their ancestral village; the baton has been passed to the second generation, who are now middle-aged with grown-up children of their own. They are the ones who bring their offspring and their grandchildren back to the ancestral village and become responsible for the religious and cultural activities there as well as those in Singapore. The extent to which they are willing to continue their support and participate in such activities will be a testimony to their understanding of Confucian moral responsibility to their ancestors and beyond. Will they continue to believe in the notion of *yinshui siyan* and persuade their younger generations to adhere to it? This is particularly important because they too will become ancestors in the years to come.

With the increase in the generation depth of the Chinese, including the Ke in Singapore, the sinking of the cultural roots and the recognition of one as a complete Singapore Chinese, identity formation of the third, fourth and other future generation, many of whom only know Singapore as their home, will be contested. Will they continue to hold true to the four sets of identities, or will individuals selectively decide on which set/sets of identity they wish to adhere to? In a modern Singapore environment, these individuals have a choice. While the individuals are prescribed two broad identities at birth by the state—as a Singaporean and a Chinese, and the surname/lineage affiliation by their family, individuals can choose to recognize or ignore their dialect and territorial ancestral homeland affiliations.

As we move towards the second decade of the twenty-first century, Singapore Chinese will assess their relationship with their ancestral village and it should come as no surprise that some form of social distancing occurs between them and their kin in the ancestral village as a result of a variety of factors. First, like all developed countries, Singapore's family structure has undergone great transformation. Nuclear family has become the norm. Second, other social and religious groupings have increasingly superseded the traditional Chinese social institutions as a source of support and networks for the younger Singaporean in general and Singapore Chinese in particular. These include professional organizations, churches and temples and other socio-recreational groupings.

The same is also true of the younger generations of Mainland Chinese in general and the Anxi Ke in particular. As China has become an economic powerhouse and many of the villagers have become wealthy and urbane, there is upward mobility and an elevation of their socio-economic status both within Mainland China and in the global sphere. As such, there is also a restructuring of the social relationship between the Anxi Chinese and their overseas counterparts.

Many of the more competent young villagers have left for the regional towns and big cities in search of economic and social opportunities. Some of them have become relatively well-off too. They no longer need assistance from their Singapore kin. Others have managed to migrate to Singapore or elsewhere, and this places them into a transnational migration network. Their new social standing has enabled them to articulate a more equitable social relationship with their Singapore counterparts.

Thus, what we are witnessing in the twenty-first century is that the new generation of Anxi and Singapore Ke members have reassessed their relationship. In this process they have discovered that a new social matrix is evolving, in which kinship revolves more around social and cultural activities, instead of the economic demands thrust upon them. Unlike the earlier years of reform, essential infrastructure and various types of economic development have already been put in place in the *qiaoxiang*. As such, the demands placed upon the Singapore Anxi Chinese to help fund these projects have eased. For those who continue the transnational kinship and lineage relationship have chosen to do so because they have found such relationship meaningful and are sentimental towards their ancestral village. For others, they will continue in a diverging direction and will lose touch with their ancestral home in time to come.

With this social transformation, there will be interesting and changing social dynamics between the source and the nodes, given that the new generations will have different outlooks and expectations. Will we see a complete break of the relationship between the two groups of Chinese? Is the thread getting thinner and will it break without reinforcement, just as what a Singapore elder has feared? For now, cultural and communal religious activities and ancestor worship hosted on a regular basis and participated by members of the Ke lineage in Penglai and Singapore help cement the transnational social relationships of those in this cultural network.

As China continues its economic ascendance and political liberalization, it is possible to predict that the traffic between the Mainland and the Chinese Diaspora will increase in the years to come and this will inevitably impact on the relationship between the source and the nodes. A growing number of the fourth and fifth-generation young Chinese in the Diaspora of America and elsewhere have already begun to search for their cultural and ancestral roots in China, with the help of the Overseas Chinese Bureau.

Likewise, there is an increasing number of younger Mainland Chinese who have moved abroad. They now feel secure and confident in their own future and have begun to reassess their own Diaspora status. Some have embarked on a journey of return migration and become the coveted returnees from across the oceans termed *haigui* (海归) that the multinational and state agencies want to recruit. They are also called the sea turtles (海龟), homonym as *haigui*, which migrate long distance and eventually return to their shores. Undoubtedly, some of the Anxi Chinese have moved back to China and are now residing in towns and cities. They would play a significant role in reshaping the dynamic relationship between the source and the nodes.

In this concluding chapter, I argue that the journey back to the ancestral village that started thirty years ago continues into the future as the Chinese carry on their journey of migration in a variety of forms, culminating in circulatory and return migration. Through their journey, each individual is confronted with issues of identity and home that are shaped by their past and present experiences, collective memories and understanding of moral duties to their family, lineage, country and humanity.

Notes

Chapter 1 Introduction

1. For a discussion of the use of Confucian ideology for statecraft and economic development, see Kuah (1990); Chua (1995: 147–168); Wong (1996: 277–293); and Kuo (1996: 294–309).
2. For a discussion on the debates supporting the 'Greater China' phenomenon, see *The China Quarterly*, December 1993, vol. 136, special issue on Greater China.
3. For a discussion on the debates supporting the 'Cultural China' phenomenon, see W.M. Tu (ed.) (1994), *The Living Tree: The Changing Meaning of Being Chinese Today* (Stanford: Stanford University Press), originally published in Daedalus, as a special issue on 'Cultural China', Spring 1991.

Chapter 2 Constructing a Singapore Chinese Cultural Identity

1. A conference entitled 'Luodi Shengen: The Legal, Political and Economic Status of Chinese in Diaspora' was held on 26–29 November 1992 in San Francisco which discussed the status of Chinese overseas during the nineteenth and twentieth centuries.
2. Straits Chinese men are called *baba* while the women are known as *nonya*. Their unique cuisine, often prepared by the women, is termed *nonya* cuisine.
3. It is to be noted here that the Malays and Indians are not homogeneous ethnic groups either, as within each group there are numerous subgroups, with a great variety of dialects. Also encouraged by the state, they are similarly embarking on a process of cultural standardization in a quest to portray ethnically unified images.

4. In 1994, the Singapore government introduced the Maintenance of Parents Act (Cap 167B) that enables Singapore citizens 60 years of age and above to claim maintenance allowance, either on a monthly basis or a lump sum payment, from their children if they are unable to sustain themselves. They could initiate a court case for this purpose. This is an attempt by the state to prevent adult children from neglecting their parents. This act requires adult children to provide financial assistance, set at S$500 a month, to their parents.

Chapter 3 The Ancestral Village in Anxi County

1. Figures provided by Anxi County Administrative Office.
2. Figures provided by Anxi County Administrative Office.
3. Figures provided by Anxi County Administrative Office.

Chapter 4 Negotiating Collective Memories and Social Experiences

1. Kaye did a sociological study of families in Singapore during this period and concluded that there was much overcrowding, with as many as five or six households living in a two-storey shophouse. See B. Kaye (1960), *Upper Nankin Street: Singapore* (Singapore: University of Malaya Press).
2. Many were able to identify members of their kinship circle: their father's elder brothers as *bofu* (伯父), father's elder brother's wife as *bomu* (伯母), mother's sister as *muyi* (母姨) or *yimu* (姨母), father's brother's sons (paternal male cousins) as *tangxiongdi* (堂兄弟), father's brother's daughters (paternal female cousins) as *tangjiemei* (堂姐妹), and mother's brother's sons and daughters (maternal cousins) as *biaoxiongdi* (表兄弟) and *biaojiemei* (表姐妹).

Chapter 5 The Moral Economy of Rebuilding the Ancestral Village

1. For a discussion on early remittances by overseas Chinese to China, see G. L. Hicks (ed.) (1993), *Overseas Chinese Remittances from Southeast Asia 1910–1940* (Singapore: Select Books).
2. For a discussion of this, see Chen Kechen (1994), *Anxi Huaqiao zhi* (Xiamen: Xiamen University Press).
3. Other uses included the starting of small businesses, the purchase of equipment and electronic goods and the financing of marriages.

Chapter 6 The Bond of Ancestor Workship

1. For a discussion on death rites and ancestor worship, see J. J. DeGroot (1964), vol. 1.

2. Among the Singapore Chinese, this is one main reason for staging large-scale communal sacrificial offerings to the wandering ghosts during the Hungry Ghost Festival (Zhongyuan Jie) during the seventh lunar month.
3. For a discussion on the relationship between space and social structure, including identity, see M. Castells (1976: 60–84); see also D. Harvey (1985).
4. Khun Eng Kuah-Pearce (2004), 'Cultural and Network Capitals: Chinese Women and the "Religious" Industry in South China', in Khun Eng Kuah-Pearce (ed.), *Chinese Women and Their Social and Network Capitals* (Singapore: Marshall Cavendish International), pp. 121–143.
5. In recent years, people with Chinese ancestors overseas who have high official titles have been given due acknowledgements by the provincial government. One example here is the restoration of the ancestral grave of the former president of the Philippines, Corazon Aquino, when she visited her ancestral village in Hongjian Village, Longhai County, Fujian.
6. For a discussion of karma and merit-making, see G. Obeyesekere (1968: 7–40).
7. The debate on whether the practice of Chinese religion is a matter of orthodoxy or orthopraxy is discussed extensively by J. L. Watson, who favours orthopraxy, while Whyte argues for the importance of orthodoxy. See Watson (1988: 3–19); see also Whyte (1988: 289–316).
8. The six Buddhist planes of existence are Heaven, Human, Azuras, Animal, Preta and Hell. See D. D. Daye (1978: 123–126).
9. See M. Freedman (1979: 296–312) for a discussion on geomancy.

Chapter 7 Religious Revivalism

1. In 2010, during a visit to the Penglai temple in Singapore, I was informed that the leasehold of the temple was coming up for renewal, there was still no decision taken on this. If members of the seven temple groups could not come to an agreement, then the land on which the temple stood would be reverted back to the government and the fate of the temple would be at stake.

Chapter 8 Rewriting Geneology and Reclaiming One's Cultural Roots

1. During my research, I discovered that many village households had more than one child; some had several, especially daughters, as many couples would continue to reproduce until they finally had a son. Under the one-child policy, they dared not risk registering all their children. As a result, many daughters and sons were not formally registered with the Bureau of Birth. Such children are called 'Japanese sons' by the locals, to differentiate them from those who have registration papers issued by the village

government. Only after giving birth to a son, or after having the desired number of children, would the family bring all the children for registration and pay the required fines. On another trip to the village, the local family planning unit had tightened their policy and for those women found pregnant with a second child, the husband was arrested and locked up until the wife aborted the child. I am aware of one such case where despite the fact that the woman was already in her second trimester of pregnancy, she had to abort her child (which turned out to be a son) so that her husband would be released from custody. They already have a daughter.

Glossary

Pronunciations of words are given in Mandarin (Putonghua,普通话) alphabetized according to the Hanyu Pinyin system, except where followed by [H] (for Fujian dialect). Proper nouns are capitalized.

anwei (安位) – positioning
Anxi Huiguan, Ann Kway Hui Guan [H] (安溪会舘) – Anxi Association

Baihuayou, Pae Hway Yew [H] (白花油) – a brand of medicated oil called White Flower Oil
bai tiangong (拜天公) – praying to Heaven
beishan wangshui (背山望水) – 'backing the hills and facing the waters', used to refer to a good geomantic location with a good view
biaojiemei (表姐妹) – first or second female cross-cousins; mother's sisters' and brothers' daughters, maternal grandmother's sisters' and brothers' granddaughters, and both grandfather's sisters' granddaughters
biaowen (表文) – a religious rite. The priest makes a submission to the deities on behalf of the supplicant.
biaoxiongdi (表兄弟) – first or second male cross-cousins; mother's sister's or brother's sons;
bishang buzu, bixia youyu (比上不足，比下有余) – 'cannot be compared to those above you (in terms of wealth and social status) but is well endowed when compared with those below one's social and economic stratum
bofu (伯父) – paternal uncle, father's elder brothers
bomu (伯母) – wife of elder brother
boshi (博士) – a person with a PhD

buhui zuoren (不会做人) – 'does not how to be a person', meaning one does not know how to behave properly

changshoudeng (长寿灯) – longevity lanterns
couwen, cho-bun [H] (凑文) – petition to the deities/gods
citang (祠堂) – lineage ancestral hall

Dabei zhou (大悲咒) – Great Compassion Sutra
daode jingji (道德经济) – moral economy
daode jingji wangluo (道德经济网络) – moral economic network
Dashiye (大士爷) – A deity, protector of the netherworld
dating (大厅) – first hall, first branch of the lineage
dawu (大屋) – 'grand house'; spirit or soul house
Da Zhonghua (大中华) – Great China Thesis
dianxie (点谢) – offering of libation to the deities or dead
difangzhi (地方志) – local gazetteer
Dizangwang pusa benyuanjing (地藏王菩萨本愿经) – Ksitigarbha Bodhisattva Sutra

erting (二厅) – second hall, second branch of the lineage

fan, huang [H] (番) – uncivilized and detribalized
fanren (番人) – uncivilized and/or detribalized person
fang (房) – 1. room; 2. a stem family
fangyan gonghui (方言公会) – dialect associations
fanke, huang-ke [H] (番客) – uncivilized guest
fashi (法事) – religious activities
feiqiao (肥侨) – 'fat overseas Chinese'; wealthy overseas Chinese
fengshui (风水) – geomancy
fengshuidi (风水地) – burial sites chosen according to geomancy
fodan (佛诞) – birthday of Buddha
fotou, puo-tau [H] (佛头) – 'buddha head', also known as stove-master; person in charge of a religious celebration
fu (符) – amulet
fugui bulizu (富贵不离祖) – 'wealth does not depart from the ancestors'

ganqing (感情) – sentiments
gen (根) – root
genyuan (根源) – source, origin
gongde (功德) – meritorious deeds. A religious ceremony to transfer merits to the dead and to increase the dead's store of good karma.

guanxi (关系) – social connection
guanxi wang (关系网) – social network
guhun (孤魂) – lonely soul
guma (姑妈) – paternal aunt, father's elder sister

haigui (海归) – return migrants to China
haigui (海龟) – sea turtles
Hanlin Academy (翰林院) – a scholarly institution within the Chinese Mandarinate
hongbao (红包) – a small sum of money placed in a red envelope
huaqiao (华侨) – overseas Chinese, Chinese overseas
huaren hua (华人化) – become Chinese, become sinicized
Hubiaoyou, Hor Piaw Yew [H] (虎标油) – a brand of medicated oil/balm called Tiger Balm Oil
huitou (汇头) – head of the credit rotation system
hun (魂) – soul

jia (家) – family
jiagen (家根) – family roots
jiapu (家谱) – family genealogy
jieyuanqian (结缘钱) – affinity money, money given to outsiders who would perform ritual mourning during the funeral rites for family who do not have a sufficiently large group of mourners for this purpose
Jingang jing (金刚经) – Diamond Sutra
jinian, ki-liem [H] (纪念) – remember, memorialize
jinshi (进士) – scholar who passed the highest level of imperial examination
jiujiu (舅舅) – maternal uncle, mother's brothers
jizu (祭祖) – worship the ancestors
juanding (涓丁) – continuous flow of descendants
junzi (君子) – gentleman
juren (举人) – scholar who passed the second-level imperial examination

kaipu (关谱) – opening the genealogy
kaipu yishi (关谱仪式) – the ceremony of opening the genealogy
kai zuzhai men (开祖宅门) – opening the doors of the ancestral house
Kuitou Keshi Zupu (魁头柯氏族谱) – Ke Genealogy of Kuitou Village
Kuitou zuzhai, kwaytau zhorchu [H] (魁头祖宅) – Kuitou Ancestral House
kuixinggong, kway-sin-gong (H) (魁星公) – Penglai District guardian deity

laojia (老家) – old home
li (礼) – propriety

ling (灵) – spiritually efficacious
lingwu, ling-chu [H] (灵屋) – soul/spirit house. See *dawu*.
liunian (留念) – have fond memories
luobi zushigong (落鼻祖师公) – 'dropping nose ancestor'
luodi shenggen (落地生根) – planting one's roots in foreign soil
luoye guigen (落叶归根) – 'the leaves return to the roots'

maowu (茅屋) – communal latrine made of planks, with thatched roof
Mazu (妈祖) – Heavenly Empress, also known as Tian Hou (天后)
Miaofa Lianhuajing (妙法莲花经) – Lotus Sutra
mingyun (命运) – fate, destiny
mixinde (迷信的) – superstitious
mubei (木杯) – small boat-shaped wooden religious item 8–10 cm long and 4 cm wide with one side concave and the other flat
muyi (母姨) – maternal aunt, mother's sister

neijiu (内疚) – remorseful
nianshou (念寿) – chant prayers for the dead

Omitojing [H] (阿弥陀经) – Amitabha Sutra

paibeifen (排辈份) – to assemble all members according to the generational order of the members, senority is based on one's generational order and not age
Penglai Si (蓬莱寺) – Penglai Temple
po (魄) – spirit
pu (谱) – genealogy
pudu (普渡) – religious rituals to provide merits for the dead

qiaobao (侨胞) – overseas compatriots
Qiaolian suo (侨联所) – Overseas Chinese Guest House
qiaoqin (侨亲) – overseas relatives
qiaoxiang (侨乡) – emigrant villages
Qingming jie (清明节) – Festival for Sweeping the Tombs
qinqing guanxi wangluo (亲情关系网络) – kinship social network
Qingshuiyan Si (清水岩寺) – Clear-Water Deified Ancestor Temple
Qingshui zushigong (清水祖师公) – The Clear-Water Deified Ancestor
qinqing (亲情) – kinship sentiments
qipao (旗袍) – traditional high-collared gown
qiyuandi (起源地) – place of origin

ren (仁) – human-ness, humanity
renao (热闹) – heat and noise; a noisy and exciting atmosphere
renjian (人间) – human plane of existence
renzu (认祖) – recognize or acknowledge the ancestors

sangli (丧礼) – mourning rites
shanqu (山区) – mountainous district
shehui wangluo (社会网络) – social networks
sihaizhinei jiexiongdiye (四海之内皆兄弟也) – 'within the four seas, we are brothers'
shouqiao (瘦侨) – 'thin overseas relatives'; those who are not wealthy
shushu (叔叔) – paternal uncle, father's younger brother
sifangqian (私房钱) – 'private room money'; a woman's private savings
sishu (私塾) – private tuition, during the nineteenth century; usually for girls who did not go to schools
siying qiyue (私营企业) – private enterprise

tangshan (唐山) – China
tangshanke (唐山客) – guests from China
tangshanxin (唐山信) – 'China letter', letter from village kin in village
tangshu (堂叔) – father's brother and father's first cousin,
tangjiemei (堂姐妹) father's brothers' daughters – paternal female first and second cousins; also, paternal grandfather's brother's granddaughters
tangxiongdi (堂兄弟) – father's brothers' sons, and paternal grandfather's brother's grandsons; paternal male first and second cousins
tianfang (填房) – 'filling the room'; taking a concubine
tongxiang (同乡) – of the same rural village or area
tongxianghui (同乡会) – same-village or same-territory-based association, also called territorial associations
tongxiang huiguan (同乡会馆) – same as tongxianghui
tudigong (土地公) – Earth God

wenhua qu (文化区) – cultural district
Wenhua Zhongguo (文化中国) – Cultural China Thesis
wugu (五谷) – mourning rites according to the five-grain categorization
Wumian zushigong (乌面祖师公) – Black-faced Deified Ancestor

xian (县) – county
xiancheng (县城) – county town
xianglu (香炉) – incense urn
xiangyou (香油) – incense and oil

xiao (孝) – filial
Xiaojing (孝经) – the *Book of Filial Piety*
xia shu wei, ae-chiu-ber [H] (下树尾) – below the tree
xiepu yishi (谢谱仪式) – The Rite of Thanking the Genealogy
xiezu (谢祖) – giving thanks to the ancestors
xiezu juanding (谢祖涓丁) – The Rite of Thanking the Ancestors for the Continuous Flow of Descendants
xin (心) – heart, spirit
xinjia (新家) – new house
Xinjiapo Fujian Anxi Huaren (新加坡福建安溪华人) – Singapore Fujian Anxi Chinese
Xinjiapo Huaren (新加坡华人) – Singapore Chinese
Xinjing (心经) – Heart Sutra
xin laojia (新老家) – renovated old house of traditional architectural style
xingshi gonghui (姓氏公会) – surname association
xinyong (信用) – trust
xitou, kway-tau [H] (溪头) – creek head, source of a river
xiucai (秀才) – scholar who passed the first level imperial examination
xiupu (修谱) – 'mending the genealogy' by adding new entries and correcting old ones
xiuxin (修心) – spiritual cultivation of the heart
xiwei, kway-ber [H] (溪尾) – downstream of a river
xuetong guanxi (血统关系) – blood ties

yangjian (阳间) – heavenly plane of existence
yangqi (阳气) – *yang* (roughly, positive or active) energy
ye (叶) – leaf
yi (仪) – rite
yimu (姨母) – mother's sisters
ying qingshui zushi (迎清水祖师) – Rite for Welcoming the Clear-Water Deified Ancestor
yingshen yinghuo (迎神迎火) – Rite for Welcoming the Deities and Fire
ying zushi (迎祖师) – Rite for the Welcoming of the Deified Ancestor
yinhun (引魂) – Rite for Guiding the Soul of the Dead
yinjian (阴间) – netherworld
yinqi (阴气) – *yin* (roughly, negative or passive) energy
yinqian (银钱) – paper money for the dead, spirits and gods
yinshui siyuan (饮水思源) – 'when drinking the water, think of the source'
yixiongdi (义兄弟) – sworn brothers

youlu wuwu (有路无屋) – There is a road but no home, meaning that a Chinese from overseas can come to the ancestral village but has no home there.
youhun (游魂) – wandering spirit

zhangcheng (章程) – petition
zhi (枝) – stem or branch
zhong (忠) – loyalty
Zhongyuan Jie (中元节) – Festival of the Hungry Ghosts
Zhouyue Miao (州月庙) – Zhouyue Temple
zijiren (自己人) – member of one's group
zong (宗) – lineage
zongci (宗祠) – ancestral hall
zongmiao (宗庙) – ancestor shrine
zongpu (宗谱) – genealogy
zongqing (宗亲) – lineage members
zongqing guanxi wangluo (宗情关系网) – lineage guanxi network
zongtang (宗堂) – lineage shrine
zongxiang hui (宗乡会) – lineage association
zoujing (做劲) – religious service, chanting of sutras
zu (祖) – ancestor
zucuo, zhor-chu [H] (祖厝) – ancestral house
zuding (祝丁) – rite of gratification for the flow of descendants
zujia (祖家) – ancestral family/home
zumiao (祖庙) – ancestral temple
zupu (族谱) – lineage genealogy
zushidian (祖师殿) – Shrine Hall Devoted to the Deified Ancestor
Zushigong Dan (祖师公诞) – Birthday of the Deified Ancestor
zuxiang (祖乡) – ancestral village
zuzhai (祖宅) – ancestral house

Bibliography

Anderson, B. (1986). *Imagined Communities: Reflections on the Origin and Spread of Nationalism.* London: Verso, 3rd. edition.

Anderson, J. N. D. (ed.) (1968). *Family Law in Asia and Africa.* London: Allen and Unwin.

Anxi County Website （安溪区划地名网）, http://ax.dmw.gov.cn. Retrieved on 30 December 2009.

Anxi Kuitou Penglai Keshi Zupu (Anxi Kuitou Penglai Ke Lineage Genealogy) (Eighth amendment 1996), Vols. 1 and 2.

Bourdieu, P. (1993). *The Field of Cultural Production.* New York: Columbia University Press.

Brook, T. (1988). Must lineages own land? *Bulletin of Concerned Asian Scholars* 20(4): 72–79.

Castells, M. (1976). Theory and ideology in urban sociology. In C. G. Pickvance (ed.), *Urban Sociology: Critical Essays.* London: Tavistock, pp. 60–84.

Chen, Jintian (1989). Zuxian shenzhu ji jisi（陈金田：〈祖先神主及祭祀〉）. *Taiwan fengwu*（《台湾风物》）39(1): 99–106.

Chen, Kechen (ed.) (1994). *Anxi huaqiao zhi*（陈克晨主编：《安溪华侨志》）. Xiamen: Xiamen University Press（厦门：厦门大学出版社）.

Chen, Luxi (1980). *Jizu wenti*（陈璐兮：《祭祖问题》）. Taipei: Xiaoyuan shufang（台北：校园书房）.

Chen, Xiangshui (1978). Zhongguo shehui jiegou yu zuxian chongbai（陈祥水：〈中国社会结构与祖先崇拜〉）. *Zhonghua wenhua fuxing yuekan*（《中华文化复兴月刊》）11(6): 32–39.

Chen, Zhongmin (1969). Jinjiangcuo de zuxian chongbai yu shizu zuzhi (陈中民：〈晋江厝的祖先崇拜与氏族组织〉). *Minzuxue yanjiusuo jijkan* (《民族学研究所集刊》) 23: 167–193.

Chua, B. H. (1995). *Communitarian Ideology and Democracy in Singapore*. London: Routledge.

Daye, D. D. (1978). Cosmology. In C. S. Prebish (ed.), *Buddhism: A New Perspective*. University Park: Pennsylvania State University Press, pp. 123–126.

De Groot, J. J. M. (1964). *The Religion of the Chinese*. Vols. 1–6. Taipei: Literature House, reprint.

Dun Jue (1980). You yige anjing de difang gen zuxian shuohua (顿觉：〈有一个安静的地方跟祖先说话〉). *Guanxi wo* (《关系我》) 1: 27–29.

Eberhard, W. (1972). Chinese genealogies as a source for the study of Chinese society. In J. Palmer (ed.), *Studies in Asian Genealogy*. Provo, UT: Brigham Young University Press, pp. 27–37.

Ebrey, P. B. and Watson, J. L. (1986). *Kinship Organisation in Late Imperial China, 1000–1949*. Berkeley: University of California Press.

Evans-Pritchard, E. E. and Fortes, M. (eds.) (1970). *African Political Systems*. London: Oxford University Press.

Faure, D. (1989). The lineage as a cultural intervention. *Modern China* 15(1): 4–36.

Fei, H. T. (1939). *Peasant Life in China*. London: Routledge Kegan and Paul.

Fei, H. T. and Chang, C. T. (1953). *China's Gentry*. Chicago: Chicago University Press.

Fentress, J. and Wickham, C. (1992). *Social Memory*. Oxford: Blackwell.

Feuchtwang, S. D. R. (1974). *An Anthropological Analysis of Chinese Geomancy*. Vientiane: Vithagna.

Freedman, M. (1957). *Chinese Marriage and Family in Singapore*. London: Her Majesty's Stationery Office, Colonial Research Studies No. 20.

Freedman, M. (1958). *Lineage Organisation in Southeast China*. London: LSE Monograph, no. 18.

Freedman, M. (1966). *Chinese Lineage and Society: Fukien and Kwangtung*. London: LSE Monograph on Social Anthropology, no. 33.

Freedman, M. (1979). *The Study of Chinese Society: Essays*. Selected and introduced by G. W. Skinner. Stanford, CA: Stanford University Press.

Fujian jingji (1987, 1989, 1990). (《福建经济》).

Fujian tongji nianjian (1992). (《福建统计年鉴》).

Fujiansheng Anxixian difangzhi bianweiyuanhui (ed.) (1994). *Zhonghua Renmin Gongheguo difangzhi: Anxi xianzhi* (福建省安溪县地方志编委员会编：《中华人民共和国地方志：安溪县志》). Vols. 1

and 2. Beijing: Xinhua chubanshe (北京：新华出版社). (Anxi County government: http://www.fjax.gov.cn/pagehtml/2008/04/b83cf92a-0887-4acd-acd4-6495256579d7.html) (安溪县政府网站信息)
Furnivall, J. S. (1980). Plural societies. In H-D. Evers (ed.), *Sociology of Southeast Asia*. Kuala Lumpur: Oxford University Press, pp. 86–96.
Geary, P. J. (1994). *Phantoms of Remembrance*. New Jersey: Princeton University Press.
Geertz, G. (1973). *The Interpretation of Cultures*. New York: Basic Books.
Granet, M. (1975). *The Religion of the Chinese People*. Oxford: Oxford University Press.
Halbwachs, M. (1992). *On Collective Memory*. Chicago: Chicago University Press.
Hannerz, U. (1992). *Cultural Complexity: Studies in the Social Organisation of Meaning*. New York: Columbia University Press.
Harding, H. (1993). The concept of 'Greater China': Themes, variations and reservations. *The China Quarterly* 136: 660–686, special issue on Greater China.
Harvey, D. (1985). *Consciousness and the Urban Experience*. Oxford: Basil Blackwell.
Hazelton, K. (1986). Patrilines and the development of localised lineages: The Wu of Hsiu-ning City, Hui-chou to 1528. In P. Ebrey and J. Watson (eds.), *Kinship Organization in Late Imperial China, 1000–1940*. Berkeley: University of California Press, pp. 137–169.
Hicks, G. L. (ed.) (1993). *Overseas Chinese Remittances from Southeast Asia 1910–1940*. Singapore: Select Books.
Hobsbawm, E. and Ranger, T. (eds.) (1983). *The Invention of Tradition*. Cambridge: Cambridge University Press.
Hsiao, K. C. (1966). *Rural China: Imperial Control in the Nineteenth Century*. Seattle: University of Washington Press.
http://ax.dmw.gov.cn/onews.asp?id=1428, website of Anxi County Government. Retrieved on 30 December 2009.
http://axpenglai.com, website of Penglai Local Government. Retrieved on 30 December 2009.
Huang, Shu-min (1989). *The Spiral Road: Changes in a Chinese Village Through the Eyes of a Communist Party Leader*. Boulder, CO: Westview Press.
Huang, Youzhi (1988). Zhongguo zuxian chongbai de yiyi tantao (黄有志：〈中国祖先崇拜的意义探讨〉). *Shijian xuebao* (《实践学报》) 19: 1–24.
Hymes, R. P. (1986) Marriage, descent groups, and the localist strategy in Sung and Yuan Fuchou. In P. Ebrey and J. Watson (eds.), *Kinship Organization in Late Imperial China, 1000–1940*. Berkeley: University of California Press, pp. 95–136.

Kaye, B. (1960). *Upper Nankin Street: Singapore*. Singapore: University of Malaya Press.

Kluckhohn, C. (1960). *Mirror of Man*. Greenwich: Fawcett Publications.

Kuah, Khun Eng (1990). Confucian ideology and social engineering in Singapore. *Journal of Contemporary Asia* 20(3): 371–383.

Kuah, Khun Eng (1998a). Maintaining ethno-religious harmony in Singapore. *Journal of Contemporary Asia* 28(1): 103–121.

Kuah, Khun Eng (1998b). Rebuilding their ancestral villages: The moral economy of the Singapore Chinese. In G. W. Wang and J. Wong (eds.), *China's Political Economy*. Singapore: University of Singapore Press and World Scientific, pp. 249–276.

Kuah, Khun Eng (1999). The changing moral economy of ancestor worship in a Chinese emigrant village. *Culture, Medicine and Psychiatry* 23(1): 99–132.

Kuah, Khun Eng (2000a). *Rebuilding the Ancestral Village: Singaporeans in China*. Aldershot: Ashgate.

Kuah-Pearce, Khun Eng (2000b). As local and global cultural brokers: A Fujianese territorial-based association in Hong Kong. In Teresita Ang (ed.), *Intercultural Relations, Cultural Transformation and Identity: The Ethnic Chinese*. Manila: Kaisa Publication, pp. 226–235 (co-author: Wong Siu-lun).

Kuah-Pearce, Khun Eng (2001). Dialect and territorial-based associations: Cultural and identity brokers in Hong Kong. In Lee Pui-tak (ed.), *Hong Kong Reintegrating with China: Political, Cultural and Social Dimensions*. Hong Kong: Hong Kong University Press, pp. 203–218 (co-author: Wong Siu-lun).

Kuah-Pearce, Khun Eng (2003). The relationship between ancestor worship and cultural capitalism in a Qiaoxiang village in Fujian, South China (Fujian Qiaoxiang jizu yu wenhua ziben de guanxi, 福建侨乡祭祖与文化资本的关系). In Zhou Daming and Khun Eng Kuah-Pearce (eds.) (周大鸣和柯群英), *Overseas Chinese and the Qiaoxiang Society* (Qiaoxiang yimin yu difang shehui, 《侨乡移民与地方社会》). Beijing: Publishing House for Nationality (北京：民族出版社), pp. 51–67.

Kuah-Pearce, Khun Eng (ed.) (2004a). *Chinese Women and Their Social and Network Capitals*. Singapore: Marshall Cavendish International.

Kuah-Pearce, Khun Eng (2004b). Cultural and network capitals: Chinese women and the religious industry in South China. In Khun Eng Kuah-Pearce (ed.), *Chinese Women and Their Social and Network Capitals*. Singapore: Marshall Cavendish International, pp. 121–143.

Kuah-Pearce, Khun Eng (2006a). The worship of Qingshui zushi and religious revivalism in South China. In Tan Chee-Beng (ed.), *Southern Fujian:*

Reproduction of Tradition in Post-Mao China. Hong Kong: Chinese Hong Kong University Press, pp. 121–144.

Kuah-Pearce, Khun Eng (2006b). Introduction: The Chinese diaspora and voluntary associations. In Khun Eng Kuah-Pearce and Evelyn Hu-Dehart (eds.), *Voluntary Organizations in the Chinese Diaspora*. Hong Kong: Hong Kong University Press (co-author: Evelyn Hu-DeHart), pp. 1–28.

Kuah-Pearce, Khun Eng and Hu-DeHart, Evelyn (eds.) (2006c). *Voluntary Organizations in the Chinese Diaspora*. Hong Kong: Hong Kong University Press.

Kuah-Pearce, Khun Eng (2006d). The cultural politics of clan associations in contemporary Singapore. In Khun Eng Kuah-Pearce and Evelyn Hu-Dehart (eds.), *Voluntary Organizations in the Chinese Diaspora*. Hong Kong: Hong Kong University Press, pp. 53–76.

Kuah-Pearce, Khun Eng (2006e). Transnational self in Chinese diaspora: A conceptual framework. *Asian Studies Review Journal*. Guest issue on 'Locating the Self in the Chinese Diaspora', 30(3) (September): 223–239.

Kuah-Pearce, Khun Eng (2006f). Locating the self in the Chinese diaspora: Introductory remarks. *Asian Studies Review Journal*. Guest issue on 'Locating the Self in the Chinese Diaspora', 30(3) (September): 217–221.

Kuah-Pearce, Khun Eng (2006g). Moralising ancestors as socio-moral capital: A study of a transnational Chinese lineage. *Asian Journal of Social Sciences* 34(2) (June): 243–263.

Kuah-Pearce, Khun Eng and Davidson, A. (eds.) (2008a). *At Home in the Chinese Diaspora: Memory and Belonging*. Basingstoke: Palgrave Macmillan.

Kuah-Pearce, Khun Eng (2008b). Collective memories as cultural capital: From Chinese diaspora to emigrant hometowns. In Khun Eng Kuah-Pearce and A. Davidson (eds.), *At Home in the Chinese Diaspora: Memory and Belonging*. Basingstoke: Palgrave Macmillan, pp. 111–127.

Kuah-Pearce, Khun Eng (2009). *State, Society and Religious Engineering: Towards a Reformist Buddhism*. Singapore: Institute of Southeast Asian Studies, second edition.

Kuchler, Susanne and Melion, Walter (eds.) (1991). *Images of Memory: On Remembering and Representation*. Washington: Smithsonian Institute Press.

Kuo, E. C. Y. (1996). Confucianism as a political discourse in Singapore: The case of an incomplete revitalization movement. In Tu Weiming (ed.), *Confucian Traditions in East Asian Modernity*. Cambridge, MA: Harvard University Press.

La Fontaine, J. S. (1985). *Initiation*. Middlesex: Penguin Books.

Lang, O. (1946). *Chinese Family and Society*. New Haven: Yale University Press.

Lau, P. C. (trans.) (1970). *Mencius*. London: Penguin.

Lau, P. C. (trans.) (1979). *Confucius: The Analects*. Middlesex: Penguin.

Le Goff, Jacques (1992). *History and Memory*. Translated by S. Rendall and E. Claman. New York: Columbia University Press.

Lee, P. H. (1978). *Chinese Society in Nineteenth Century Singapore*. Singapore: Oxford University Press.

Leo, J. B. (1976–77). *Confucianism in Singapore*. Singapore: University of Singapore, Department of Sociology, Academic Exercise, unpublished.

Liao, Kuntian (1979). Cong shenxue de guandian yanjiu dangqian Taiwan hanren shehui zuxian chongbai zhi zongjiao benzhi (廖昆田：〈从神学的观点研究当前台湾汉人社会祖先崇拜之宗教本质〉). *Yazhou jinxinhui shenxue yanjiuyuan shuoshi lunwen* (《亚洲浸信会神学研究院神学硕士论文》).

Lim, J. H. (1967). Chinese female immigration into the Straits Settlement, 1860–1901. *Journal of the South Seas Society* 22: 58–95.

Lin, Luo (1986). Gen—Tan jizu de liyi ji qita (林洛：〈根 — 谈祭祖的礼仪及其它〉). *Minsu yu Xinyang* (《民俗与信仰》) 102: 82–85.

Lin, Meirong (1990). Zupu zhong youguan jizu de wenshu (林美容：〈族谱中有关祭祖的文书〉). *Minzu yanjiusuo ziliao huibian* (《民族研究所资料汇编》) 3: 181–194.

Lin, Shuguang (1990). Zushigong shi shidao erjiao zhi shen (林曙光：〈祖师公是释道二教之神〉). *Guanxi wo* (《关系我》) 37: 78–83.

Lin, Wenbin (ed.) (2003–04). *Anxi Nianjian* (凌文斌主编：《安溪年鑒 2003–04》). Fuzhoushi, Fujian: Haifeng Publishing House (福建省福州市：海风出版社).

Lin, Wenbin (ed.) (2005–06). *Anxi Nianjian* (凌文斌主编：《安溪年鑒 2005–06》). Fuzhoushi, Fujian: Haifeng Publishing House (福建省福州市：海风出版社). Retrieved from http://www.axdfz.gov.cn/showtext.asp?ToBook=17008&index=4&.

Lin, Y. H. (1947). *The Golden Wing: A Sociological Study of Chinese Familism*. London: Kegan Paul, Trench, Trubner.

Liu, Guoguang (1973). Taiwan minjian sizu zhi fengsu (刘国光：〈台湾民间祀祖之风俗〉), *Taiwan funu yuekan* (《台湾妇女月刊》) 202: 3–5.

Lo, H. L. (1972a). The history and arrangement of Chinese genealogies. In J. Palmer (ed.), *Studies in Asian Genealogy*. Provo, UT: Brigham Young University Press, pp. 13–26.

Lo, H. L. (1972b). The preservation of genealogical records in China. In J. Palmer (ed.), *Studies in Asian Genealogy*. Provo, UT: Brigham Young University Press, pp. 38–55.

Lou, Zikuang (1969). Zushigong Chen Zhaoying (娄子匡：〈祖师公陈昭应〉). *Taibei wenxian* (《台北文献》) 6–8: 1–3.

Lou, Zikuang (1977). Qingshui zushi de lailongqumai（娄子匡：〈清水祖师的来龙去脉〉）. *Taiwan wenxian*（《台北文献》）22: 49–52.
Lyons, T. P. (1992). *China's War on Poverty: A Case Study of Fujian Province, 1985–1990*. Hong Kong: Chinese University of Hong Kong.
Lyons, T. P. (1994). *Poverty and Growth in a South China County: Anxi, Fujian 1949–1992*. Ithaca: Cornell University East Asia Series.
Mak, L. F. (1981). *The Sociology of Secret Societies: A Study of Chinese Secret Societies in Singapore and Peninsular Malaysia*. Kuala Lumpur: Oxford University Press.
Mei, J. (1975). Socioeconomic origin of emigration: Guangdong to California, 1850–1882. *Modern China* 5: 463–501.
Nosco, P. (1990). *Remembering Paradise: Nativism and Nostalgia in Eighteenth-Century Japan*. Cambridge, MA: Harvard-Yenching Monograph 31, Harvard University.
Nyce, R. (1969). Chinese folk religion in Malaysia and Singapore. *The Southeast Asia Journal of Theology* 2: 81–91.
Obeyesekere, G. (1968). Theodicy, sin and salvation in a sociology of Buddhism. In E. R. Leach (ed.), *Dialectic in Practical Religion*. Cambridge: Cambridge University Press, pp. 7–40.
Ong, A. and Nonini, D. (eds.) (1997). *Ungrounded Empires: The Cultural Politics of Modern Chinese Transnationalism*. New York: Routledge.
Ong, T. C. (1979). *Report on Moral Education, 1979*. Singapore: Ministry of Education.
Palmer, J. (ed.) (1972). *Studies in Asian Genealogy*. Provo, UT: Brigham Young University Press.
Parish, W. L. and Whyte, M. K. (1978). *Village and Family in Contemporary China*. Chicago: Chicago University Press.
Peng, Jingyuan (1977). Tantan guanyu jingtian jizu de yiyi（彭敬元：〈谈谈关于敬天祭祖的意义〉）. *Hengyi*（《恒毅》）26(8): 2–3.
Perry, R. B. (1909). *The Moral Economy*. New York: Charles Scribner's Sons.
Png, P. S. (1969). The Straits Chinese in Singapore: A case study of local identity and socio-cultural accommodation. *Journal of Southeast Asian History* 10(1): 95–114.
Potter, S. H. and Potter, J. M. (1990). *China's Peasants: The Anthropology of a Revolution*. Cambridge: Cambridge University Press.
Purcell, V. (1951). *The Chinese in Southeast Asia*. London: Oxford University Press.
Purcell, V. (1967). *The Chinese in Malaya*. Kuala Lumpur: Oxford University Press.
Quah, J., Chan, H. C. and Seah, C. M. (eds.) (1985). *Government and Politics of Singapore*. Singapore: Oxford University Press.

Rawski, E. S. (1988). A historian's approach to Chinese death ritual. In J. L. Watson and E. S. Rawski (eds.), *Death Rituals in Later Imperial and Modern China*. Berkeley: University of California Press, pp. 20–36.

Reid, A. (ed.) (1996). *Sojourners and Settlers: Histories of Southeast Asia and the Chinese*. St. Leonard, NSW: Allen and Unwin and ASAA Southeast Asia Publication Series.

Rodan, G. (ed.) (1993). *Singapore Changes Guards*. Melbourne: Longman Cheshire.

Scott, J. (1985). *Weapons of the Weak*. New Haven: Yale University Press.

Simoniya, N. A. (1961). *Overseas Chinese in Southeast Asia: A Russian Study*. Ithaca: Cornell University Southeast Asia Programme.

Soothill, W. E. (1973). *The Three Religions of China*. London: Curzon Press, reprint.

Tamney, J. (1996). *The Struggle over Singapore's Soul*. Berlin: Walter de Gruyter.

Tan, T. T. W. (1984). Modernisation: A study of traditional Chinese voluntary associations in social change. Ann Arbor: Microfilms International, University of Virginia PhD dissertation, 1983.

Tan, T. T. W. (1986). *Your Chinese Roots: The Overseas Chinese Story*. Singapore: Times Books International.

Tong, C. K. (1982). Funerals, ancestral halls and graveyards: Changes and continuities in Chinese ancestor worship in Singapore. National University of Singapore, Department of Sociology, M.A. dissertation, unpublished.

Topley, M. (1961). The emergence and social function of Chinese religious associations in Singapore. *Comparative Studies in Society and History* 3(3): 289–314.

Tu, W. M. (1985). *Confucian Thought*. Albany: State University of New York Press.

Tu, W. M. (1994a). Cultural China: The periphery as the centre. In W.M. Tu (ed.), *The Living Tree: The Changing Meaning of Being Chinese Today*. Stanford: Stanford University Press, pp. 1–34.

Tu, W. M. (ed.) (1994b). *The Living Tree: The Changing Meaning of Being a Chinese Today*. Stanford: Stanford University Press.

Turnbull, C. M. (1972). *The Straits Settlement 1926–67*. London: The Athlone Press.

Turnbull, C. M. (1977). *A History of Singapore, 1819–1975*. Kuala Lumpur: Oxford University Press.

Turner, V. (1969). *The Ritual Process*. Ithaca: Cornell University Press.

van der Sprenkel, Otto Berkelbach (1973). Genealogical registers. In D. D. Leslie, C. Mackerras, and G. W. Wang (eds.), *Essays on the Sources for Chinese History*. Canberra: Australian National University Press, pp. 83–98.

Van der Veer, P. (ed.) (1995). *Nation and Migration: The Politics of Space in the South Asian Diaspora*. Philadelphia: University of Philadelphia Press.

Van Gennep, A. (1960). *The Rites of Passage*. Chicago: Chicago University Press.

Vaughan, J. D. (1972). *The Manners and Customs of the Chinese of the Straits Settlements*. Kuala Lumpur: Oxford University Press, reprint.

Wang Jianzhu (1980). Jizu yu baishen（王建柱：〈祭祖与拜神〉）. *Guanxi wo*（《关系我》）1: 14–20.

Wang, G. W. (1958). The Chinese in search of a base in the Nanyang. *Journal of the South Seas Society* 14 (Parts 1 and 2): 86–96.

Wang, G. W. (1981). *Community and Nation: Essays on Southeast Asia and the Chinese*. Singapore: Heinemann.

Wang, G. W. (1991). *China and the Chinese Overseas*. Singapore: Times Academic Press.

Wang, G. W. (1993a). Greater China and the Chinese overseas. *The China Quarterly* 136: 926–948, special issue on Greater China.

Wang, G. W. (1993b). Migration and its enemies. In D. Mazlish and R. Buultjens (eds.), *Conceptualizing Global History*. Boulder, CO: Westview Press, pp. 131–151.

Wang, G. W. (1996). Sojourning: The Chinese experience in Southeast Asia. In A. Reid (ed.), *Sojourners and Settlers: Histories of Southeast Asia and the Chinese*. St. Leonard, NSW: Allen and Unwin and ASAA Southeast Asia Publication Series, pp. 1–14.

Wang-Liu, H. C. (1959). *The Traditional Chinese Clan Rules*. New York: Locust Valley.

Watson, J. L. (1975). *Emigration and the Chinese Lineage: The Mans in Hong Kong and London*. Berkeley: California University Press.

Watson, J. L. (1982). Chinese kinship reconsidered: Anthropological perspectives on historical research. *The China Quarterly* 92: 589–622.

Watson, J. L. (1986). Anthropological overview: The development of Chinese descent groups. In P. Ebrey and J. Watson (eds.), *Kinship Organization in Late Imperial China, 1000–1940*. Berkeley: University of California Press, pp. 247–292.

Watson, J. L. (1988). The structure of Chinese funerary rites: elementary forms, ritual sequence, and the primacy of performance. In J. Watson and E. S. Rawski (eds.), *Death Ritual in Late Imperial and Modern China*. Berkeley: California University Press, pp. 3–19.

Watson, J. L. (1991). *The Renegotiation of Chinese Cultural Identity in Postmodern Era*. Hong Kong: University of Hong Kong; Social Sciences Research Centre Occasional Paper, vol. 4, 27 pp.

Watson, J. L. (2004). Virtual kinship, real estate and diaspora formation: The Man lineage revisited. *The Journal of Asian Studies* 63(4): 893–910.

Watson, J. L. and Rawski, E. S. (eds.) (1988). *Death Ritual in Late Imperial and Modern China*. Berkeley: California University Press.

Watson, J. L. and Watson, R. S. (2004). *Village Life in Hong Kong: Politics, Gender and Ritual in the New Territories*. Hong Kong: The Chinese University Press.

Watson, R. S. (1982). *The Creation of a Chinese Lineage: The Teng of Ha Tsuen, 1669–1751*. London: Cambridge University Press.

Watson, R. S. (1985). *Inequality Among Brothers: Class and Kinship in South China*. Cambridge: Cambridge University Press.

Watson, R. S. (ed.) (2000). *Marriage and Inequality in Chinese Society*. Boulder, CO: Netlibrary, Inc.

Watson, R. (ed.) (1994). *Memory, History and Opposition*. Santa Fe, NM: School of American Research Press.

Weber, M. (1951). *The Religion of China*. New York: Free Press.

Weber, M. (1966). *The Sociology of Religion*. London: Associated Book.

Whyte, M. K. and Parish, W. L. (1984). *Urban Life in Contemporary China*. Chicago: Chicago University Press.

Whyte, M. K. (1988). Death in the People's Republic of China. In J. L. Watson and E. S. Rawski (eds.), *Death Rituals in Late Imperial and Modern China*. Berkeley: University of California Press, pp. 289–316.

Wickberg, E. (1985). Chinese organisations and ethnicity in Southeast Asia and North America since 1945: A comparative analysis. Canberra: Australian National University, Symposium on Changing Identities of the Southeast Asian Chinese Since World War Two.

Willmott, W. E. (1964). Chinese clan associations in Vancouver. *MAN* 94(49): 33–37.

Wilson, H. (1978). *Social Engineering in Singapore*. Singapore: Singapore University Press.

Wolf, A. P. (ed.) (1974). *Religion and Ritual in Chinese Society*. Stanford, CA: Stanford University Press.

Wong, J. (1996). Promoting Confucianism for socioeconomic development: The Singapore experience. In W. M. Tu (ed.), *Confucian Traditions in East Asian Modernity*. Cambridge, MA: Harvard University Press, pp. 277–293.

Woon, Yuen-fong. (1989). Social change and continuity in South China: Overseas Chinese and the Guan Lineage in Kaiping County, 1949–87. *China Quarterly* 118: 324–344.

Xiamen jingji tequ nianjian (1990) (《厦门经济特区年鉴》).

Xinjiapo Anxi huiguan (1988–1996) (《新加坡安溪会馆》).

Yang, C. K. (1961). *Religion in Chinese Society*. Berkeley: University of California Press.

Yang, M. M. H. (1994). *Gifts, Favors and Banquets*. Ithaca: Cornell University Press.

Yen, C. H. (1981). Early Chinese clan organisations in Singapore and Malaya 1819–1911. *Journal of Southeast Asian Studies* 12(1): 62–87; edited by C. F. Yong (ed.), Ethnic Chinese in Southeast Asia, independent issue.

Yen, C. H. (1986). *A Social History of the Chinese in Singapore and Malaya 1800–1911*. Singapore: Oxford University Press.

Yong, C. F. (1968). A preliminary study of Chinese leadership in Singapore 1900–1941. *Journal of Southeast Asian History* 9(2): 258–285.

Yong, C. F. (1977a). Leadership and power in the Chinese community of Singapore during the 1930s. *Journal of Southeast Asian Studies* 8(2): 195–209.

Yong, C. F. (1977b). Pang, Pang organisations and leadership in the Chinese community of Singapore during the 1930s. *Journal of the South Seas Society* 32(1 and 2): 31–52.

Yong, C. F. (1987). *Tan Kah Kee: The Making of an Overseas Chinese Legend*. Singapore: Oxford University Press.

Yong, C. F. (ed.) (1981). Ethnic Chinese in Southeast Asia. *Journal of Southeast Asian Studies* 12(1), independent issue.

Yu Guanghong (1987). Meiyou zuchan jiumeiyou zuzong paiwei—E. Ahern Xinan ziliao de zai fenxi (余光弘：〈没有祖产就没有祖宗牌位 — E. Ahern 溪南资料的再分析〉). *Minzuxue yanjiusuo jijkan* (《民族学研究所集刊》) 62: 115–177.

Zhenxiang zazhi bianjibu (1987). Qingshui zushi de chuanqi yu lingji (真相杂志编辑部：〈清水祖师的传奇与灵绩〉). *Zhenxiang zazhi* (《真相杂志》) 40: 57–59.

Zhongguo xiangzhen qiye nianjian bianji weiyuanhui bian (1992). *Zhongguo xiangzhen qiye nianjian* (中国乡镇企业年鉴编辑委员会编：《中国乡镇企业年鉴》). Beijing: Nongye chubanshe (北京：农业出版社).

Zhou Fengjun (1978). Shenzhong zhuiyuan de jizu yishi (周丰君：〈慎终追远的祭祖仪式〉). *Guohun* (《国魂》) 387: 26–27.

Index

administrative village 55, 58
adoption 29, 194
affinity money 146, 257
altruistic motivation 13
Amitabha Sutra 148, 258
ancestral burial ground 108
ancestral graves 108, 150, 153
ancestral halls 132, 136, 191, 219, 219, 270
ancestral tablets 133–35, 138, 146, 149, 152–53
Anderson, B. 263
animism 164
anti-poverty campaign 66, 109, 117, 120
Anxi Association 3, 24, 50, 69, 169, 203, 232–33, 236, 255
Anxi County Administrative Office 252
aristocratic families 194

baba 39, 42, 47, 50, 201, 204, 251
bodhisattva 13, 148, 256
Book of Filial Piety 13, 260
Bourdieu, P. 263
bridges 69, 83, 102, 109–11, 128, 167, 208, 233–34
British colonialism 20
Brook, T. 263
Buddha 13, 131, 148, 169, 175, 256
buddha head 175, 256
Buddhist monks 143–45, 179

Buddhist morality 13
Buddhist sutras 148
burial grounds 108, 133, 150

China guests 93
China letter 74, 259
Chinese calligraphy 207
Chinese cosmology 131–32
Chinese Federal Republic 18
Chinese medicine 77, 118
Chinese nationalism 41, 230
Chinese opera troupe 172
Chinese religious orthodoxy 163–65
Chinese transnationalism 20, 269
Christianity 43–44
Christians 184
circulatory migration 249
citizenship 21–22, 37–38, 52
clan association 33, 43, 46, 50, 134, 267, 272
clan registers 189
collectivization 60, 107–08
commercialization 66–67, 120
communal ancestral worship 127, 133, 136–37, 139, 152, 154–55, 157, 160, 165, 175, 224, 243
communal religious fairs 16, 125, 128, 165, 174, 176–77, 183–86
communication 18, 22, 25, 69, 74–76, 92, 97, 109, 111, 182, 195, 235, 244

concubines 193
Confucian ethic 10
Confucian ideology 10–11, 251, 266
Confucianism 11–12, 161, 164, 185, 228, 267–68, 272
conjugal families 32
construction industry 102, 128
corporate property 222
corruption 110, 123–24, 135, 179
Cosmic Rite of Renewal 213
cosmocrat 52
cottage industries 88, 120–21, 234
credit rotation system 35–36, 257
cultural authenticity 17, 162
cultural bankers 17
cultural capital 17, 127, 161, 266–67
Cultural China 18–21, 251, 259, 270
cultural dilution 43–44
cultural districts 112–13, 259
cultural integration 19
cultural orthodoxy 41, 43
cultural reintegration 42–43
cultural reinvention 14–15, 17, 42
cultural renaissance 162, 246
cultural representation 41–42
Cultural Revolution 30, 38, 60, 74, 108–09, 150, 156, 175, 184, 195, 197, 207, 227
cultural time 21

Dao 14
Daoism 14, 164, 185
Daoist priests 143–44, 172, 178–79
daughters 36, 44, 49, 73, 112–13, 137, 149, 151, 174, 190, 192, 194, 208–13, 252–53, 255, 259
death rituals 141, 270, 272
decollectivization 107–08
decolonization 33–34, 37
deified ancestor 166–68, 172, 176, 258–61
descent group 220–22, 265, 271
detribalized 47, 90, 256
dialect organizations 33–34
Diamond Sutra 148, 257
diaspora 18, 20–21, 29, 233, 239, 248, 251, 267, 271–72

diversification 67
divinization 4

Eberhard, W. 264
Ebrey, P. 264
economic integration 18–19
economic rationalism 122
English education 34, 46
enterprise development 117, 121–22
ethnic memory 5
ethnic pluralism 197
ethnic segregation 39
Evans-Pritchard, E. 264

face 48, 69–70, 72, 75, 81, 84, 92, 96–97, 103, 116, 132, 136, 151, 157, 164–65, 167–68, 177, 181, 184, 186, 204, 213, 259
family business 34–36, 45, 95, 171, 174, 209
family registers 189
family roots 257
Faure, D. 264
Fei, H. T. 264
female infanticide 192
Fentress, J. 264
fieldwork 26
folk beliefs 164
Fortes, M. 264
Freedman, M. 264
fruit orchards 60, 65, 68
functionalist 221
Furnivall, J. S. 265

Geary, P. J. 265
Geertz, G. 265
geomancy 166, 256, 264
gift-giving 74
global lineage flows 236
global migration history 21
globalization 22, 24, 45, 84, 121, 244
Granet, M. 265
Great Leap Forward 60
Greater China 18–19, 21, 251, 265, 271
group identity 163
guilt 3, 71, 126, 181, 213, 217, 241–42

Halbwachs, M. 265
Hannerz, U. 265
Harding, H. 265
Hazelton, K. 265
heat and noise 259
Hicks, G. L. 265
higher-order lineage 219, 221
historical memories 4
historical records 134
home tuition 34
hospitalization 119
Huaqiao Hospital 117, 119
human capital 66
Hymes, R. P. 265

imagined community 15, 24, 245
inclusive strategy 205
industrialization 60, 120, 123–24
inner source 227–29, 231–33
inner-worldly asceticism 12
insiders 23, 51, 172, 183, 196, 245
inter-lineage guanxi network 236
interviews 25–26, 122
intra-lineage network 235
invented tradition 14

Jackson Plan 39
joint-venture investments 68

Kapitans China 32
karma 13–14, 141–42, 148, 228, 252, 257
Kluckhohn, C. 266
Kuah, Khun Eng 266

La Fontaine, J. S. 267
labelling 127
land degradation 66
letters 4, 21, 73–75, 89, 91–92, 242
liminal stage 141
Lin Y. H. 268
lineage ancestral house 133–34, 136, 154–55, 157, 224
lineage genealogy 142, 189, 197, 203, 207, 234, 261, 263
lineage registers 189
lineage school 116
Lo, H. L. 268
localist strategy 220–21, 265

locality registers 189–90
localized lineage 218–19
Long Men Tunnel 110
longevity lanterns 149, 256
Lotus Sutra 148, 258
Lyons, T. 269

Mahayana Buddhism 13
Malay Federation 37
Mandarinate 191, 257
manufacturing 45, 122–24
market economy 62, 66, 122–23
memoirs 4
memorial halls 132–34
memory specialists 5
meritorious deeds 14, 131, 133, 140–42, 257
methodology 25
microcultures 223–24
mistresses 125
modern homes 102
moral consciousness 2, 126
moral duty 2, 11–12, 14, 126–27, 129
moral economy network 234
moral persuasion 126, 128
mourners 143–49, 257
multiculturalism 39, 246
multi-ethnic population 24, 35, 245
multi-ethnicity 24, 38, 246
multiple identities 24, 53
mythology 4

Nanyang 30, 34, 71, 127, 156, 196, 271
national identity 23–24, 38–39, 215, 233, 245–46
nation-building 24
nation-states 19, 29–30, 227, 230, 245
negative representations 82, 86–87, 90
Neo-Confucian scholars 10
new elite 6–8
nodal links 224–25, 240
Nonini, D. 269
Nosco, P. 269
nostalgia 8, 104, 239, 241, 269

occupational specialization 45
old family house 102
one-child policy 205, 209, 253

Oolong Quality Control Centre 67
Oolong Tea Research Institute 67
Open Door Policy 61, 84
oral stories 11
oral transmission 4, 9
orthopraxy 142, 164, 174, 252
outer source 228–30, 233
outsiders 50–51, 64, 84, 153, 174, 176, 183, 196, 219, 222, 224, 245, 257
Overseas Chinese Guesthouse 89
overseas comrades 84

participant-observation 25
People's Action Party 37
Peranakan 39
Perry, R. B. 269
phenotype 39
philanthropy 12, 136, 229
politics of space 20, 271
pre-capitalist societies 221
primogenitor 103, 190
primordial guanxi network 233
primordial kinship network 3
principal wife 193–94
private room money 77, 259
prostitution 125
public health 117

questionnaires 26

Ranger, T. 265
rationalization 4, 175
Rawski, E. S. 270, 272
rebirth 14, 142, 149
Reformist Buddhism 164, 267
refugee mentality 72
Regional Chinese Cultural Centres 230
religiosity 165–66, 173, 183, 187, 244
religious fairs 16, 27, 125, 128, 158, 160, 163, 165, 169, 171, 174–77, 179–81, 183–86
religious legitimacy 185
religious orthodoxy 163–65, 174
religious paraphernalia 125, 140, 144, 146, 165, 178, 180, 185, 187
religious procession 179

religious revivalism 27, 131, 163, 165, 167, 169, 171, 173, 175–77, 179, 181, 183–85, 187, 266
reminiscences 10–11
remittances 2, 21, 60, 73, 87–88, 90, 101–02, 105, 241, 252, 265
Republic of China 125, 190, 272
residence committee 58
residual Chinese communities 226
retailing 64, 102, 121, 124, 128, 187
Rite of Gratification 133, 136, 138, 261
rite of passage 143, 153
ritual adoption 194
ritual land 191, 219
ritual weeping 146
road construction 60, 109–10

sacrificial offerings 132, 191, 252
schools 26, 33–34, 46, 83–84, 89–90, 112–16, 128, 159, 180, 182, 191, 200, 208, 259
scriptural purity 164
secret societies 33, 36, 269
Secret Societies Ordinance 33
secularization 4
shop houses 70, 128
social engineering 11, 266, 272
social historians 220
social memories 5
social networks 30, 33, 35–36, 45, 52, 73, 121, 187, 233, 259
sojourner 22, 31–32, 38, 270–71
source 15–16, 21, 24–25, 36, 47, 55, 57, 60–61, 66–67, 73, 93, 98, 103–04, 114–15, 120–21, 126–28, 132, 135, 141, 159, 162, 168–70, 186, 192, 197, 199, 204, 214, 219–20, 225–40, 242–43, 245, 247–48, 256, 260, 264, 270
South China Economic Periphery 19
storytelling 4, 9
Straits Chinese 34, 39–40, 251, 269
structural time 20
subcultures 223–25
subjective thought-process 4
subsistence farming 62, 69–70

superstition 16, 158, 176, 183, 186
surname associations 36, 40, 165, 230, 235
sworn brotherhood 36
symbolic capital 17

tablet carriers 139
telecommunication 18, 22, 69
temples 33, 43, 84, 90, 127, 131, 133–34, 148, 152–53, 165, 169–73, 182–83, 247
this-worldly asceticism 13
transitional economy 124
transnational networks 242
Tu, W. M. 270
Turner, V. 270

uncivilized guests 182
unemployment 63, 122–23
universal suffrage 38
upward mobility 190, 194, 247
utilitarian morality 7
uxorilocal marriage 194

Van der Veer, P. 271
Van Gennep, A. 271
village committees 58
village letter-writers 73

Wang, G. W. 19, 22, 31
Watson, J. L. 164, 219, 220, 221, 222, 252–53n
Watson, R. 4
Weber, M. 12
Western medicine 77, 118
Whyte, M. K. 133, 141, 253n
Wickham, C. 9
World Anxi Association 203, 233

Xiamen Economic Zone 61

Yang, C. K. 273
Yong, C. F. 273

Zhong Yuan Festival 43

For Product Safety Concerns and Information please contact our EU
representative GPSR@taylorandfrancis.com
Taylor & Francis Verlag GmbH, Kaufingerstraße 24, 80331 München, Germany

www.ingramcontent.com/pod-product-compliance
Lightning Source LLC
Chambersburg PA
CBHW071157300426
44113CB00009B/1238